TECHNOLOGY AND MARKETS FOR KNOWLEDGE

KNOWLEDGE CREATION, DIFFUSION AND EXCHANGE WITHIN A GROWING ECONOMY

Economics of Science, Technology and Innovation

VOLUME 22

The titles published in this series are listed at the end of this volume.

TECHNOLOGY AND MARKETS FOR KNOWLEDGE

KNOWLEDGE CREATION, DIFFUSION AND EXCHANGE WITHIN A GROWING ECONOMY

edited by

Bernard Guilhon
Université de la Méditerranée, France

KLUWER ACADEMIC PUBLISHERS
Boston / Dordrecht / London

Distributors for North, Central and South America:
Kluwer Academic Publishers
101 Philip Drive
Assinippi Park
Norwell, Massachusetts 02061 USA
Telephone (781) 871-6600
Fax (781) 871-6528
E-Mail <kluwer@wkap.com>

Distributors for all other countries:
Kluwer Academic Publishers Group
Distribution Centre
Post Office Box 322
3300 AH Dordrecht, THE NETHERLANDS
Telephone 31 78 6392 392
Fax 31 78 6546 474
E-Mail <services@wkap.nl>

 Electronic Services <http://www.wkap.nl>

Library of Congress Cataloging-in-Publication Data

Technology and markets for knowledge : knowledge creation, diffusion, and exchange within a growing economy / edited by Bernard Guilhon.
    p. cm. -- (Economics of science, technology, and innovation ; v. 22)
   Includes bibliographical references (p.) and index.
   ISBN 0-7923-7202-6 (alk. paper)
   1. Intellectual capital. 2. Intellectual capital--Case studies. 3. Knowledge--Economic aspects. 4. Knowledge--Economic aspects--Case studies. I. Guilhon, Bernard. II. Series.

HD53 .T43 2001
338.4'7001--dc21   00-048694

CONTENTS

vi

LIST OF FIGURES

Chapter 1, 2 & 3

Figure 1: Modes of knowledge conversion.
Figure 2: Place and role of specialized firms in knowledge production.
Figure 3: Knowledge production and knowledge flows.
Figure 4: The changing shape of innovation process.
Figure 5: The management of knowledge by firms.

Chapter 4

Figure 1: Use of proprietary technologies (largest European, North American and Japanese companies).

Chapter 5

Figure 1: Growth in U.S domestic R&D and abroad, 1980-2000.
Figure 2: New products approved in USA from 1987 to 1998.
Figure 3: Improvement in research methodology.
*Figure 4:*The drug development and approval process in the '90s.
Figure 5: Total development time from synthesis to approval.
Figure 6: Complementary knowledge bases and knowledge transfer.
Figure 7: Evolution of biotechnological agreements with reference to different types of partnerships for the period between 1982 and 1999.
Figure 8: Knowledge exchange in 1999.

Chapter 6

Figure 1: Semiconductor market segments in 1999.
Figure 2: The three paradigms in the semiconductor industry.
Figure 3: From simple product to complex system.
Figure 4: Disintegration of IC production.
Figure 5: Young's cumulative dynamics.
Figure 6: The design gap crisis.
Figure 7: The growing trend of IP reuse.
Figure 8: Pervasiveness of IP in ASICs.
Figure 9: Internal creation *vs* purchase of physical libraries.
Figure 10: IP Market Evolution.

Chapter 7

LIST OF TABLES

Chapter 1, 2 & 3

Chapter 4

Chapter 5

Chapter 6

Chapter 7

LIST OF CONTRIBUTORS

Suma ATHREYE is Lecturer in International Business at the Manchester School of Management, UMIST, Manchester. She obtained her doctoral degree from the SPRU, University of Sussex, in 1996. Current research interests lie in the field of technology markets, innovation and competition policy in the software sector, and comparative studies on the determinants of innovative activity.

Rajà ATTIA is PhD candidate at CEFI-CNRS, University of the Mediterranean Aix-Marseille II (France). She is working in the area of the semiconductors in the Pays d'Aix region. She is teaching assistant at the University Institute of Technology and at the IUP–Public Management, (Aix-en-Provence).

Fabrizio CESARONI is attending the PhD programme in Economics and Management of Innovation at the Sant'Anna School of Advanced Studies, Pisa (Italy). His main research interests are in the Economics of Technical Change, Technological Management, and Science and Technology Policy.

Isabelle DAVY is PhD candidate at CEFI. Her research interest lies in the competitiveness and the innovation competencies in the European semiconductor industry.

Bernard GUILHON is Professor and Director of the Doctoral Training at CEFI. He is in charge of the "Innovation and Performance" program.

Myriam MARIANI is PhD candidate at MERIT (The Netherlands) in the programme "Economics and Policy Studies of Technical Change". Her main research interests concern the geographical and institutional aspects of the processes of production and diffusion of innovations.

Daisy RHUGUET is PhD candidate at CEFI, in the field of the pharmaceutical industry. She is teaching assistant at the Faculty of Economics, University of the Mediterranean Aix-Marseille II.

Roland RIZOULIERES is PhD candidate at CEFI. His research area is the semiconductors industry. He is teaching assistant at IUP – Public Management (Aix-en-Provence).

Christophe SILVY is PhD candidate at CEFI, in the field of the economics of innovation and human capital. He is teaching assistant at the Faculty of Economics, University of the Mediterranean Aix-Marseille II.

ACKNOWLEDGEMENTS

We would like to acknowledge Professor Cristiano Antonelli who encouraged us to undertake this work.

The CEFI team is grateful to Professor André Cartapanis for the financial and moral support of the CEFI. We also thank Philippe Antomarchi whose advises related to the final set up were precious.

Fabrizio Cesaroni and Myriam Mariani would like to thank Ashish Arora, Andrea Fosfuri, Alfonso Gambardella, Fabio Pammolli and Massimo Riccaboni for helpful suggestions and advice, and Walter Garcia-Fontes and Manuel Fernández Bagüés for help in data elaboration and analysis.

FOREWORD

This book provides a unique set of empirical and theoretical analyses on the conditions, determinants and effects of the exchange and trade of technological knowledge. This work delivered by the research team lead by Bernard Guilhon shows that technological knowledge is more and more traded and exchanged in the market place. When and where contractual interactions are implemented by an institutional set-up which makes_the exchange better reliable for both parties. The new evidence provided by the book moreover makes it possible to appreciate the positive role of major knowledge rent externalities provided by the new quasi-markets for technological knowledge. Trade in technological knowledge leads in fact, as the book shows, to higher levels of division of labor, specialization and efficiency in the production and distribution of new technological knowledge.

This dynamics is considered a part of a broader process where the generation of technological knowledge is itself becoming closer to the production of goods so that the division of labour among learning organization plays a growing role. Exchange of technological knowledge takes part because the conditions for appropriability are now far better that currently assumed by a large traditional literature. The analysis carried out through the book builds upon the notion of localized technological knowledge and suggests that the exchange of technological knowledge is not a spontaneous 'atmospheric' process. It can take place successfully because technological knowledge is localized and embedded and as such better appropriable and only if both parties, vendors and customers, are actively involved. Moreover an actual transaction can take place only if and when in an appropriate institutional context. Arm's length transactions are being implemented by an array of contractual devices such as long-terms contract, membershiop in technological clubs and joint-ventures, equity-agreements, interlocking__directorates, patents' swaps, bundling of licencies and goods. Institutional and contractual ingenuity helps the emergence of quasi-markets for technological knowledge.

The theoretical analysis conducted in the first chapters of this book by Bernard Guilhon also highlights the important role of external disembodied technological knowledge purchased by firms in the market place as an intermediary input in the production of new knowledge. Firms that have been able to take advantage of the opportunity offered by the new emerging quasi-markets for technological knowledge can complement their internal R&D expenditures and recombine external disembodied knowledge with internal competence and formal research activities. The supply of external knowledge clearly makes it possible to acquire inputs at lower costs than those generated internally with major rent knowledge externalities. Technological outsourcing from firms specializing in the provision of technological knowledge as well as from other 'industrial' firms willing to sell disembodied knowledge hence becomes an important source of technological knowledge and thus adds to the general efficiency of the generation of new knowledge.

The appreciation of rent knowledge externalities, as distinct from the more traditional technical knowledge externalities, is a major achievement of this book. Rent knowledge externalities stem in fact from the opportunity to take advantage from trade in technological knowledge and hence to purchase bits of knowledge at costs that are lower than the internal product. Technical knowledge externalities instead consist in the opportunity to directly benefit, without any actual transaction, from the low appropriability of technological information. The Arrovian tradition of analysis values technical knowledge externalities. The evolutionary approaches focus technological knowledge, instead of technological information, regard it as an appropriable mix of generic and localized knowledge, and pay more and more attention to rent knowledge externalities.

The detailed empirical analyses provided in the second part of the book on the actual quasi-markets for knowledge in software, chemicals, bio-pharmaceuticals and semiconductors confirm that the emergence of such markets for technological knowledge is the result of a complex institutional process with a strong collective character. These empirical analyses also confirm that the acquisition of external knowledge in dis-embodied technology markets and its recombination with internal research and development activities and competencies is emerging as an effective way to increase the total amount of technological knowledge each company can generate. Transactions in technological knowledge take place among industrial firms as well as between industrial firms, universities and knowledge-intensive-business-services specializing in the generation of technological knowledge to be delivered and sold to third parties.

Recombination, assembling, specialization and division of labour are now spreading into the organization of the production of knowledge, after much experience in the production of manufactured goods. The large empirical evidence at the company level, made available through the book, confirms that external knowledge is becoming an important source of technological knowledge as a key input in the process generating technological knowledge and eventually technological change and productivity growth.

As a result of the detailed analysis provided in this book, a new framework with important policy implications becomes evident in conclusion. Until now, the economic importance of formal intramural R&D conducted by firms and scientific activities conducted by universities, as the unique and single input into the generation of technological knowledge has been exaggerated. As a consequence too much emphasis has been put upon R&D policies and more generally science policies as the basic tools to sustain the rates of accumulation of new knowledge. In the generation of new technological innovations, firms rely more and more on technological communication which is conducive to the acquisition of external knowledge by means of formal interactions between themselves, sharing learning opportunities and experience, and with other established sources of knowledge, such as universities and other public research centres. Outsourcing of research activities and the procurement of knowledge intensive business services plays an increasing role in assessing the innovative capabilities of each firm.

The levels of technological procurement from other 'industrial' firms and the outsourcing of knowledge intensive business services should be accounted for when assessing the actual amount of inputs invested in the process of research and learning. The procurement of technological knowledge from third parties, both at the international level and within countries, is an important component of the general process of accumulation of new knowledge.

Public policy interventions to support technological communication at large and specifically the emergence of new quasi-markets for trade in technological knowledge, the acquisition of external disembodied technological knowledge might be especially successful. Institutional and contractual relationships, elaborated to support the outsourcing of knowledge-intensive services and the purchase of technological knowledge from other industrial firms and research-intensive organizations should become an area for public policy analysis and a perspective recipient for policy interventions.

CRISTIANO ANTONELLI
DIPARTIMENTO DI ECONOMIA
UNIVERSITA' DI TORINO

PREFACE

The purpose of this book is to reconcile two terms that the economic tradition has opposed for a long time: market and knowledge. Market exchange is difficult, if not impossible, as far as the nature of knowledge is concerned (Nonaka et al., 2000). First, knowledge creation is characterized by a high degree of uncertainty which results cannot be evaluated a priori. To this first feature can be added the tacit dimension, that renders knowledge largely non-transferable. Besides, even codified, knowledge cannot be easily evaluated if we do not know its content. But, once this content is revealed to the buyer, market exchange needs not to occur. At last, appropriability problems strongly arise when, for example, general and specific know-how are accumulated due to numerous R&D contracts.

Nevertheless, economic agents are not reasoning as economists do. The empirical data indicate without ambiguity that transactions on specialized technological inputs have continuously increased to reach several billion $.

The first part of this book analyzes knowledge markets basis. The first three chapters (B. Guilhon) rely on the idea that knowledge is the organizations' fundamental capital. This capital possesses very specific properties, especially those related to production and accumulation. Thus, to accumulate knowledge, must the firm produce it itself? We think technological and scientific knowledge is becoming more fragmented: pieces of knowledge may be articulated due to sophisticated R&D technologies (modeling, computer-aided simulation, etc). Of course, a part of tacit knowledge, embedded in organizational routines, values and beliefs, is not transferable. Markets for knowledge solely concern individual knowledge units which form the knowledge base of the firm. These knowledge units are capitalizable and adaptable to different contexts.

Economic thought on markets invites us to consider at the same time demand-side and supply-side factors (Geroski, 1998). Markets for knowledge can be used to secure the functioning of production activities and their outlets: manufacturing, logistics, sales and distribution. Also, they participate to the product and process innovations in the form of R&D, design contracts and licensing. Knowledge producers (Knowledge-Intensive-Business-Services-Firms) increase the connectivity and the receptivity of the economic agents. Indeed, knowledge is a relationship structure: knowledge producers play an interface role between basic knowledge and applied knowledge. Moreover, they favor the R&D orientation of the user firms. As such, markets for knowledge express an increasing specialization inside the industrial organization of knowledge production. Market for knowledge lead firms to manage the 'knowledge-gap' (P. Huard, forthcoming) when the value chain is subject to frequent technological improvements.

The second part of this book extends these developments by providing sectoral illustrations. Chapter 5 (F. Cesaroni and M. Mariani) deals with markets for knowledge in the chemical sector. The large size of the chemical sector, its strong science base and its long history favor a comprehensive study of the determinants and effects of such markets. Chapter 6 (D. Rhuguet, C. Silvy) outlines the coexistence of two paradigms, respectively grounded on chemistry and biotechnology. It analyzes knowledge transfers which take place within the bio-pharmaceutical field and witnesses the preponderant character of market exchanges with respect to multiple contractual agreements and financial operations. Chapter 7 (R. Attia, I. Davy and R. Rizoulières) deals with the intellectual property market in the semiconductors. These authors emphasize that the evolution of both the technological knowledge base and the organization of the industry have been intertwined sine the early 50s. The study reveals a progressive separation between manufacturing and design and further within design activities, leading to a deep division of labor and to the emergence of a market for knowledge. The 8th and last chapter (S. Athreye) analyzes the emergence conditions of knowledge markets in the software industry. The constraints stemming from supply side and mostly demand side are the growth engine of the software industry and its important segments.

Bernard GUILHON

REFERENCES

Huard P. Market, firm and knowledge gaps. Forthcoming.

Geroski PA. Thinking creatively about markets. International Journal of Industrial Organization 1998; 16:677-95.

Nonaka I, Toyama R, Nagata A. A firm as a knowledge-creating entity: a new perspective on the theory of the firm. Industrial and Corporate Change 2000; 9:1-20.

PART I

THE THEORETICAL ANALYSIS OF THE MARKETS FOR KNOWLEDGE

The first part will be made up of three chapters. The first chapter aims to analyze the markets for knowledge by highlighting their specificity. The second chapter analyzes the emergence conditions of these markets. The third chapter approaches the issue of markets for knowledge running and provides quantification elements.

Chapter 1

HOW TO CHARACTERIZE MARKETS FOR KNOWLEDGE ?

Bernard Guilhon
CEFI-CNRS, Aix-en-Provence, Université de la Méditerranée, France

Knowledge is at the heart of organizational forms as it lays the fundamental questions of its production, of its transfer and of its utilization (Lundvall, 1999). The answers to these questions depend on the formulated hypothesis as to properties attributed to knowledge.

Standard neo-classical approach is a theoretical construction of a resources allocation plan, in which supply and demand conditions assumed to be given on all markets. In this context, it is crucial to suppose that consumers have a complete knowledge of their own preferences as well as of market prices of goods being part of their utility function. As far as producers are concerned, knowledge is also assimilated to information, as it possesses the properties to be codified, homogenous and free access to all (public good). In such a competitive market, knowledge (or information) is perfectly transmissible and identifiable and there is no need to question how it is produced and acquired. Suppliers distinguish themselves from consumers by the fact that they 'possess in proper a technological know how' (Thévenot, 1989) on the production function, they use to answer instantaneous and anonymous demands.

A much richer approach was suggested by Hayek (1960, 1978, 1988). Competition is a 'discovery process' of scarce goods and things as well as their degree of scarcity. On this point of view, knowledge is imperfect (due to labor division between autonomous economic agents), intrinsically partial (as it is linked to implementation of individual plans of action) and not easily communicable: 'nobody can communicate to another all that he knows, because much of the information he makes use of himself will elicit only in the process of making plans of action' (1988, p.27). The economic problem of society is 'in its essence' the problem of knowledge: as dispersed *knowledge*, as one is to use at best knowledge distributed among individuals linked to contextual factors, and as *process* that will favor economic agents which will discover and apply new organizational/institutional technical tools ('social tools').

The central question of *transferability of knowledge* is asked in two ways:

- spatial dimension is articulated to a conception of labor division conceived as 'division of knowledge'. Then, we ask ourselves on mechanisms that make possible coordination of action plans of economic agents, as they only possess fragmented and partially not transferable knowledge. If agents have knowledge, even limited to the actions of others, they may coordinate their action plans by market mediation, without necessarily communicating among themselves;

- the intertemporal dimension is linked to the efficient use of knowledge and experience that accumulates with time as 'new ways of doing things' are discovered and tried. The possibility of accumulating knowledge in time opens the way to 'adaptation and learning processes' understood as review processes of individual cognitive capabilities. These processes enable an improvement of practices on a technological as well as organizational/institutional level.

For evolutionist authors, knowledge is cumulative as well as learning which uses for support. Knowledge embedded in organizational routines (Nelson and Winter, 1982) that cannot be codified and are consequently tacit. Besides, they are not easily observable in use (intangible), they are more or less complex (according to what field they are linked to) and we have to take into account the degree of interdependence that links different cognitive elements of a system (Winter, 1987). As such, we are to take into account instrumental knowledge (inputs), and interpretative knowledge that enables to define situations and serve to elaborate representations. These dimensions of knowledge imply that technological assets (knowledge and know-how) are specific to each firm that produces them, and are difficult to replicate and transfer (Nelson and Winter).

Consequently, these different analytical perspectives (knowledge transmissible without cost, dispersed and not easily transferable knowledge, knowledge embedded in organizational routines of tacit nature specific to each firm) have only a limited utility to conceive and characterize the markets for knowledge.

To progress in our analysis, we will first put in evidence the notion of market applied to knowledge. Then, we will clarify the underlying hypothesis and the content of exchanged services. Finally, we will propose a definition of these markets.

1. THE NOTION OF MARKET FOR KNOWLEDGE WOULD BE A PRIORI CONTRADICTORY

1.1   The Two Suggested Arguments

At first, the creation of knowledge is often analyzed in the literature, as a by-product of firm's other activities. From this viewpoint, codified knowledge is opposed to tacit knowledge that would be predominant.

Codified knowledge is explicit knowledge, i.e. formalized and transmissible due to different supports: concepts, graphics, diagrams, formulas, etc. This knowledge type has circulatory properties (of duplication), under constraint that economic agents possess the code allowing its access: to get hold of a formula does not mean that the economic agent knows how to exploit it. This is the reason why one can admit that the transmission cost of knowledge is the summation of duplication cost (that tends toward zero) and the acquisition cost that can be very high (Foray, 1995). In fact, it corresponds to an investment in training for an individual or to the development of a learning capability for a firm.

Tacit knowledge is inseparable of the person or group that holds it: it is difficult to formalize and as such to communicate. As conceptualized by Polanyi (1966), it makes reference to the fact that we are generally conscious of the existence of certain objects or of certain acts, without our attention being fixed on them. They are no less important as they favor the development of 'context knowledge' inseparable of productive activities and of persons and that can only be transmitted by experience. As such, tacit knowledge is a practical knowledge, acquired by and through practice; it corresponds then to know-how. But it is not only reduced to that. Nonaka (1994) specifies that tacit knowledge includes at the same time technical and cognitive elements, i.e. mental models, diagrams and beliefs that structure the representations as well as the know-how and practical abilities articulated to contexts. Pressure is put on the importance of tacit knowledge embedded into routines, procedures and organization codes and that knowledge is not subject to ubiquity (Maskell and Marmberg, 1999).

For our analysis, it is important to retain that codified aspect is above all connoted to knowledge as outcome or end product and embedded in database or a knowledge list. When it results of R&D under the shape of principles or patterns, it can be used to predict definite performances before reaching the production stage. Tacit knowledge calls for process aspect, to the continuous activity of knowing and it is basically located in the experience base of the firm.

These two forms of knowledge interweave in the organizations and are often produced on the locus of their utilization. The creation and transfer of new knowledge requires knowledge conversion processes that Nonaka did particularly well analyze.

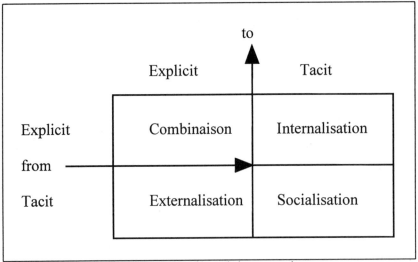

Figure 1: Modes of knowledge conversion.
Source: Nonaka (1994)

Knowledge markets suppose the activation of two processes of conversion. Externalization that takes place inside the firm enables to transform a tacit knowledge into an explicit knowledge, by shifting from an embodied knowledge in a context to an encoded knowledge and expressed by the means of abstract symbols and alienated from its context (Blackler, 1995). The second mode of conversion is the combination of different pieces of explicit knowledge. This operation, in the suggested analysis, links two firms: a specialized firm transmits codified knowledge that could combine with explicit knowledge of the firm using it.

The first mode of conversion implies a knowledge codification, a condition necessary to its transfer. The second mode of conversion expresses the increasing separation between the supply of knowledge by specialized firms and their accumulation by user firms.

Secondly, a market of codified knowledge will always be imperfect because the market is not a suitable mechanism to knowledge allocation. Kenneth Arrow (1962) was the first to underline the deeply contradictory character of this type of market. It is difficult to determine a market price for a piece of knowledge: the buyer wants to know the value of what he is buying and the seller do not wish to disclose this information for nothing. If the buyer can obtain this information, the market exchange does not need to occur. The sub-optimal character of supply is more increased by the fact that the knowledge producer has the right to restrain the use of the knowledge sold, but he may have difficulty to have this right respected. There is a risk of expropriation of explicit knowledge by the potential purchaser (Grant, 1996a).

The buyer, contrarily to what happens on the product market, lacks information both on producers of knowledge and their reputation, and on the quality of the piece of knowledge he wishes to buy. In fact, he does not have the possibility to compare two pieces of knowledge because, to make this comparison, he has to buy for example two exploitation licenses of a patent.

Far from constituting an objection to knowledge markets, these considerations may be used to admit the idea that the supply of scientific or technological knowledge cannot be assimilated to the supply of a material component for production. The operation cannot be reduced to a *make or buy* trade-off. From this point of view, the outsourcing practices could be defined in different way. Either they represent the externalization of an activity that was before internalized (in this case the firm knows how to do, but for costs reasons, it prefers to have it done by another firm), or they represent a service purchase the firm did not need previously (Coombs and Battaglia, 1998). If the firm acquires knowledge in a specific field, it means that it cannot or do not wish immediately affect resources to develop an in-house capability there. Also, we may consider that the firm which buys knowledge must develop indirect capabilities (Loasby, 1998): to select, learn and coordinate knowledge by integrating the different pieces they represent, while reducing the absorption costs. We will see later how the model suggested by Cohen and Levinthal (1990) can be enhanced by taking into account the knowledge markets.

1.2 Summary

The knowledge production tends to constitute a separate activity, distinct of production and the created knowledge can be expressed under abstract form and alienated from its context. Besides, a part of tacit knowledge is likely to be codified thanks to expenditure explicitly oriented toward different forms of codification: artificial intelligence and expert-system, transmission of data, etc. This knowledge is then potentially transferable toward firms that seek to enhance their knowledge base and to extend their competences. By the way, the analytical approach in terms of *make or buy* trade-off is not adapted to knowledge transfer. The lengthening of the period of production of knowledge and the growth of development costs that accompany it, and the impossibility to master different technological fields lead firms to concentrate their resources on 'core technologies' and to call for other mechanisms, among which the market, to acquire technological assets that they need.

These remarks conduct to analyze knowledge markets, not as pure markets, but as *rather organized markets* (Lundvall). On my side, I will use the expression of *quasi-markets*:

- they are not 'spot' markets, but most often they are long-term relations between suppliers and users built on trust based on common experience;
- there is not, on one side, a supply ready-to-use and on the other side, a well-defined demand. In fact, even if technological knowledge can be codified 'the code which makes sense to the codifiers may not make relevant sense to the recipient of the message' (Loasby, 1998, p.148). Knowledge transfer often implies the definition of co-conception and constant interaction procedures that enable to articulate the demand of solving problem capabilities and the services supply in the framework of contracts on research, development, engineering, production, supplying, etc. The customer becomes as such an input of the production (Nachum, 1999).

2.   THE HYPOTHESES UNDERPINNING MARKETS FOR KNOWLEDGE

2.1   Statement of Hypotheses

- The lengthening of production processes and their break down into knowledge blocks are responsible for the rise of intermediate inputs and the promotion of productive relations materialized by market links or co-operations (Richardson, 1998). Inputs that make technological progress visible at the intermediary level are composed by products and services that firms supply to other firms (Carter, 1970);
- industrial development in the context of technology dynamics, 'leads to wholly new patterns of specialization both by firm and by industry' (Rosenberg, 1982, p.71). The production of knowledge is itself subject to an increasing process of specialization that favors mediation of knowledge by the market. The process of specialization can be inferred from Autio (1997) who argues that scientific knowledge can undergo two transformations, in basic technology and in application specific technologies. In the first case, the transformation is realized by *science-based firms* suited to take advantage of scientific discoveries and by drawing from them a generic interpretation. Whereas, in the second case, transformation is realized by *engineering-based-firms* that extract from basic technologies the specific applications necessary to exploit market opportunities. Science-based firms have intensive R&D relations with their users as they represent the link with public research, the channel by which scientific and technological knowledge can be exploited. These firms constitute as such an external resource for other producers 'in complementing the technological pool through the development and the application of new basic technologies'[1] (ibid., p.275). By contrast, engineering-based firms essentially sell consultancy and logistics services, etc., as such reinforcing efficiency of other firms' production, distribution and administration. Autio's empirical analysis results confirm the existence of an increasing specialization process

of knowledge production, in which small firms supply specialized technological inputs.

The idea that science-based firms are more active to transform scientific knowledge into basic technologies rather than in application specific technologies allows us to draw the figure 2.

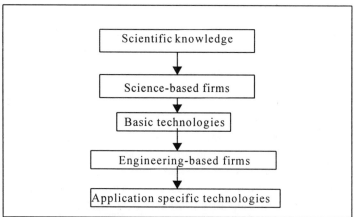

Figure 2: Place and role of specialized firms in knowledge production.
Source: diagram adapted from Autio (1997)

2.2   Specialized Technological Inputs

They are constituted of the following elements (Arora, Fosfuri and Gambardella, 1999): chemical and pharmaceutical molecules, new products concepts or prototypes, algorithms and software, studies, logistics services. To those are added data processing services, database activities, advanced communication services, technical testing and quality control, economic and management services, training activities. These inputs involve all forms of intangible knowledge that can be embedded in patterns or concepts and sold by Knowledge-Intensive-Business-Services-Firms (KIBSFs). One of these forms most frequently used to transfer these technological inputs is the licensing. It is a way of creating revenues in technological-intensive industries (chemistry, semiconductor, software, pharmaceutical, etc.) and this enables to rapidly expand the use of a technology as a substitute to a production growth. But if the competing firms are very few and if products differentiation is weak, then licensing can induce profits erosion on product market (Arora and Fosfuri, 1999).

The identification of these intermediary technological inputs allows these authors to distinguish three markets vertically embedded:
- *the innovation market* (Gilbert and Sunshine, 1998) that rests on firms' R&D investments in an industry, aiming at producing new or improved products and processes and to patent the proprietary knowledge;

- *the technology market*: once scientific and technological knowledge is patented, each holder of patents evaluates the number of licenses to sell to established or potentially entering firms. In this case, intellectual property rights are separately sold from products likely to embody new knowledge. Bayh-Dole Patent and Trademark Amendments Act of 1980 enables to grant exploitation licenses to developers for patents protecting the results of basic research. Basic knowledge is as such converted into technological input. We need to take into account firms' heterogeneity to analyze the propensity to sell licenses. If economic agents have non-existent or very limited production capabilities (laboratories, small firms), licensing becomes very attractive since revenue effect is very strong in the absence of profits erosion. This may bring large firms to adopt more aggressive behaviors of licensing.

- The *product market* on which firms who acquired technology compete.

The articulation of these markets is significant in two ways. In one way, it implies that upstream positioning on technological assets production have downstream consequences on product market. This proposition does not have a determinist content. It does not mean that technological assets acquisition permits by itself new markets entry. Many authors have insisted on the importance of complementary assets required: manufacturing capabilities, marketing capabilities, services and sales, etc. (Gambardella and Torrisi, 1998) The link between technological assets and product market rather means that knowledge intensity of activities contributing to products realization increases. Knowledge intensity can be measured by R&D expenditure, patent applications, and training expenditure. In the pharmaceutical industry, the steady increase in R&D expenditure is given by table 1:

Table 1. Expenditure on R&D as a % of sales (ethical medicines), American pharmaceutical companies, 1970-1998

Year	R & D Turnover
*1998	20,0 %
*1997	20,3 %
1996	19,8 %
1995	19,4 %
1994	20,4 %
1993	19,9 %
1992	17,9 %
1991	16,6 %
1990	16,2 %
1989	16,8 %
1988	16,7 %
1987	16,1 %

1986	15,1 %
1985	15,1 %
1984	14,6 %
1983	14,7 %
1982	14,0 %
1981	13,3 %
1980	11,9 %
1979	11,2 %
1978	10,9 %
1977	11,1 %
1976	11,0 %
1975	11,3 %
1974	10,9 %
1973	11,2 %
1972	11,6 %
1971	11,2 %

* Estimated - Source : Pharmaceutical Research and Manufacturers of America, (1998)

Besides, increased knowledge intensity would produce a shift of labor division principle in firms and between firms (Moati and Mouhoud, 1998), that would move from yield and technical logic to a competence and learning logic. The splitting of activities along the value chain would be founded on blocks' segmentation of homogeneous knowledge. These knowledge blocks may be defined 'as a whole set of knowledge tied up to the same body of technical and scientific principles. These knowledge are subject to a common evolution dynamics boosted by a research and transformation activity of new knowledge information, obeying to certain heuristics shared by a community of specialists' (ibid., p.36). The specialization in knowledge blocks favors the blooming of knowledge markets.

3. DEFINITION OF MARKETS FOR KNOWLEDGE

Now we can define markets for knowledge as places where transactions for scientific and intangible technological assets occur. These assets are protected by intellectual property rights in the form of patents, copyrights, licenses, patterns. These markets are likely to transfer knowledge already established or on the way to be. To some extent, they shape relationships between instrumental knowledge and activities that represent the firm's value chain: research, development, conception, production, marketing. Markets are the expression of an increasing specialization of knowledge industrial production. The technological proximity is preponderant to understand the meaning of these transfers (aeronautics sells knowledge to automotive sector though no product exchange takes place between these two activities).

3.1   Valorizing Intangible Technological Assets

Knowledge owned by firms can first be valorized on product markets under the form of marketing applications. CIS I inquiry on European industry (Calvert et al., 1996) made on 12 countries and 17 sectors indicates that product innovations greatly contribute to sales (42%) and exports (48%). Innovations are those introduced by firms during the three years preceding the realized inquiry.

It is possible to move upstream in the innovation chain and seek to evaluate knowledge embedded in individuals as well as in R&D departments. The underlying hypothesis is that the firm has a value on the market that can considerably exceed the value of its physical assets, (Artus et al., 1998) thanks to these two constituent elements of its knowledge base. Therefore, we resort to Tobin ratio, i.e. the ratio of market value of a firm over the value of its capital. More exactly, we use the following ratio:

$$q = \frac{\text{Stock market val ue} + \text{Long - term debt value}}{\text{Gross fixed assets (outside intangible assets)}}$$

Calculated values of q vary according to sectors:
• q >> 1 in the media and wholesale distribution (high growth and low fixed assets)
• q ≅ 1 in traditional industry (automotive sector)
• q > 1 in technology-intensive industries (patents) or having a reputation of know-how linked to the brand.

The point is to identify exogenous variables specific to firms that could explain their market values fluctuations, apart from explications in terms of speculative movements. To econometrically estimate q, we use the following variables:
R_a= R&D expenditure/gross tangible assets
R_b = total wage bill/number of employees
d = liabilities/stockholder's equity

Human capital is estimated by R_b which represents the value of an employee for the firm. The average wage reflects knowledge embedded into individuals: the higher the average wage is, the more limited the employee mobility is, and the more durable the relation between employees and the firm is. If competition does not exercise more on employees, it is because there exists a firm-specific human capital which itself owns specific knowledge (Arrow, 1996). The resulting regression model is applied to large firms belonging to the following sectors of French economy: aeronautics, agribusiness, automobile, building, energy, distribution, primary goods.

$$q_{est.i} = \alpha_i.R_a + \beta_i.R_b + \delta_i.d + \Delta_i d^2 \qquad \text{with } i = 1985, ..., 1996$$

d^2 is introduced to indicate a non-linear relation between debt ratio and Tobin's q. For the years 1994, 1995 and 1996 it is observed that q depends of R_a with a factor close to 4, of R_b with a factor close to 20, of d and d^2 with factors of -35 and 40.

For the year 1996, firms could be brought into two categories (q < 0.9 and 2 < q < 10) and the above defined variables could be used to explain the gap with respect to 1 of Tobin's q:
- R_a explains 40% of the gap
- R_b explains 15% of the gap
- d explains 45% of the gap

Overall, we observe that intangible assets (R&D and human capital) play a key role. Markets increase the value of these assets that accounting policies do not register. The analysis could be deepened by breaking down intangible assets into three categories: those linked to technology (R&D), those linked to human capital and those linked to marketing (advertising). This would be a way to take into account knowledge as innovation input and knowledge as running input (production and marketing). Markets can reinforce these three types of knowledge and, for leading companies, the technological balance must be positive: i.e. the number of patents and licenses sold must exceed technological assets bought.

3.2 The Channels of Knowledge Circulation

Patents and licenses constitute one of the possible channels for knowledge to circulate among firms. The set of possibilities for the firm B to obtain information contained in an innovation realized by the firm A is indicated in the figure 3 (Arundel, Smith, Patel and Sirilli, 1998). All will depend on the ways firm A used to capture innovation outcomes.

This figure brings the following remarks:
- secrecy blocks knowledge disclosure;
- knowledge can be embedded in a product. Firm B resorts to reverse engineering that could be combined to other possible sources, when information is partly conveyed by specialized newspapers;
- if firm A decides to patent knowledge, this decision 'also opens up additional routes for the flow of knowledge' (ibid., p.15). For firm B, the possibility to exploit this knowledge requires to have access to an

'undisclosed complementary information' through a license purchase. Patents and licenses purchase is one way by which knowledge spreads in the economic system.

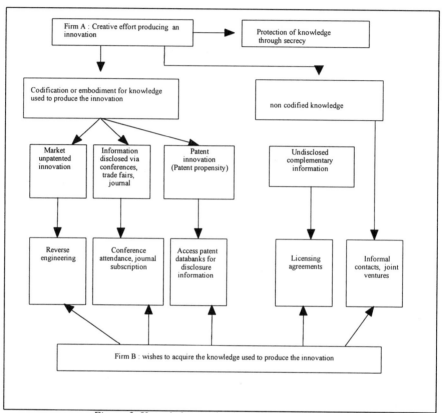

Figure 3: Knowledge production and knowledge flows.
Source: Arundel, Smith, Patel and Sirilli, 1998, p.16

The market relationship established between firm A and B implies that these two entities must be identifiable in terms of ownership and especially in terms of distinctive competences resulting in the products and/or services sales to other firms. 'Disembodied technology is the «product» and familiar principles of market definition can be applied to «market» transactions. Examination of demand-side and supply-side criteria can be tapped to identify market boundaries and participants […].' (Gilbert and Sunshine, p.599) Many scenarios exist. In electronic industry, disembodied technologies sale is linked to that of equipments. In pharmaceutical industry, sales are not coupled and exclusively concern licenses and R&D services. Some firms offer R&D services to firms which activity is limited to production. If durable relationships between entities exist, they cannot alter the market character since both a buyer and a seller are identified and since a transaction involving a specialized technological asset is observed.

3.3 Markets for Knowledge and the Traditional Model of Innovation

In this model, innovation acts linearly from scientific research and is then applied to development, conception, production, and marketing. Feedback effects and possible overlapping between the various steps do not exist, contrary to the chain-link model (Kline and Rosenberg, 1986) that introduces chaining and feedback phenomena between downstream and upstream stages and that implies a constant interaction between knowledge and the innovation process within each phase that structures this process from innovation to marketing.

The traditional model overestimates the importance of scientific research and research in general and eliminates the difficulties linked to the organization of the innovation process. It proposes a vertical representation of this process, in which the necessary *complementary assets* may be provided by the firm itself or by market processes (Jorde and Teece, 1990): 'Indeed, the serial model relies on an implicit belief that arms-length contracts between unaffiliated firms in the vertical chain from research to customer will suffice to commercialize technology' (ibid., p.80). If knowledge appropriability regime is well established and if technology can be transferred at zero cost, then 'the market for intellectual property is likely to support transactions enabling the developer of the technology to simply sell its intellectual property for cash, or at least license it to downstream firms who can then engage in whatever added value activities are necessary to extract value from the technology. With a well running market for know-how, markets can provide the structure for the requisite organization to be accomplished' (ibid., p.81). *In fact*, these authors estimate technological knowledge markets are being probably inefficient. Their deficiency (market failures) brings to establishing complex contractual arrangements, to create hybrid organizational design or to coordinate activities inside firms.

Nevertheless, the previous analysis implies a stable technological regime. Often, firms are faced with a strong technological discontinuity that declassifies their knowledge, lessens their competences (included those involved in sales and distribution) and reduces to zero the value of owned assets. Therefore, firms cannot use their competences of in-house existing research in order to survive within a new paradigm. Two possibilities are offered to them (Teece, 1988): 'the relevant competence may have to be purchased *en masse,* or technology transfer programs must be employed to educate existing personnel in the assumption and logic of a new paradigm' (p.266). In these circumstances, licensing and collaboration with universities or other emerging firms represent efficient mediations so that the organization is able to run. Consequently, when a paradigm change occurs which deeply modifies the knowledge base content, and if the new knowledge required is strongly appropriable and difficult to copy, then the recourse to market and to other forms of collaboration becomes legitimate. We shall show the pertinence of this proposition in sectoral applications (chapters 5, 6, 7 and 8 in this volume).

3.4   The Notion of Complementary Assets

Besides its principal assets and its core competence, a firm owns a relatively set of secondary assets or complementary assets to the former ones. They correspond to 'those assets and capabilities that need to be employed to package new technology so that it is valuable to the end user' (Jorde and Teece, p.83). These complementary assets are articulated to principal assets and are present in complementary technologies, i.e. manufacturing, marketing, distribution, sales, and services. On the analytical level, complementary assets show rather strong analogies with specialized technological inputs that we enumerated. Nevertheless, in connection with the conceptualization suggested by evolutionist scholars, differences exist on three levels:
- complementary assets are only present in the added value chain downstream of products or processes development (Dosi, Teece and Winter, 1990). They differ from specialized technological assets that intervene along the firm activity cycle, from the R&D to the market. Knowledge exchanges between economic agents and especially between suppliers of high value added services and users imply a retooling of the whole firms productive process, which frontiers become more permeable, without losing their distinctive competences;
- complementary assets include both physical assets (production capability, distribution channels) and immaterial technological assets;
- firms create complementarities over time, i.e., very often complementary assets are developed within the firm. In this framework, the technological opportunities that characterize the immediate environment of the firm may lead itself to develop more rapidly its secondary competences. *It is then only a transfer inside a positioning system of assets and skills.* Assets, secondary so far, become more strategic and allow the firm to change its principal activity. If we adopt the classification of firms' technological profiles suggested by Granstrand, Patel and Pavitt (1997), we can say that some background and even marginal competences will become core or distinctive competencies.

During periods of technological turbulence, evolutionist scholars admit that complementary knowledge assets can be bought. But as the market for complementary assets is itself riddled with imperfections, the market mediation to acquire these assets can entail a loss of competitive advantage.

4. CONCLUSION

To conclude this chapter, we can underline that knowledge transmitted by the market may be used in two ways by user firms:
- some knowledge represents intermediary inputs necessary to the running of productive processes, for instance, data processing software, databases services, consultancy services, market management studies, and training services, etc.;
- intermediary technological inputs may be useful from another point of view. They facilitate the innovation process of the firm by causing a recombination of this process toward disintegration. Mang (1998) developed this idea from the hypothesis that a technological option may be realized by two ways: either firms perform internal development or have recourse to a market transaction. In some sectors, notably bio-pharmaceutical, small biotechnological firms may transfer the project development of a molecule to incumbent large firms, because they lack sufficient resources to do it. The trade-off between internal and external development depends, among other things, on the level of their own resources and on the more or less specific character of knowledge linked to the R&D project. Chapters devoted to sectoral applications witness the importance of these mechanisms with respect to other channels of knowledge transfer.

To sum up, the production of knowledge is acquiring an industrial logic and is associated to a more complex social distribution than before. Not only because the places where knowledge is created are multiplying (laboratories, research centers, universities, firms of all sizes), but also because the specialization process at work enables to isolate 'know-how' companies offering suited solutions to issues faced by firms in their daily running and in innovations they wish to develop. The presence of 'knowledge-intensive firms' (Alvesson, 1993) is important from a double point of view: they produce an abstract knowledge based on a specialized expertise, that differs from knowledge and skills possessed by incumbent firms. At the same time, they influence the innovative behavior of the latter by providing guidelines to interpret the events taking place in the environment.

NOTES

[1] Even when science-based firms offer manufacturing services, it is not the supply of standard assembly services, but services that request specialized technical skills (p.275).

REFERENCES

Alvesson M. Organization as rhetoric : knowledge-intensive firms and the struggle of ambiguity. Journal of Management Studies 1993; 30:997-1016.

Arora A, Fosfuri A, Gambardella A. Markets for technology (why do we see them, why don't we see more of them and why we should care). Working paper 99-17, Universidad Carlos III de Madrid, 1999.

Arora A, Fosfuri A. Licensing the market for technology. Discussion paper series n°2284, CEPR, 1998.

Arrow KJ. Technical information and industrial structure. Industrial and Corporate Change 1996; 5:645-52.

Arrow, Kenneth. "Economic Welfare and the Allocation of Ressources for Innovation." In *The Rate and Direction of Inventive Activity*, R Nelson, ed. Princeton University Press : Princeton, NJ, 1962.

Artus P, Hubert F, Verlé N. "En 1997, les entreprises françaises étaient valorisées normalement : une approche par le Q de Tobin et le capital immatériel". CDC Marchés 1998; 20:1-13.

Arundel A, Smith K, Patel P, Sirilli G. The futur of innovation measurement in europe. Concepts, problems and pratical directions. STEP group, IDEA Paper Series, 3, 1998.

Autio E. New technology-based firms in innovative networks symplectic and generative impacts. Research policy 1997; 26:263-81.

Blackler F. Knowledge, knowledge work and organizations: an overview and interpretation. Organization Studies 1995; 16/6:1021-46.

Calvert J, Ibana C, Patel P, Pavitt K. "Innovation outputs in european industry : analysis from CIS. " Part of report submitted to DG XII (Contrat : EIMS 93/52). European Commission, 1996.

Carter Anne, P, *Structural Change in the American Economy*. Cambridge, Massachussetts, 1970.

Cohen WM, Levinthal DA. Absorptive capacity : a new prospective on learning and innovation. Administrative Science Quarterly, 1990; 35:128-52.

Coombs R, Battaglia P. Outsourcing of business services and the boundaries of the firms. CRIC Working Paper 5, The University of Manchester, 1998.

Dosi G, Teece DJ, Winter SG. Les frontières des entreprises : vers une théorie de la cohérence de la grande entreprise. Revue d'Economie Industrielle, 1990; 51:238-54.

Foray D. "Innovation, connaissance et information : un rapide tour d'horizon." Séminaire *Economie de l'Information*, Commissariat Général du Plan, 1995 novembre 14, Paris.

Gambardella A, Torrisi S. Does technological convergence imply convergence in markets ? Evidence from the electronic industry. Research policy 1998; 27:445-63.

Gilbert RJ, Sunshine SC. Incorporating dynamic efficiency concerns in merger analysis: the use of innovation markets. The Journal of Reprint for Antitrust Law and Economics 1998; XXVIII (2):449-81.

Granstrand O, Patel P, Pavitt K. Multi-technology corporations: why they have "distributed" rather than "distinctive core" competencies. California Management Review 1997; 39:8-25.

Grant RM. Towards a knowledge-based theory of the firm. Strategic Management Journal 1996a; 17 (Winter Special Issue): 109-22.

Hayek, Friedrich, *The Fatal Conceit: The Errors of Socialism.* London: Routledge and Kegan Paul, 1988.

Hayek, Friedrich, *The Constitution of Liberty.* Chicago: University of Chicago Press, 1960.

Hayek, Friedrich. "Competition as a Discovery Process." In *New Studies of Philosophy, Politics, Economics, and the History of Ideas,* Chicago of University Press, 1978.

Jorde TM, Teece DJ. Innovation and cooperation :implications for competition and antitrust. Journal of Economic Perspectives 1990; 4:75-96.

Kline, S, Rosenberg N. "An Overview of Innovation." In *The Positive Sun Strategy.* Rosenberg N and Landau R, eds., Washington, DC : National Academy Press, 1986.

Loasby B. The organization of capabilities. Journal of Economic Behavior & Organization 1998; 35:139-60

Lundvall, Bengt-Åke. "What Constitutes the Knowledge Base in the so-called Knowledge-Based Economy." In *Indicateurs Prospectifs de Science et de Technologie,* Rapport final dans le cadre du contrat n° ERBRIST – CT 970013 entre le CEFI et la DG XII, Commission Européenne : Cefi, 2000.

Mang PY. Exploiting innovation options : an empirical analysis of R&D intensive firms. Journal of Economic Behavior & Organization, 1998; 35:229-42

Maskell P, Marmberg A. Localised learning and industrial competitiveness. Cambridge Journal of Economics, 1999; 23:167-85.

Moatti P, Mouhoud EM. Connaissances, logiques productives et modes de division du travail : une contribution à la réflexion sur les mécanismes d'exclusion. Revue d'Intelligence Economique 1998; 2:31-42.

Nachum L. Measuring the productivity of professional services : a case study of swedish management consulting firms. Working paper series, ESRC Centre for Business Research, WP 120, University of Cambridge, 1998.

Nelson, Richard R, Sidney G, Winter, *An Evolutionnary Theory of Economic Change.* The Belknap Press of Harvard University Press, Cambridge, Massachussetts, and London, England, 1982.

Nonaka I. A dynamic theory of organizational knowledge creation. Organization Science, 1994; 5:14-37.

Polanyi, Michael, *The Tacit Dimension.* London, Routledge & Kegan, 1966.

Richardson GB. Production,planning and prices, Druid Working Paper, 98-27, 1998.

Rosenberg, Nathan, *Inside the Black Box: Technology and Economics.* Cambridge University Press, 1982.

Teece DJ. Capturing value from knowledge assets : the new economy, markets for know-how, and intangible assets. California Management Review 1998; 40:55-79.

Thévenot L. Equilibre et rationalité dans un univers complexe. Revue Economique (Special Issue) 1989; 40:147-97.

Winter, Sidney G. "Knowledge and Competence as Strategic Assets." In *The Competitive Challenge: Strategies for Industrial Innovation and Renewal*, David J Teece, ed. Ballinger : Cambridge, MA, 1987.

Chapter 2

THE EMERGENCE OF THE QUASI-MARKETS FOR KNOWLEDGE

Bernard Guilhon
CEFI-CNRS, Aix-en-Provence, Université de la Méditerranée, France

In the first chapter, we wished to put the strength on the specific character of knowledge markets. The term *quasi-markets* expresses the idea that they are not pure markets by which firms could put at work 'fully explicit blueprints by purchasing homogeneous inputs on anonymous markets' (Nelson and Winter, p.119). Rather, firms seek to acquire specific instrumental knowledge resting on a specialized expertise, allowing them to increase the efficiency of their daily operations and of their innovation behavior. These markets are far from being a recent phenomenon: Arora, Fosfuri and Gambardella (1999) make reference to the research of Lamoreaux and Sokoloff acknowledging an active technological knowledge market in the USA at the end of the 19th and 20th century. The glass industry, according to these authors, did already experiment at that time a 'division of innovative labor' between invention activity and its marketing, on the basis of a specific organizational and geographic differentiation.

Other research works state of a 'new division of labor' as a recent characteristic of U.S. innovation system (Mowery, 1998). According to this author, the development of market exchanges is not linked to the externalization of industrial R&D that is analyzed from the point of view of the increasing creation of consortia, joint ventures and strategic alliances. Market transactions are a consequence of the Bayh-Dole Act which postulates that the restriction brought to the diffusion of basic research results that could be bought, will favor the pace of commercial innovation. 'Emphasis on patenting, rather publishing, the results of research may well reduce the volume of information flowing through conventional channels of dissemination in favor of marked-based transactions' (ibid., p.649). This strongly questions the previous model.

It is possible to mark out the evolution of industrial organization of knowledge production by distinguishing five steps (Antonelli, 1999):

- entrepreneurship has been the dominant mode of knowledge production during and immediately after the industrial revolution. The creation of a new firm by schumpeterian entrepreneur is the privileged way to introduce new knowledge in the economic system. Innovative entrepreneurs apply knowledge they have produced or developed themselves from other activities or academic studies;

- at the end of the 19th century, the mode of 'institutional variety' prevails and rests on a division of labor well established between universities and industrial firms: 'universities generate technological externalities which firms absorb and translate into economic value' (ibid., p.142);

- after 1945, vertical integration becomes the preponderant characteristic of industrial organization of knowledge production, notably in the U.S.A. and the U.K., while some European countries (France, Italy, Germany) remain closer to institutional variety and to the role of universities. Industrial firms create internally their own R&D labs and they produce applied knowledge and basic scientific knowledge. There are many theoretical and practical justifications. In-house R&D allows the exploitation of cumulativeness and complexity of technological knowledge, to monitor the economic and temporal management of research programs. Meanwhile, the firm's independence is secured with respect to contractual research, which is subject to transfer costs between developer and user. Besides, firms preserve themselves from a possible credit rationing since banking sector is often reluctant to finance scientific and technological research;

- technological cooperation represents an intermediary form of organization (consortia, joint-ventures, strategic alliances). Thereby, economies of scale may be realized by avoiding duplication of R&D efforts and by mutualizing costs and risks between some participants. Besides, cooperation enables to save time, and, as such, to shorten research cycles. It might be considered as a means to upgrade the degree of knowledge appropriability and to capture research results that firms can independently valorize. Hence we talk about pre-competitive research;

- the increasing specialization is linked to the introduction of new information and communication technologies. As such, a distinctive industry of knowledge production can emerge, that is no more linked to firms productive activities. Therefore, market exchanges of knowledge and know-how are likely to develop.

Identifying these different steps does not mean they follow a linear trajectory. Overlapping occurs, indicating the complex character of organization of knowledge production. For instance, institutional variety coexists with entrepreneurship and specialization in many countries. Consequently, connections between the academic world and the industrial one shift and modify economists' representations. Rather than considering that firm exists as an exogenous entity and creates new knowledge from R&D that will be used as input in the innovation process, it is possible to reverse the causality. When scientists leave the academic world to create a firm, they possess an established knowledge (exogenous variable) in a specific field. In order to valorize this knowledge and to capture returns, they create a new firm that becomes the endogenous variable (Audretsch and Stephan, 1998). This matches with the diagram suggested by Autio (see figure 2, chapter 1), in which the existence of new knowledge of scientific and technologic nature does favor the KIBSFs interface activities .

Knowledge markets emerge under the influence of four factors that we shall analyze successively: increased complexity of firms' knowledge base, disintegration of the innovation process, technological convergence and transactions frequency.

1. INCREASING COMPLEXITY OF FIRMS' KNOWLEDGE BASE

1.1 Knowledge Base

This notion may be defined in many ways:
- the functional definition outlines the whole set of cognitive resources (information inputs, knowledge and capabilities) that inventors may use to define new solutions concerning products, processes, marketing, etc. (Dosi, 1988);
- the second definition is more focused on knowledge base features: complex, cumulative, appropriable and enabling to seize technological opportunities (Malerba and Orsenigo, 1993). Cumulativeness expresses the learning effects on a product or when moving from a product to another. Technological opportunities take into account key knowledge development which allows to apply technological knowledge to a broader range of products and markets. The complexity of the knowledge base is linked to products complexity. Such complexity affects the firm's organization, since it implies the integration of complementary knowledge stemming from various scientific and technological fields. Finally, the degree of appropriability expresses the relative possibility of knowledge transfer to other firms and this possibility is itself determined by the tacitness of knowledge. In this perspective, the knowledge base highlights the properties of knowledge from the point of view *of transferability*: tacit/codified and tangible/intangible (Wright, 1996). The consequences following from this analysis tend to privilege learning that takes place in manufacturing (learning by doing) and to locate firms' competitive advantage in the existence of an experience-based and tacit knowledge base;
- the third definition outlines knowledge acquisition procedures and the knowledge base maturity (Pisano, 1997). From this viewpoint, we distinguish empirical procedures of knowledge acquisition resting on a trial / error approaches and the more abstract ones that enables to identify

relationships between causes and effects. That is to predict future the performances of future knowledge uses. Here, the tacit / codified debate is secondary and the central property of knowledge lies in its capacity to indicate precisely enough how the events will occur in a given environment. The locus of learning changes: the importance of manufacturing shrinks to the benefit of laboratory or design office.

We will thus refer to these different conceptions to analyze the reasons that drive firms to spread their technological resources. This tendency is often observed (Patel and Pavitt, 1997; Granstrand, Patel and Pavitt, 1997). Starting from a sample of 440 large firms in which patents are listed in 34 technical fields, we notice that firms' technological competences measured by patents granted in the USA are dispersed among a larger range of sectors than production activities. Inventoried large firms are building and maintaining wide technological bases by becoming multi-technologies. Thus, technological portfolios are more diversified than products portfolios. Diversification even increases within firms which reduce their product diversification.

1.2 The Complexity of Production Systems

The increasing complexity of production systems is first linked to technical interdependence that develops and involves blocks of complementary knowledge. Also, we are to take into account the creation of new products which technological functions are more extended and the rise of emerging technological opportunities that push firms to spread their technological resources via internal R&D expenditure and the acquisition of external knowledge. Technological opportunities take into account scientific progress and technological advances realized inside the industrial chain via inputs and capital goods (Nelson and Wolff, 1997). Technological opportunities coming from science play a preponderant role that witnesses increasing integration of science and market.

Indeed, a new mode of knowledge production emerges – corresponding to the stage of specialization analyzed in the introduction of this chapter – which implies that a great part of scientific knowledge is produced in the application context (Gibbons et al., 1994). The proof is the increasing importance of the industry in the university research funding. This is reflected in the increasing number of research institutes in American universities developing research on areas directly interesting the industries. Close to 45% of research institutes established during the 80s 'involve 1-5 firms as members, and more than 46% of them rely on government funds for support in addition to (or in some cases, in lieu of) support from industry' (Mowery, p.648).

Besides, scientific developments offer new technological opportunities and propose new solutions to known problems. Moreover, science offers a great variety of theoretical models, techniques of data-building and problem-solving capabilities used in the industrial R&D (Klevorick et al., 1995). These elements favor the emergence of an R&D market.

The contractual R&D is defined as a 'work of an innovatory nature undertaken by one party on behalf of another under conditions laid out in a contract agreed formally beforehand' (Ringe quoted by Howells, 1997, p.3). This work includes R&D in its narrow sense, but also design, prototype-debugging and specific studies. Nevertheless, the content of R&D activity in this research could be enlarged[1].

The growth of contractual R&D in the UK is indicated the table 2.

Table 2. The growth in Contract Research and Development in the UK: 1985-1995* (millions of £)

	1985	1990	1991	1992	1993	1994	1995
a) Extra-mural R&D	450	757	711	727	887	821	935
b) Total BERD **	8,195	10,022	9,161	8,138	9,467	9,421	9,379
a) as a % of b)	5.5	7.6	7.8	8.0	9.4	8.7	10.0

Source : Howells (1997, p.5)
* (Constant 1995 Prices)
** BERD : Business Expenditure on Research and Development

The reasons for growth of contractual R&D, according to this author, are in two categories:
- *push*-type factors emphasize the increasing complexity of research process and the incurred risks. Large firms do not always dispose of scientific resources necessary to exploit fundamental knowledge. At Stevenage (U.K.), where the central R&D laboratory of Glaxo Wellcome is located, half of the personnel present on the site is employed by a firm under contract. The overall management of cognitive resources through R&D function becomes more flexible: it favors the emergence of a 'central' work force and a 'peripheral' personnel;
- *pull*-type factors involve financial costs that must be incurred by firms compelled to reduce innovation cycles. Meanwhile, these firms are trying to improve the interface between fundamental research, applied research and development while resorting to specialized expertise. Contractual research also constitutes a general supervision mechanism of technological opportunities (it increases receptivity) and a way to become part of a larger network within a research community (it increases connectivity).

Moreover, complexity is linked to modifications that affect knowledge acquisition procedures. Trial / error empirical approaches and learning types focused on *learning by doing* tend to create concrete information in real production environment (factory). Both are substituted by deductive modes of problem-solving that enable – by the means of sophisticated technologies (computing capacity, computer-aided simulation) – to point out theoretical patterns, principles, algorithms, heuristics, etc. Therefore, they give birth to a more abstract knowledge, more universal (Arora and Gambardella, 1994), *which central property will be to predict performances in real environments.* The learning type is modifying to the benefit of *learning before doing*, responsible in discovering problems before reaching the factory and to master the gap variables between the laboratory and the production (Pisano, 1997).

The possibility to undertake experimentations from simplified representations (models), at different product- or technology-levels (systems, sub-systems, components) or to proceed to virtual experimentations causes in the long run a decrease in costs and time devoted to iteration. This leads to improve the products and processes design in sectors such as chemistry, pharmaceuticals, semiconductors, and automotive (Thomke, 1998). The computer-aided simulation affects the performances and the corresponding learning processes: learning is rendered more efficient, creates information available for other development tasks; knowledge transfer toward manufacturing takes place more rapidly. The locus of learning shifts insofar as product and process design can be simulated. 'In process development, some experiments are conducted in laboratories, others are performed in pilot plans, and still others are run in full-scale commercial plants' (Pisano, p.43)[2].

In fact, knowledge bases are enhanced by deeper and more theoretical knowledge, especially on processes and on the development of processes architectures. The processes development is narrowly articulated to products development and firms possess specific knowledge that has predictive capacities potentially benefiting to several development projects.

The evolution of knowledge acquisition modes permits to extract general principles giving rise to different applications available for users. More deeply, it allows the passage from tacit to explicit knowledge 'and, as a result, making it transferable within and between firm boundaries' (Thomke, p.72). Here, the potential alienation of knowledge from its context gives such knowledge the quality of a tradeable good. The result of codification itself transforms knowledge into an information that can be communicated to other decision-makers. Dasgupta and David (1994) outline that codification is a necessary condition to exchange knowledge as a good: it facilitates the conversion, the transmission, the verification, the storage and the reproduction of this information at a lower cost.

The contemporary period would be characterized by an expansion of the codified knowledge base. This tendency needs to be clarified. On the one hand, firms' strategies become more complex to understand. Codification eliminates the specificity of some knowledge held by the firm since it increases the diffusion of such knowledge. At the same time, firms re-create scarcity: codification creates new tacit elements (Senker, 1995). On the other hand, firms patent more in order to control the diffusion of recently codified knowledge. They can also elaborate esoteric codes that create diffusion barriers (encryption) and benefit from the technical complexity of productive operations when knowledge is located in productive processes (Cohen and Klepper, 1996).

Furthermore, possibilities to codify knowledge heavily depend on the knowledge base maturity. From this viewpoint, chemistry and chemical engineering are mature activities, while biotechnology is characterized by a relatively immature knowledge base. Within this activity, new knowledge is produced and the degree of scarcity of this knowledge diminishes because new scientists are motivated to undertake researches and publish their results. But the tacitness diminishes more slowly for a 'technological transfer' is necessary from experienced scientists to newcomers (Zucker and Darby, 1998). These authors observe that 81% of publications between 1969 and 1982 are made with "star" scientists. The co-publication is thus considered as a proxy of the of the knowledge tacitness degree.

In sectors characterized by a mature knowledge base, technology producers are incited to operate the alienation since the knowledge context of application may vary, and thus may cause high adaptation costs. Because the alienation cost, i.e. outlining the theoretical structure of a problem, is incurred once and for all, economies of scale may be realized as soon as the demand for services increases. The same technological knowledge could be used by many firms; it 'is an extreme form of increasing returns' (Arrow, 1996, p.648). More precisely, what is sold by the knowledge producer is the application of knowledge to a specific context. The adaptation cost is reduced for to modifying the parameters of the theoretical model is sufficient.

2. SEGMENTATION DEGREE OF INNOVATIVE ACTIVITY

Whether we consider technology as embodied (in the processes) or disembodied (licenses, patents), we have to admit that factors specific to a technology cannot be disconnected from organizational choices. Organizational action deeply affects the potential implementation of an innovation. The way an organization is structured reflects the way productive resources are combined so that the various tasks are accomplished.

2.1 The Division of Labor

One of the major teachings of A. Smith lies in the idea that breaking down a productive activity in distinctive tasks and sub-tasks increases productivity of operations. This is also true for R&D activity and, more generally, for any problem-solving activity. In the chain-link model, the division of innovative labor takes place, *inside the firm*, along with a path starting from the invention (radical invention) or from the analytical model (incremental innovation) and goes on through the successive steps of detailed design (prototyping, tests, re-design), production, marketing and distribution.

The division of labor between these functions may be more or less deep. In some large firms, the innovation path may be sequentially organized on the basis of the independence of each step. The standardization, considered as the coordination of the distinct elements (methods, results, etc.), is realized upstream from the design stage relying upon technological and economic criteria (Mintzberg, 1990). Other firms, more in accordance with the Kline and Rosenberg model, organize overlapping between stages, build inter- and intra- activities feedbacks.

Until recently, the predominant model was characterized by a close integration of R&D activities and of the engineering function within firms. If this organization leads to reduce transaction costs, it presents nevertheless some disadvantages:

- the under-utilization of technology. 'Technology, once created, can be transferred elsewhere at only a fraction of the cost of developing it in the first place' (Arora, Fosfuri and Gambardella, p.3). The dissemination of technologies may benefit to other firms or to other countries and procure substantial revenues to knowledge producers. Large firms neglected these potential revenues because the technological knowledge market was not developed yet. Another reason consists of cultural attitudes that favored what was invented in-house;

- the second argument is also suggested by Arora, Fosfuri and Gambardella: the rate of technological innovation is weaker when technology markets do not exist. Indeed, firms endowed with weak marketing capabilities are penalized by these organizational arrangements;

- the efficiency of a specific organizational arrangement must be appreciated with respect to environment conditions. A high risk or uncertainty level implies that 'internalization of transactions is foregone in favor of subcontracting with independent producers' (Aldrich and Mueller, 1982, p. 70). These considerations concerning manufacturing activities may be spread to knowledge activities without assimilating technological input purchase to that of tangible good.

Many sectors record a tendency toward innovative processes disintegration that favors the division of innovative labor. The division of labor may exist between the upstream and downstream innovative path, i.e., between inventors and users of this invention (Arora and Gambardella). The division of labor might be deeper within the inventive activity itself.

2.2   The Glaxo-Wellcome Case

The example of Glaxo-Wellcome firm is significant to this respect
(Guilhon, 1999). At Glaxo-Wellcome the first function (discovery) is taken
by 'Group Medical regulator and Product Strategy' (GMRPS) which has
defined six therapeutic development groups and the collaboration networks
with other departments of the firm. This is like saying that the R&D function
has been more and more prioritized, since it reached in 1997 a budget close
to 1.2 million pounds (see table 3).

Table 3. Expenditure on R&D (millions of £)

Year	R&D	R&D / turnover
1992	595	14,5%
1993	739	15,0%
1994	858	15,2%
1995	1130	14,8%
1996	1161	13,9%
1997	1185	15,0%

Source: Glaxo-Wellcome document (1998)

The research projects are selected thanks to a procedure which hinges
on the following steps:
- identification of medical needs and the biological opportunities. This first
step defines the technical and scientific feasibility of the project;
- legitimization: a critical finance sum is assigned to the project;
- evaluation of the relationship of costs to results; the cost of treatment to
therapeutic efficiency and the cost of treatment to social utility;
- the commercial potential of the new product and its adaptation to
differentiated regulatory contexts. The innovation process is illustrated in the
figure 4.

The firm aims to increase its R&D productivity in such a way as to
produce twenty new molecules each year which would enable the launch of
three major new products per year. The development step assumes specific
importance owing to the growing costs which can be attenuated by partial
outsourcing and the multiplication of collaborations (the budget for
collaborations represents 20% of the R&D budget).

The development costs are first and *foremost the costs of new product
validation*, in other words the costs associated with transforming theoretical
and practical knowledge into product innovation. The development costs
also include *the validation costs of new processes*. Pisano justifiably remarks
that a large part of the knowledge associated with biotechnological processes
is tacit by nature. Given this characteristic difficulties can arise at the
production stage because the different variables between the laboratory and
the factory have been mastered sufficiently: the scale-up, the plant, the
aptitudes of the workforce, etc.

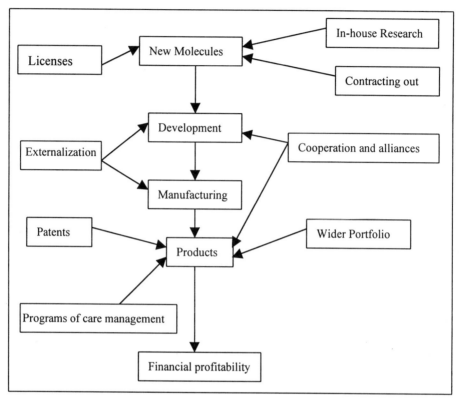

Figure 4: The changing shape of innovation process.
Source: Glaxo-Wellcome document (1998)

This is the reason why a medicine's creation cycle corresponds in biotechnology to an *integrated organization* of development and manufacture. 'Process research is not organizationally split from pilot development and manufacturing start-up, and the scientists who develop the process in the pilot plant are responsible for starting up the process in the commercial plant' (Pisano, 1997, p.141).

The emphasis placed on methodology by Glaxo-Wellcome and the importance of manufacture and new process configuration indicate the particularity of development problems of products coming from biotechnology, as much with respect to the *degree of maturity* of the knowledge base as to the type of training. The knowledge acquisition procedures remain quite empirical and they require learning by doing (the pilot plant supplies the information which corresponds to the real production environment)[3].

The R&D function is managed by allowing forever increasing flexibility. More specifically some technical tasks and research are taken on by research and technology organizations working under contract (CRTO). The development of a knowledge base by recourse to sophisticated R&D

technologies, (modeling, simulation, etc.) creates a *knowledge market* for the design of new chemical and pharmaceutical molecules. 'Here a group of new firms including Chemical Design, Oxford Molecular and Cambridge Combinatorial are providing what has been termed «discovery research services» to pharmaceutical and chemical companies in the search of new drugs and chemical compounds' (Howells, p.11). As the case study seems to indicate, the stakes for large pharmaceutical firms consist of dealing with production problems before going into production and having recourse to conceptual models, scientific principles, algorithms and heuristics that will profoundly influence development strategies. Moreover, a specialization process is emerging in the production of knowledge which cannot be interpreted in terms of supply and demand, but which assumes an active user-producer collaboration calling into question the distinction between fundamental research and applied research.

Analogous trends are being drawn in the computer industry, whom the new model based on the decline of software and the rise of service, shifts the gravity center of this industry toward the servers and business services. Sun Microsystems illustrates this new model. This is what indicates the Vice-President G. Papadopoulos in charge of technology at Sun Microsystems:

'Something extraordinary is happening in the information technologies. For the first time, the Moore's law, which states that computer power doubles every eighteen months, is no longer relevant. The bandwidth, i.e. the capacity to transmit information on the Internet network, doubles every six to nine months! That is, to benefit from the network capacities, we will not only need more powerful computers, but mainly more and more computers and servers' (Le Monde, March the 22nd, 2000).

To create the indispensable service to Internet, developers resort to Silicon Valley's start-ups such as the Inktomi company specialized in the development of tools for Internet site operators. Many firms, such as AOL, need applications of Traffic Server's type that give the possibility to store information highly required by its subscribers in servers close to Internet providers. This application gives the Internet providers a greater speed and a better quality on-line video.

2.3   The Costs of the Division of Labor

The disintegration of the innovation process amplifies the division of innovative labor and, consequently, market mediation can develop. It may concern research (pharmaceuticals) or the development and the conception of new tools (computers). The costs of division of labor may nevertheless be heavy because the user firms, according to the technological innovation type, must be able to choose and efficiently fit together several pieces of knowledge. Furthermore, more upstream factors that may intervene to thwart the disintegration process must be mentioned:

- first the cognitive aspects linked to production and utilization of knowledge must be taken into account. Users may have difficulty in admitting the utility or the superiority of a technology when it is not developed by them and strictly adapted to their needs (Arora, Fosfuri and Gambardella). In addition, even out of its context and codified, a technological knowledge must be combined to tacit knowledge of an organizational type which makes its utilization difficult;

- a contract of knowledge acquisition is often incomplete and is as such subject to important transaction costs. The make or buy static trade-off, as we said in chapter one, is inadequate on the analytical level to characterize the specialized technological assets acquisitions. In fact, firms are building core competences that they try to reinforce and extend by having recourse to intellectual assets whose costs and objective qualities (notably concerning R&D) are sometimes not well known and whose marketing potential remains uncertain. It is well-known that unlike investments in fixed capital in factories and equipment, the result of R&D is only a new knowledge 'that can have or not have a value' (Grabowski and Vernon, 2000, p.207). This remark which applies to pharmaceutical industry and more specially to biotechnology is useful to admit that an R&D contract is often a long-term recurrent transaction that can comprise significant contractual uncertainties. The re-negotiation of the contract terms, when it is scientific knowledge, is the result of cost overrun of R&D and / or the difficulty to establish with precision the services achievement dates. Difficulties may crop up concerning property rights distribution (Pisano, 1990).

It should not be forgotten that the relation between knowledge and technological application is *asymmetrical* (Guilhon, 1998). An R&D contract can create knowledge in a specific technical field and at the same time favor the development of capabilities to exploit other fields. For example, technological platforms (Kim and Kogut, 1996) represent key-knowledge that favors the development of tools enabling many directions to be exploited and giving rise to many applications. Consequently, knowledge produced very much upstream has an application field that is sometimes difficult to detail precisely. Around a technological asset is created a cognitive potential of diversification (offered technological opportunities), representations and beliefs that firms learn to exploit and that will be at the origin of a cumulative knowledge likely to give rise to many medium-term applications. The perimeter of the exploitation field depends on the accumulated in-house activities and on know-how, general and specific, that user firms will seek to acquire and protect from rival firms. This is one of the reasons why an exclusive license acquisition is often preferred to an R&D contract, i.e. to the financing of R&D expenditure of a specialized firm by a user firm.

The concept of dynamic transaction costs (Langlois, 1992) is useful to characterize relations between industrial firms and knowledge producers, notably scientific ones. If it is acknowledged that the re-negotiation of a contract's terms can give rise to opportunistic behaviors (Williamson, 1985) and if the change of supplier can be impeded by inevitable learning and experience losses that take place ('switching costs', Teece, 1988), then contractual partnership and cooperation agreements find their 'raison d'être'. In fact, transfer costs exist that could impede or delay the assimilation of new knowledge if actors remain independent (innovative division of labor). The dynamic transactions costs are admittedly negotiation costs, but they mainly represent knowledge acquisition costs (implied by the transfer of knowledge and know-how) and coordination costs. These costs could be considerable enough to block market mediation.

Two other emergence conditions remain to be analyzed whose role has been indicated by several researchers (cf. for example Athreye, 1998).

3. TECHNOLOGICAL CONVERGENCE

Technological convergence facilitates the appearance of knowledge markets. Technological convergence is the process by which the application of the same scientific concept allows the putting together of two or many fields of activity. For example, digitization caused the near-fusion of computer science and telecommunications. The resulting effects in knowledge markets affect at the same time supply and demand of knowledge.
- from a supply point of view, when activities share similar technological bases, technological knowledge might be more easily taken out of its context and it might be sold under an abstract form to expertise ends. This situation allows the supplier of knowledge to enlarge his intervention field and to reduce adaptation costs. For example, the technological knowledge on resistant materials allowed firms located in this activity to sell consulting and process design services to small firms producing steel and metals;
- from a demand point of view, when technological convergence happens on a rapid growth path, firms are confronted with the risk represented by the partial detention of knowledge capital. Two possibilities are offered to them (Dosi, Teece and Winter, 1990). It may be supposed that, with rapid learning, convergent path constraints and a narrow selection, the firms concerned will create network relations between enterprises (network firms) 'involving investments in other companies or joint learning' (p.248). With rapid learning, convergent path constrains and a narrow selection, 'opportunities appear for entrepreneurs to use contractual mechanisms to rapidly gather different capabilities oriented toward development and marketing of a specific product. We designate the corresponding entities by the term "hollow enterprises" ' (p.248).

Firms, facing the necessity to accumulate new knowledge, are confronted with the exploitation / exploration dilemma (March, 1991). The exploitation strategy is intended to improve production processes and, more largely, running routines. The exploration strategy aims to integrate external knowledge to create for oneself additional technological opportunities. If firms develop joint learning while staying independent, the diversity of specialized profiles in R&D teams will increase, but it is necessarily limited by coordination imperatives of team members. 'The observation that the ideal knowledge complemented by non-overlapping knowledge suggests an organizational trade-off between diversity and commonality across individuals' (Cohen and Levinthal, 1990, p.134).

Besides, deadlines assigned to research projects are subject to strategic considerations, temporal horizons may be more or less limited and, consequently, explored directions are more or less restrained. With regard to these considerations, knowledge markets may be used to manage convergent technological paths and to gain access to external knowledge.

4. KNOWLEDGE MARKETS MAY NOT APPEAR IF A CONTINUOUS AND MINIMAL FREQUENCY OF TRANSACTIONS DOES NOT EXIST

The standard economic approach defines the market by pre-supposing a hypothetical encounter between a supply and a demand existing before the exchange. These presuppositions enable the size of a market to be delimited and its properties to be defined in terms of static scale. The size of a market is the product of the number of participants multiplied by the number of realized transactions. Consequently, a market dynamics implies the modification of one and / or the other variable: the increase of the number of participants and the multiplication of the transactions (Athreye).

Concerning knowledge markets, one is to take into account two elements. The 'knowledge-product' may or may not exist before to the exchange. A license may exist and cause a demand, it can also be the result of a user's implication and be responsible for a dedicated service. The exchange of 'knowledge-product' implies that for such a market to be operating, it 'must be endowed with an information device' (Petit, 1999) that specifies to the interested parties the places and conditions of the supply. Compared to a competitive mechanism that uses less information than any other mechanism to realize an efficient allocation of resources (Jordan, 1982), technological assets markets use much more.

Information devices may be of varied nature. They may be *institutions* that take the form of 'distinctive service spaces' localized in information rich environments (Bryson, 1997). They are constituted of information intensive firms 'running as innovation, information and expertise transfer agents. Effectively they operate as pivotal information nodes in the global economic system' (p.11). They are the privileged places in which a 'co-present interaction' may develop, that is richer than the traditional face-to-face, and that is likely to create externalities from which firms that are localized in such environments may benefit.

Information devices can equally take the form of *codes* that emerge under the form of technical standards or management norms that channel and direct the demands in the most targeted directions. The quality norms in processes and products (ISO 9000) have favored the acquisition of services of quality control by firms that want to obtain the quality certification. Firms offering complex logistics services spread, through professional associations and specialized reviews, circulation norms of intermediary and final products between units belonging to the same enterprise and between firms and distribution networks. In other fields, specialized firms intervene as prescribers concerning the adoption of automated procedures by industrial firms. The devices that concretely organize markets indicate that a considerable amount of resources must be devoted to the acquisition of information and its analysis, thus influencing the setting of prices. These become the outcome of negotiations between firms and they cannot be conceived as anonymous signals that could be observed in an autonomous way by any economic agent.

To synthesize our thoughts, it appears that the transactions on the different knowledge markets develop according to the degree of segmentation more or less marked by the innovation process, according to the transversal nature of the application (that could be linked to the technical convergence), but also according to the obtained information on knowledge producers and their reputation. Knowledge markets not only depend on the size but also on the quality of the users. They can only develop if firms have the capability to identify and use the expertise knowledge offered by KIBSF. From this viewpoint, knowledge markets do not have only positive effects: in fact, they favor segmentation between firms. They facilitate the development and the reinforcement of the knowledge base of large enterprises, while many small and medium enterprises and very small enterprises do not feel concerned by these markets, because their organization does not allow them to manage a too important tension of knowledge.

In addition, the weakness of their technological base as regards information technologies, i.e. their 'infostructure', does not allow them to increase their connectivity and receptivity capability. We must remember that KIBSF interface activity increases the tacit knowledge and competence exchange localized between firms, i.e. their inter-connections. Moreover, each firm becomes more receptive as it can benefit in some fields from the experience of other firms.

Knowledge markets analysis poses the problem of their emergence linked with the mutation of productive organizations. Firms must adapt their structures and their organization to allow the selective intervention of experts for which large firms are better prepared than small firms. Besides, access to a deeper knowledge notably as regards R&D, is discriminating for smaller structures. In these firms, knowledge production is not linked to the existence of a formally organized R&D department. It is achieved in a very informal way by production engineers, autonomously or in relation with commercial services. The link with external service suppliers is made more difficult.

5. CONCLUSION

All things considered, compared to instrumental knowledge (specialized technological inputs) firms' strategies appear complex. Globally, being firms whose performances narrowly depend on creation and application of new knowledge, the strategy takes instrumental knowledge as its objcct, by seeking to extend and deepen it, but also to control it (Guilhon and Huard, 1996). If the priority is its extension / deepening, firms seek to increase 'direct producer goods' of knowledge by in-house R&D, training, learning, even cooperation. Previous developments lead us to admit that the strategic dimension also concerns 'indirect producer goods' held by specialized firms (cognitive division of labor) and activated by autonomous behaviors of these firms and by demands emanating from users. Knowledge enable technological complexity to be managed, to create for oneself technological opportunities and to adopt new management norms conveyed by specialized firms.

Markets can equally be used by customers to master the creation of pertinent knowledge in relation to the organizational tasks they fix themselves: to increase the efficiency of production, create new products, and conquer new markets. This strategy refers back to two fundamental questions: the role of information technologies because they restrict the demand regime; the question of property and of protection of knowledge, from the producer's as well as from the user's point of view.

NOTES

[1] For example, Ringe (1992) excludes 'testing houses' in his definition of contract R&D, stating that testing and accreditation, are too routine an activity to be included in the process of research and development. However, 'testing houses' do increasingly undertake certain applied development work. There are, therefore, a wide range of organizations and activities which are on the fringes of contract research and technical activity where contract work may not represent their central activity is still an important element of their work and which should not be excluded from a comprehensive study of the CRT market. Individually such organizations may not be key actors in the CRT industry, but cumulatively they can have a significant impact on the whole sector" (Howells, p.4). CRT: Contract Research and Technology.

[2] Consulting firms must equally be mentioned insofar as that available abstract knowledge for many applications could be put in evidence in the development, the conception, engineering, but also in logistics services and distribution networks of products.

[3] As noted by PISANO, the acquired knowledge in the production stage before mass production remains difficult to comprehend, and does not enable the deduction of what the performances will be in full-scale production.

REFERENCES

Aldrich H, Mueller S. The evolution of organizational forms : technology, coordination and control. Research in Organizational Behavior 1982; 4:33-87.

Antonelli, Cristiano, *The Microdynamics of Technical Knowledge*. Routledge, London, 1999.

Arora A, Fosfuri A, Gambardella A. Markets for technology (why do we see them, why don't we see more of them and why we should care). Working paper 99-17, Universidad Carlos III de Madrid, 1999.

Arora A, Gambardella A. The changing technology of technological change : general and abstract knowledge and the division of innovative labour. Research Policy 1994; 23:523-32.

Arrow, Kenneth. "Economic Welfare and the allocation of ressources for innovation." In *The Rate and Direction of Inventive Activity*, R Nelson, ed. Princeton Univesity Press : Princeton, NJ, 1962.

Athreye S. On markets in knowledge. Working Paper Series, WP 83, ESRC, University of Cambridge, 1998.

Audretsch DB, Stephan P. How and why does knowledge spill over ? the case of biotechnology. Discussion Paper n°1991, CEPR, 1998.

Bryson JR. Business service firms, service space and the management of change. Working Paper Series, WP 62, ESRC, University of Cambridge, 1997.

Cohen WM, Klepper S. Firm size and the nature of innovation within industries: the case of process and product R&D. The Review of Economics and Statistics 1996; 78:232-43.

Cohen WM, Levinthal DA. Absorptive capacity : a new perspective on learning and innovation. Administrative Science Quarterly, 1990; 35:128-52.

Dasgupta D, David P. Towards a new economics of science. Research Policy 1994; 23:487-521.

Dosi G, Teece DJ, Winter SG. Les frontières des entreprises : vers une théorie de la cohérence de la grande entreprise. Revue d'Economie Industrielle 1990; 51:238-54.

Dosi G. Sources, procedures and microeconomic effects of innovation. Journal of Economic literature 1988; XXXI:1120-71.

Gabrowski H, Vernon J. The determinants of pharmaceutical research and development expenditures. Journal of Evolutionary Economics 2000; 10:201-15.

Gibbons, Michael et al. The New Production of Knowledge : the Dynamics of Science and Research in Contemporary Societies. Thousand oaks: Sage publication, London, 1994.

Granstrand O, Patel P, Pavitt K. Multi-technology corporations : why they have "distributed" rather than "distinctive core" competencies. California Management Review 1997; 39:8-25.

Guilhon B, Huard P. Economie de la connaissance et organisation : quelques perspectives. Document de Travail, CEFI, n° 17, 1996.

Guilhon, Bernard. "Les théories économiques de l'innovation." In *Dix Ans d'avancées en Economie de la Santé*, Saillly JC, Lebrun T, eds, John Libbey EUROTEXT, 1997.

Guilhon, Bernard. "The dynamics of knowledge in the pharmaceutical industry. A microeconomic illustration." Paper to the Druid conference on *National Innovation systems, Industrial Dynamics and Innovation policy* 1999, June 9-12 ; Rebild / Denmark.

Howells J. Research and development externalisation, outsourcing and contract research. Paper presented at the collaboration & competition in R&D and Innovation Programs: Lessons for the Public and Business Sectors'Conference, Judge Institute of management Studies ; Cambridge 1997; 9-11 June.

Jordan JS. The competitive allocation process is informationally efficient uniquely. Journal of Economic Theory 1982; 28:1-8.

Kim DJ, Kogut B. Technological platforms and diversification. Organization Science 1996; 7:283-301.

Klevorick AK, Levin RC, Nelson RR, Winter SG. On the sources and significance of interindustry differences in technological opportunities. Research Policy 1995; 24:185-205.

Langlois RN. Transaction-cost economics in real time. Industrial and Corporate Change, 1992; 22:99-127.

Malerba F, Orsenigo L. Technological regimes and firm behavior. Industrial and Corporate Change 1993; 2:45-71.

March JG. Exploration and exploitation in organizational learning. Organization Science 1991; 2:71-87.

Mintzberg, Henry, *Le Management : Voyage au Centre des Organisations.* Paris: les Editions d'Organisation, 1990.

Mowery DC. The changing structure of the US national innovation system: implications for international conflict and cooperation in R&D policy 1998 ; 27:639-54.

Nelson RR, Wolff EN. Factors behind cross-industry differences in technical progress. Structural Change and Economic Dynamics 1997; 8:205-20.

Nelson, Richard R, and Sidney G Winter, *An Evolutionnary Theory of Economic Change.* The Belknap Press of Harvard University Press, Cambridge, Massachussetts, and London, England, 1982.

Patel P, Pavitt K. The technological competencies of the world's largest firms :complex and path dependent, but not much variety. Research policy 1997; 26:141-56.

Petit P. "L'Economie de l'Information à la Lumière des Théories de l'Information: Eléments pour une Première Synthèse des Travaux du Séminaire CGP." Séminaire *Economie de l'Information,* Commissariat Général du Plan, 1996, 18 juin, Paris.

Pisano GP. The R&D boundaries of the firm : an empirical analysis. Administrative Science Quarterly 1990; 35:153-76.

Pisano, Gary P, *The Development Factory. Unlocking the Potential of Process Innovation.* Havard Business School Press: Boston, Massachusetts, 1997.

Senker J. Tacit knowledge and models of innovation. Industrial and Corporate Change, 1995;4 : 425-47.

Teece, David J. "Technological Change and the Nature of the Firm." In *Technical Change and Economic Theory*, Dosi G, Freeman C, Nelson R, Silverberg G, and Soete L. Pinter Publishers, London and New-York, 1988.

Thomke SH. Simulation, learning and R&D performance : evidence from the automotive development. Research Policy 1998; 27:55-74.

Williamson, Oliver, *The Economic Institutions of Capitalism.* New-York: Free Press, 1985.

Wright, Richard W. "The role of imitable vs inimitable competences in the evolution of the semi-conductor industry." In *Dynamics of Competence-Based Competition*, R, Sanchez, A Heene, H. Thomas, eds., Oxford, New-York: Pergamon, 1996.

Zucker LG, Darby MR. Capturing technological opportunity via Japan's star scientists : evidence from Japanese firm's biotech patents and products. Working Paper Series n°6360, NBER, 1998.

Chapter 3

THE WORKING OF MARKETS
FOR KNOWLEDGE

Bernard Guilhon
CEFI-CNRS, Aix-en-Provence, Université de la Méditerranée, France

The first two chapters' aim was to define knowledge markets compared to transactions on specialized technological assets and to analyze the factors favoring the appearance of these markets. We must now pose the problem of the running of these markets, i.e. their consolidation. Therefore we would be advised to question ourselves on the devices that favor the market circulation of knowledge in the economic system.

One of the hypotheses of our research is the increased complexity of the knowledge base of industrial firms which, by becoming multi-technological, seek to increase their technological resources. At the same time, we have advanced the idea of a specialized organization of knowledge production that takes on an original form in this contemporary period. Specialization leads us to acknowledge the existence of two fundamental modalities of the labor division (Pavitt, 1998):
- a cognitive division of labor in the production of knowledge that can be located by the multiplication of technological specialized fields and bodies of knowledge attached to them;
- a functional division of the firm resting on cognitive division. Referring to Nelson's research, Pavitt identifies first the technological competences in specific fields materialized by technical personnel qualifications, number of patents and publications in these fields. Technological competences are at the origin of fundamental concepts that represent, according to us, a knowledge that could be capitalized and contextual (for example, the properties of pharmaceutical or chemical molecules). This knowledge possesses at the present time strong abstraction and codification properties: consequently, embodied knowledge in individuals is relatively immobile, whereas disembodied knowledge may more easily circulate. Secondly, the firm is a depository of practical technical knowledge that renders operational fundamental concepts and translates them into commercial applications.

The link between these two forms of labor division poses an essential question. Must we view the firm organized as a closed system or enclosed one, or must we view it as an open and socialized structure? (Azoulay and Weinstein, 2000). These two authors acknowledge that the firm is in fact characterized by learning processes and competences that are specific to it, but that it is also subject to institutional and social determinants that 'decompartmentalize' it in a way. As far as we are concerned, it inserts itself equally in an industrial organization of knowledge production. It is a difficult problem to understand where are the interfaces between inside knowledge and outside knowledge (Pavitt, 1998) and the second part of this book will tackle this question.

Knowledge is the central capital of the firm. If the first role of the firm is to integrate knowledge in view to use it (Grant, 1996b) and if integration of knowledge is an element of the absorptive capacity (Van den Bosch, Volberda and de Boer, 1999), one is to admit that knowledge production is not uniquely regulated by internal actors of the firm. The reason is simple: the capital-knowledge possesses specific depreciation, obsolescence, accumulation and appropriation properties. One of the questions that concerns us is the following: to accumulate knowledge, does one need to produce it oneself? Or must we rely upon externalities' dynamics as in the industrial variety model? Competitive pressures force firms to redesign their frontier along narrower activity spheres, but by expanding their technological resources (Patel and Pavitt; Gambardella and Torrisi). In this context, strategic alliances and the market deserve the same analytical interest (Whittington et al., 1999).

The market mediation in knowledge production is justified, on a theoretical level, by the fact that the firm is embedded in a larger 'activity system' called market and by the fact that markets evolve also along historic and technological trajectories (Spender, 1996). As such, one is to consider the firm and the market as linked elements inside a more general economic mechanism that leads us to analyze their interactions and their complementarities. These phenomena can be considered on two levels. First, when the market learns, vertical disintegration of firms accelerates. Secondly, 'organization by firm is reducing variety. The great power of the market is not only its information properties, but also its function as a generator of variety in innovations and capabilities that are subject to selection. The «market», as an assemblage of firms pursuing different visions and organized by distinct identities, generates a variety that individual firms cannot manufacture internally without decrement to division of labor and the salience of focal rules, i.e., to the organizing principles (...) by which work is coordinated' (Kogut, 2000, p.408).

To go in this direction, we will study the devices that ensure the running of knowledge markets. We will retain two of them:

- a technological device, information technologies, that offers the potentiality of multiplying transaction possibilities and of reducing costs;
- an institutional device that exercises its influence, through innovation and production systems or, more restrictively, through intellectual property rights.

In a third step, we will seek to evaluate the differentiated running of knowledge markets by country and by size of firms, starting from empirical evaluations.

1. INFORMATION TECHNOLOGIES

The influence of information technologies is difficult to delimit because they affect at the same time the form and the object of transactions.

First, they constitute a technical support allowing multiplying and coordinating transactions. They increase the transaction possibilities by introducing reinforced competitive services. These technologies modify information flows by provoking information costs decrease and a coordination improvement. In this perspective, information is said, 'to adjust' (Paulré, 1998) and the resulting consequences are the reduction of informational asymmetries and the more competitive running of the markets. If this proposition is incontestable, it is nevertheless far from characterizing all the markets (Petit).

Second, information technologies affect the object of the transaction itself. For example, computerized databases contribute to knowledge production and their accumulation. In biotechnology, the technical ways of sequencing and of treatment of bio-computerized data have led some firms to specialize in the building of databases, the scientific and technical information becoming the principal object of their commercial activity (Orsi et al., 2000). In this perspective, information technologies are narrowly linked to the nature of technological knowledge that is a 'systemic activity' (Antonelli, forthcoming) i.e. which is made to construct and modify, because it is composed of specialized components, which could be combined and capitalized.

These two aspects of form and object are narrowly interwoven when one seeks to evaluate the running of information technologies on the knowledge market.

A remarkable property is ascribed to these technologies: they enable to increase separability, exchangeability, divisibility and transportability of information (Antonelli, 1999). They offer new organizational possibilities inside and between firms that result in the following two observations.

1.1   Knowledge Codification

Codification enables knowledge supply to be separated from the know-how that created it. In this 'passage from informal to formal, information technologies constitute a learning task support, of relations or knowledge that lead to the codification of information (Caby et al., 1999, p.162). Tacit knowledge, let us recall, is constituted of two elements: the knowledge used or embodied and the knowledge not yet embodied and which is linked to imagination, to intuition, to beliefs and to values. Knowledge-in-use exceeds know-what to include know-how (i.e. the ability to do something), and know-why that is rarely established in totality due to the imperfect understanding of underlying cause to effect relations. It is the relation between a fact, a doing capability, and the highlighting of causality links, that could be clarified by expert-systems and computerized databases. Consequently, codification concerns only a part of tacit knowledge (Lundvall, 1999).

This restriction being made, questions must be asked about codified knowledge production. Codification cannot be reduced to a modification of the form under which knowledge is presented, 'it interferes and transforms «prior» knowledge' (Paulré, p.18). It enables initial knowledge to be readjusted, to be enriched and systematized, making it an available resource for building. Codification is a specific investment to give knowledge an appropriate productive form. 'Computerization can be applied to knowledge: through the constitution of computerized databases, the enterprise can systematize knowledge accumulation... .' on operating modes, of products characteristics or else research processes (Caby et al., p.138).

Therefore, knowledge and know-how codification offer possibilities in terms of new professions. Firms develop resources and know-how that become exchangeable. Parting from an EDI linkage between an automobile producer, suppliers and dealers, complex logistics services concepts may be elaborated to better coordinate the upward information circulation and the downward products circulation. This can also concern the sale of engineering services, of access services to computerized databases or else of know-how marketing acquired by the building of a computer system (this is the case, for example, of software sold by airline companies).

1.2   The Specific Market Interaction Mode

'On-line' interaction between producers and users of knowledge constitutes a specific market interaction mode. Electronic mail service and information exchange favor the setting-up of dialogues based on questions / answers modes. The issue is not negligible: an uncoupling take place between scientific and technological knowledge production and their accumulation by firms. This moves away from the narrow integration diagram that linked together knowledge production and their accumulation inside firms. 'The corporate organization of the production of knowledge is shifting away the «intramuros» model upon well specified and self-contained research and development activities. A variety of tools are nowadays used by corporations to take advantage of external knowledge and minimize the tragedies of intellectual enclosures' (Antonelli, forthcoming).

To communicate, communication codes must be established. They are of two types:
- codes that use appropriate and sophisticated technical languages to facilitate exchanges between partners and block the disclosure of information;
- codes that organizations develop to increase the running efficiency of information channels (Arrow, 1974). Codes of this type are often implicit and they represent an accumulation of 'irreversible' capital for an organization. These codes favor the implementation of a 'non-structured, non-systematized, generally verbal' dialogue (Monteverde, 1995, p. 1629) and that demands a face-to-face communication. Organizational codes are, consequently, difficult to establish between independent firms. 'Where unstructured technical dialog is necessarily high, communication in firm-specific dialect should be particularly efficient' (p.1629). As such, the firms' boundaries according to this author correspond to transactions that have a particularly rich non-structured content.

It is possible to put this point of view into perspective by indicating that a knowledge contract is an expertise contract. That is to say that the object of the contract is relatively well established (to achieve a determined result), but the activities that it implies are complex and difficult to describe. In this context, information technologies make possible this exchange by facilitating the building of 'technical grammar' (Argyres, 1999) between independent entities. 'One can interpret the technical grammar... As precisely a system of communication codes useful for transmitting informal and partly tacit knowledge from one engineer to another....' (p.171). The exchange between independent firms becomes possible: communication is favored by the definition of rules to manipulate and make the syntax of used terms. From this viewpoint, information technologies create an obstacle to the expropriation of the knowledge producer and they as such limit opportunistic behavior[1].

Besides, communication codes used create irreversibility phenomena insofar as exchangers progressively improve knowledge by spreading them and / or by deepening them in a constructed technical language. The message quality is improved by the recourse to common research standards and to evaluation protocols. Thanks to information technologies, user firms have access to know-how and, indirectly, to producers' competences. So, it is the content of the transaction that is affected by information technologies. The embeddedness of know-how in software capable of executing a procedure and to facilitate its comprehension leads to the idea that 'competence materialize as it were' and this materialization enables competence to be 'duplicated' and sold (Brousseau, 1993, p.207)[2].

In this way, KIBSF transfer codified knowledge that will be converted into localized competences by user firms. Codified knowledge thus transmitted is put into relation with explicit existing knowledge (process of combination and capitalization) and is progressively, with tacit and implicit knowledge, embedded in working teams and organizational routines. More generally, information technologies enable diverse and fragmented forms of complementary and localized knowledge to be mobilized and integrated (Cohendet et al., 1999).

1.3   The Consequences of the Analysis

From this analysis follow several remarks.

First, an organizational design can be characterized starting from coordination modes of activities or starting from integration mechanisms of economic agents' actions (Langlois and Robertson, 1995). If one chooses the second possibility, the organization of knowledge production is analyzed according to two dimensions: ownership and coordination. If the activities of knowledge production are integrated within the firm, one will say that the ownership dimension is predominant[3]. On the other hand, if the technological assets are the product of an in-house activity and a contractual activity resting on the market and / or on cooperation, it is the coordination dimension that becomes predominant. It is possible to characterize the steps that have marked out the knowledge production organization by using these two dimensions. The two integration mechanisms – ownership and coordination – present the advantage of being at the same time separable and combined according to these authors. This signifies that knowledge production may be in part realized inside the firm while at the same time, diverse contractual agreements and market relations allow to access to complementary knowledge. Each case designates a particular mode of organizing knowledge production and must be *interpreted ceteris paribus*.

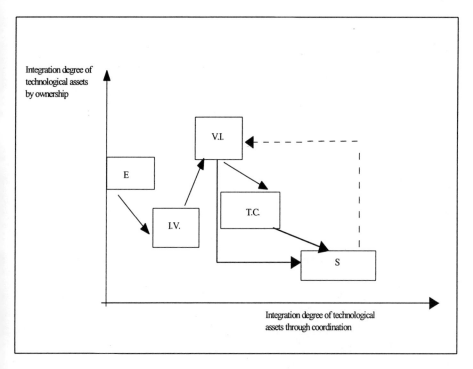

Figure 5: The management of knowledge by firms.

E = Entrepreneurship
I.V. = Institutional variety
V.I. = Vertical Integration
T.C. = Technological Cooperation
S = Specialization

An organizational trajectory is drawn from the characterized entrepreneurship situation by the full ownership of technological assets that merge with physical assets and that in the 19th century required a weak coordination. The institutional variety corresponds to a clear sharing of 'attributions': to universities basic knowledge, and to industrial firms technological applications. Externalities' dynamics that underlines this organization mode demands a higher degree of coordination, as one is to interweave different pieces of knowledge. With vertical integration, R&D and design activities are developed and articulated in-house, firms spreading their activities to the production of basic knowledge.

Technological cooperation is a modality of commitment of previously constituted intellectual assets and of creation of technological assets produced in common with two or more firms, which increases the degree of coordination. Finally, specialization accentuates the combination between internal knowledge and external knowledge. It expresses the fact that 'knowledge is costly to produce, maintain and use' (Demsetz, 1991, p.171).

Knowledge management is characterized by a strong intensity of required coordination, according to this author, by the fact that market exchange of knowledge necessitates interface services (p.174).

Information technologies, as we have seen, improve coordination possibilities and favor knowledge combination. Consequently, what is important is not so much the development of market links as the form taken by those links and their signification from the point of view of vertical disintegration possibilities and of knowledge production[4]. The access to producer knowledge base and the development of customized transactions play an essential role.

Some points can be made about the interpretation of figure 5. First, it is not a linear organizational trajectory insofar as organization codes can coexist. Secondly, vertical integration can evolve directly toward the specialization without passing through technological cooperation. Empirical studies on European firms rather indicate that outsourcing and long-term strategic alliance formation increased in the same proportions (+ 65%) over the 1992-1996 period (Whittington et al.). Besides, the feedback line going from specialization toward technological cooperation means that technological assets acquired by the market can put a firm in a favorable situation to conclude an R&D agreement with another firm. The cooperation object can be different and can be realized by an agreement oriented toward commercial applications of knowledge acquired, in part, by the market (co-production agreement).

If the relations between producers and users are established in time, which is often the case for R&D and design activities and which is not for when there is acquisition of license to use a brand name, we have to deal with something more complex than the buying of a material component for the production. In fact, a learning of cognitive nature on tools and techniques is doubled by a relational learning between the two firms.

At the risk of irritating certain researchers, we might try to transpose the Argyris and Schön thesis (1978) that identifies two possible anchorage places from learning outcomes: the espoused theory and the theory-in-use. The espoused theory is the theory advanced to explain and justify a certain action mode. The theory-in-use includes procedures, operating modes, but also the set of know-how. We can say that knowledge acquisition that brings into play two entities favors in time a process of learning in simple loop by allowing espoused theory to coincide with theory-in-use, i.e. an expected 'collaboration' and an effective 'collaboration'. Of course, it must be collaboration in time, which excludes knowledge immediately usable and ready-to-use, for example a special knowledge embedded in a program.

Secondly, information technologies pose the problem of costs that could be considered in two ways:
- reciprocal investigation and communication costs will be diminished in cases where the two partners have a well understood interest to achieve this

objective, i.e. it is in their interest to improve the productivity of their relation (Brousseau). Generally, recurrent exchanges favor costs decrease, which is the case of dedicated technological assets that represent different applications of the same knowledge;

- knowledge absorption costs will probably be reduced. In fact, if the providers of knowledge are in competition on well identified market segments, there results an acceleration of the codification of knowledge and a decrease in the costs as compared to a narrow integrated diagram of R&D and design activities inside firms. Absorption costs may be limited to another viewpoint. Competitors might benefit from advice and orientations supplied by KIBSF. The Cohen and Levinthal model might be as such enriched. The concept of absorptive capacity does not indicate in which way firms will select research directions that will influence their capacity to learn. To make up for this shortcoming, the idea can be put forward that some knowledge 'persists long enough to be recognized and exploited' by other firms (Steinmuller, 1995). In this context of knowledge markets, KIBSF not only play a particular role of connection agents by specializing in knowledge transfer from universities toward industrial firms (see Autio diagram). Equally, they direct the absorption capacity of firms by 'guiding' them toward technological developments that appear to be the more promising. A knowledge-based economy tends to multiply intermediation forms.

Nevertheless, knowledge fragmentation poses acute problems to firms. First, complex and modular products often include multiple systems, sub-systems and components. Intellectual assets may correspond to important technological progress and be the place where the added value tends to be localized. A firm holding a patent on a strategic intermediary asset may have a 'hold-up' behavior by trying to capture for its profit a large part of the added value of the innovation (Arora, Fosfuri and Gambardella). Besides, if information technologies improve the coordination between a producer and a user of knowledge, coordination costs of several pieces of knowledge may be increased. Along the same line, if knowledge is held by a multiplicity of different agents, this means that the final user runs the risk of bearing extensive transaction costs to gather all utilization rights of technological knowledge. This is what leads us to analyze institutional devices.

2. INSTITUTIONAL DEVICES

The influence of institutional devices may be spotted at several levels: that of institutional architecture of economies and that, more restricted, of intellectual property regimes.

2.1   The Institutional Structure

Production and acquisition knowledge strategies require specific configurations of institutional arrangements. The notion of national system of innovation (Lundvall, 1992) refers to the existence of diverse actors (firms, technological institutes, universities, training systems, venture capital) whose interrelations constitute a context which directs and channels as it were the production of new knowledge. 'The specificity of knowledge production reflect unique combinations of technological specialization and institutional structures' (Lundvall, 1999, p.12). This is to say that *institutional architecture* of economies lights up the paths of knowledge development and the specialization processes that result from it.

The radical innovation / incremental innovation couple thus becomes decisive in characterizing *comparative institutional advantages* (Hancké, 1999). Radical innovation is synonymous of breakdown (in terms of products, processes and organizations) in relation to accumulated experiences and existing knowledge. The production of new knowledge and the emergence of new activities require *deregulated* labor markets, a strong mobility of the qualified labor force, substantial rewards attributed to inventors and innovators and a capital market open enough so that venture capital have free access to it.

An institutional architecture of this type is in phase with particularly active knowledge markets. It multiplies the places of creation of scientific and technologic knowledge, it favors mobility of persons between firms or else from universities to firms, it valorizes the creation of new firms and facilitates the access to funding sources. Besides, in science-based sectors the constant technological renewals imply deep reorganizations of R&D laboratories. For example in biotechnology, one is to meet particularly high R&D costs (knowledge intensity) and substantial commercial risks. Structured knowledge markets find their justification in this institutional architecture because they favor the firms' *exploration strategies*. This characterization corresponds to '«liberal» market economies of the Anglo-Saxon type' (Hancké, p.2).

The analysis that has just been made is directly in phase with the notion of *innovation and production system* (Amable, Barré and Boyer, 1997). These authors use descriptors (economic-industry, technology, science, human resources, financial system) that enable the market system to be characterized (USA, U.K., Canada). Framed by a strict definition of property rights, the market logic is diffused along the whole chain that starts from basic research to the creation of new firms, by putting in competition universities, laboratories and research centers, products, processes, organizations, and by supplying required resources to the funding of radical innovations thanks to the existence of sophisticated financial markets.

These propositions differ from observations resulting from approaches taken in terms of institutional dimensions and management practices (Lewin, Long and Carroll, 1999) which consider, among other things, that US capitalism favors short-term orientations and adaptations by exploitation. The running of financial market is assessed only in turns of the mergers and acquisitions they enable to be realized, a proposition which seems too restrictive.

If we formulate the hypothesis that industrialized countries are at the *technological frontier*, i.e. they no longer dispose of technological reserves, on which it is possible to draw (catching up situations), the market logic plays a significant role in allowing an economy to create new knowledge, prepare new technologies and create productivity gains (Guellec, 1998). In this context, entrepreneurial initiative and competition constitute privileged vectors. The market creates information on the technological ways that could be efficient and profitable and it favors the dispersed creation of explicit knowledge by prospector agents who will progressively explore a whole set of potentialities. Three conditions are required so that processes converge: market and competition must function well, (no entry barriers and no private and public monopolies), the financial system must favor innovation and risk-taking by newcomers, and external frontiers must be opened to allow firms to capitalize and to develop their technological capabilities by having access to larger markets allowing R&D costs to be spread.

Conversely, incremental innovation rests on a cumulative knowledge that does not improve existing products and processes. In Germany, the production of new knowledge remains conditioned by new long-term labor contracts, well-established educative and professional trajectories, stabilized research teams inside firms, wage negotiation systems to the scale of the branch aiming to homogenize rather than differentiate. Training is ensured thanks to relations between firms and capital suppliers, established in time. Knowledge production leads to a technological specialization in terms of patents which is the inverse image of the technological specialization of the USA. The outcome is that cumulative knowledge is produced inside firms. 'Long-term contracts,..., provide the human resources conditions for cumulative knowledge, while the relative lack of venture capital does not pose problems for financing research into new products' (Hancké, p.3)[5].

This does not means that knowledge markets do not exist in Germany. They simply fill a different function that could to a large extent be attributed to the socio-institutional context. Insofar as the qualified labor market is not organized to allow individual mobility between organizations, engineers will consider that it is more important to belong to a firm than to leave it for an already existing start-up or one in the making. These macro-institutional aspects may be observed at a finer level: that of regional work markets and networks differentiated organizations that underpin them inside market economies (Silicon Valley vs Route 128, Kogut).

While in the market system knowledge markets have primarily an exploration function, they realize slower and more coordinated changes in the system qualified as 'European integration' (Amable, Barré and Boyer). That is, they contribute to give more flexibility and adaptation capability to innovation potentials constituted by R&D, design and manufacturing activities, which are strongly structured and articulated inside large firms.

This framework can be transposed, *mutatis mutandis*, to characterize differentiated behaviors of US and Japanese firms. Two split lines clearly appear in the semiconductors industry (West, 2000). First, knowledge bases appear deeper and more structured and make development the key-step in American firms (the process yield reaches almost 60% at the end of the development stage). This role is devoted to manufacturing in Japanese firms, the process yield reaching only 16% at development end (learning by doing is preponderant). Besides, American firms present more numerous interfaces with external knowledge sources: more widespread research (universities, specialized organizations, research consortiums) and a particularly dynamic labor market. 'US employees are only partially integrated into their firms. They are integrated also in a professional or scientific community, and an associated distinctive labor market that assigns a specific market value to their skills' (p.356)[6].

2.2   Knowledge Protection Forms

Production of new knowledge is a source of externalities. If knowledge is not appropriable, i.e. if knowledge is a non-rival and non-exclusive commodity (technological knowledge is then reduced to information from which all firms can benefit), the outcome is an over-use of this knowledge that impedes its improvement and development (Maskus, 1998). The value of this knowledge is lessened, which could lead to behavior limiting the production of new knowledge, for example under-investments in R&D behavior. The 'congestion problem' (p.188) is combined with an additional difficulty due to the fact that social value may differ from private knowledge value, due to insufficient institutional devices allowing firms to capture the totality of social gains coming from their activity.

In this perspective, the patent represents a property right on an invention. This is the case particularly for new technological functions embedded in products because their distinctive features are easier to define than processes innovations (Levin et al., 1987). New or improved products are likely to cause an accelerated and discontinuous growth of production. Market positions, when firms' productive capabilities are in a position to respond to an increasing demand, are principally defended by patents that confer to a producer the right to forbid other producers and for a determined period, to manufacture, sell or use the described product without authorization. The new knowledge – characteristics that a patent must satisfy are newness, the non-evident character and industrial utility – can be transferred via licensing (exclusive or not) along with more or less considerable fees.

In technological intensive industries, this is a powerful way to create revenues and it enables the use of a technology as substitute to production increase to be rapidly diffused (Cohen and Klepper). The two aspects, revenues creation and substitution effect, characterize clearly enough the behavior of some firms producing semiconductors (Grindley and Teece, 1997). This expresses a clear evolution of firms' behavior. The idea of privative rights on an innovation transforms the strategic stakes: it is a matter of exploiting market positions by elaborating a domination and diffusion strategy. Whereas for Schumpeter, giant enterprise is the driving force to technical progress and size is considered as the key element of the appropriation.

The links between intellectual property rights and novelty creation nevertheless deserve to be specified:
- patents serve more to measure invention activity than concretely realized innovation. Links between patents and market are frail as some European inquiries indicate that only 20% of patents are exploited, the other 80% are explained by defensive considerations. 'When a company has an important technological advance it may attempt to patent around it to obtain «defensive patents» on the periphery of the advance... Important innovations are often represented by a cluster of patents and not just a single patent' (Wright, p.335);
- patents constitute only one of the knowledge protection elements among which one notes secrecy, temporal advantages or else technical complexity in sectors producing complex products difficult to copy and that rest on high investment costs and expertise levels (Arundel and Kabla)[7];
- patents only approximately measure knowledge appropriability. This would be more correctly estimated by the time taken by a competitor to duplicate a patented product innovation. This time could be inferior to that of the legal period defined by the patent (generally 20 years). This leads to the idea that patents are not destined to protect new knowledge, but rather their embeddedness in new products or new industrial processes.

Problems linked with the running of knowledge markets are different. Knowledge can only be bought or sold if it is protected. If intellectual property rights are not firmly established and if confidence in non-disclosure agreements is lacking, transactions could be hampered due to the perceived risks. When intellectual property is bought and sold in the form of licenses by example, the object of the transaction is a 'bundle of rights' (Teece, 1998): for the seller, the knowledge value is narrowly linked to the definition of its property right, to the capacity to have utilization restrictions respected and to evaluate and collect royalties.

Starting from here, very specific problems arise particularly because new forms of creative activity do not correspond properly to established protection forms. Everybody agrees to acknowledge that 'the patent protects property rights on a way of making (whereas) copyright protect the expression of an idea rather than the idea itself' (Amable, Barré and Boyer, p.21). In that case, considering that computer software includes elements that concern at the same time expression and industrial utility, does it concern a copyright or a patent protection? Along the same line, Maskus mentions some aspects of semiconductor chip design for which specific hybrid forms 'sui generis protection' were constituted (p.190). One can equally note that, as far as software is concerned, the copyright protection is combined to the existence of costs that must be incurred to modify exploitation systems and to compatibility problems. One then can ask oneself if the economic content of a patent corresponds really to an invention activity. For example, intellectual property rights may protect genes as soon as their therapeutic function is identified. But is it an *invention* or the *discovery* of an information whose existence is not imputable to the activity of a scientific team? One observes that private ownership is not limited to the application of scientific knowledge progress. From now on it concerns 'the source' of knowledge itself, liable to give birth to industrial developments.

These arguments can lead to the consideration that intellectual assets have specific characteristics that render market exchange difficult. This is what the table 4 significantly expresses.

Table 4. Inherent tradability of different assets

Characteristics	Know-How/IP	Physical Commodities
1. Recognition of trading opportunities	Inherent difficulty	Posting frequent
2. Disclosure of attributes	Relatively difficult	Relatively easy
3. Property rights	Limited (patents, trade secrets, copyright, etc.)	Broad
4. Item of Sale	License	Measurable units
5. Variety	Heterogeneous	Homogeneous
6. Unit of consumption	Often Unclear	Weight, volume, etc.
Inherent Tradability	Low	High

Source: Teece, 1998, p.68

Let us comment on the different rubrics:
- recognition of trading opportunities. Undeniably regarding to software secret attitudes exist, for example concerning the access to code source. It might be objected that all firms do not adopt the same attitude (see for example Linux). Besides, generally, the multiplication of «Distinctive Services Spaces» progressively informs on the quality of knowledge producers and on their reputation;

- disclosure of performance features. Knowledge producers may be reluctant to exchange because of knowledge dissemination risks, which are not easily controllable. Nevertheless, this objection could be partly removed if one admits the idiosyncratic mode of market interaction (building of a dedicated service) and if the definition of suited communication codes strongly diminishes the probability of opportunistic behaviors;
- uncertain legal rights. The argument is not easily questionable. It is evident that a weak definition of property rights along with a relative confidence in non-disclosure agreements is an obstacle to market exchange;
- item of sale. In the case of knowledge, one does not sell a commodity but a know-how or a 'knowledge-product'. When it is an R&D contract, the enterprise that buys a result wants to acquire the general and specific know-how linked to a project. But this know-how may be inextricably linked to know-how developed by other projects. The 'imputation problem' is such that it is difficult to agree on 'who owns what' (Pisano, 1990). It becomes evident that confidence in a partner and in the legal system becomes crucial;
- variety. The intellectual property is by definition extremely 'variegated' (Teece, p.69), which might complicate evaluation difficulties and impede the running of markets. Besides, supplementary difficulties reside in the proliferation of property rights that concern more and more tenuous elements or fragments of knowledge. To avoid high transaction costs linked to the creation of a patent portfolio, several solutions are conceivable: cross licensing agreements and / or the constitution of a patent pool (Arora, Fosfuri and Gambardella)[8];
- unit of consumption. Must royalties concern the component value or the value of the system in which it is embedded? If knowledge is a systemic activity, it only has value in narrow interaction with other assets. On the other hand, one might admit that income sharing will depend on the scarcity of technological assets (because it constitutes a 'bottleneck technology') and rules that define relations between firms (Kogut, p.418). In microprocessors, technologies sharing coexists with a control on 'bottleneck technologies', knowledge markets enable the entry of new firms to be stimulated by selling licenses, which limits the risks of monopoly position. In the pharmaceutical industry, property rights firmly established and the absence of bottleneck technology lead to durable relations between biotechnological firms and pharmaceutical firms constituted from research programs (see, chapter 2, The Glaxo Wellcome case).

These remarks bring us to formulate three ideas. First, some researchers consider that intellectual assets have properties such that knowledge markets cannot develop. In this perspective, firms to protect themselves will choose to exert their property rights in an anti-competitive way by reducing the diffusion of technological knowledge and by increasing the prices and the royalties to pay for licenses. This is a static position that does not correspond to the idea that knowledge is a systemic activity, which is subject to expansion processes, capitalization, deepening and recombination. In the context of specialization, one must admit that markets (which are not pure markets) may learn (Langlois, 1992; Kogut) and they actively participate in the permanent reconstitution movement of the knowledge capital of different industries.

Secondly, adopted attitudes depend on properties that one attributes to knowledge. If one considers that technological knowledge is not easily transferable, it is normal to maintain that patents and licenses are imperfect ways of knowledge protection. This is the basis of the evolutionist approach which collides with the following difficulty: to reintroduce the patent into the analysis, one is to admit that knowledge has an exogenous character, that some technological assets are directly evaluated by the market and that organization is not uniquely defined in relation to performances.

Lastly, and more generally, the analysis of knowledge markets emphasizes the equivalent of a paradox. First, information technologies improve markets' efficiency, that of technology as well as that of products, and favor knowledge transformation in commercial applications. In this perspective, information technologies impose constraints on the system, i.e. for a firm the cost of being late becomes greater. Second, part of the patented knowledge has an exploratory character and, if used with precipitation, it may create the destruction of capitalized values by firms downstream from the value chain (markets knowledge, commercial practices, network economies,...). Firms, in knowledge intensive sectors, must constantly manage the trade-off between new knowledge acquisition and commercial application.

3. KNOWLEDGE MARKET RUNNING: SOME QUANTITATIVE REFERENCE MARKS

The evaluation statistics of knowledge markets are either not very abundant or are of a more general nature. Being unable to check technological assets transfers taking place between domestic firms inside a country, we have first considered technological payments registered by the balance of payments. We will then try to evaluate the extent of outsourcing from diverse studies, notably those carried out by OECD.

3.1 Technological Payments as Partial Indicators of Knowledge Markets

Since 1983, international technical transfers statistics distinguish five rubrics (INPI, 1998):
- transferred amounts on the basis of a buying contract or patent cession or licenses and patents concessions;

- transferred amounts on the basis of a buying contract or brand, design and models cession or license concessions of brand, design and models;
- transferred amounts on the basis of a contract concerning operations relative to know-how or software;
- transferred amounts on the basis of 'studies expenses', i.e. studies expenses (technical and economic) and of research, engineering, buying or selling of plans;
- transferred amounts on the basis of 'technical assistance': personnel training, consulting for factories exploitation, commercial assistance, organization and management of enterprises operations, etc.

Statistics established for the EU and OECD countries (outside EU) stretch from 1981 to 1996. We have retain two countries: France and U.K., for which we have related the amounts of technological payments (T.P.) to the R&D expenses of enterprises (BERD). The existing statistics enable a more exhaustive sample to be used. We have limited, to illustrative ends, our investigations to two countries which are those for which we uses data concerning services supplied to enterprises (see, 3.2).

Table 5. Technological payments and BERD in France and United Kingdom
Ratio T.P./BERD in % 1981-1996

	U.K.	France
1981	10,5 %	14,6%
1982	-	15,1%
1983	11,6%	14,4%
1984	-	16,1%
1985	14%	15,4%
1986	11%	14,3%
1987	15%	14,6%
1988	15,2%	14,3%
1989	16,5%	13,8%
1990	18,5%	14,4%
1991	16%	13,8%
1992	19,6%	14%
1993	19,5%	13,5%
1994	22,5%	13%
1995	24,2%	13,7%
1996	24,8%	14,4%

Source: MSTI, OECD, 1998/2

The recourse to external knowledge by enterprises accelerated clearly from the end of the 80's in the UK while it represents a fairly stable proportion of the BERD in France. A priori, one can think that the UK's 'market system' favors the acquisition of knowledge produced outside more than the French economy which is more 'administered'. In fact, these figures must be interpreted with caution. A part of technological payments may represent sale flows going from head office toward subsidiaries localized in the UK. Subsidiaries buy technological knowledge from head office.

It may equally be a deeper phenomenon. Firms aiming at spreading their technological resources seek to exploit for the best the complementarity potential existing between non-similar intellectual assets holders. If this proposition is true, one must have a wider conception of R&D expenditure. The notion of used research (internal research + absorbed external research) becomes crucial to analyze industrial performances (Patel and Pavitt, 1995).

3.2   Outsourcing Market

The figures that emerge from surveys carried out in different countries concern the whole set of outsourcing practices put in place by firms, including those relative to traditional subcontracting (subcontracting of capacity in production, of accounting, etc.).

The outsourcing market, in its larger significance, is strongly growing. Surveys made in the USA reveal that firms whose annual sales are higher than 80 million $, increased their external expenses of 26% in 1997 for a total of 85 billion $ (Outsourcing Institute, 1997). Among the most significant expenses, services linked to information technologies emerge (30% of the overall expenses). A significant part of this market corresponds to knowledge-Intensive-Business-Services (KIBS) which represent activities aiming to create, to accumulate and to sell specialized technological knowledge. The list of services concerned is given in the table 6:

Table 6. Categories of KIBS

I.   Traditional Professional Services, liable to be intensive users of new technology :
- Marketing/Advertising
- Training (other than in new technologies)
- Design (other than involving new technologies)
- some Financial services (securities and stock-market related activities)
- Office services (cleaning and new technology excluded)
- Building services (architecture, surveying, construction engineering)
- Management consultancy (new technology excluded)
- Accounting and bookkeeping
- Legal services
- Environmental services

II.   New Technology-based KIBS :
- Computer networks/telematics (VANs, on-line databases)
- some Telecommunications (especially new business services)
- Software
- Facilities management
- Training in new technologies
- Design involving new technologies
- Office services involving new technology equipment

- Building services involving (based on IT or new technologies sush as Energy Management Systems)
- Technical engineering
- Management consultancy involving new technologies
- Environmental services involving new technologies
- R&D Consultancy and 'high-tech boutiques'

Source: Coombs and Battaglia, p.199

Individual statistics of firms that sell KIBS are fairly scarce and, when they exist, they are sometimes difficult to isolate from other activities. An estimation of the activity of the larger enterprises is given in the table 7.

Table 7. Sales of the ten first world suppliers of services (million dollars)

Information services			Software		
Firm	(1995)	Revenues	Firm	(1997)	Revenues
IBM	(US)	20 143	IBM	(US)	12 844
EDS	(US)	12 422	Microsoft	(US)	12 208
Digital Equipment	(US)	6 498	Oracle	(US)	4 486
Hewlett-Packard	(US)	6 258	Computer Associates	(US)	4 332
CSC	(US)	3 895	Hewlett-Packard	(US)	2 438
Andersen Consulting	(US)	3 798	SAP	(D)	2 360
Fujitsu	(JPN)	3 752	Fujitsu	(JPN)	1 915
Cap Gemini Sogeti	(F)	3 614	Hitachi	(JPN)	1 499
Unisys	(US)	3 535	Novell	(US)	958
ADP	(US)	3 157	Siemens Nixdorf	(D)	916
Advertising			Management consultancy		
Firm	(1995)	Revenues	Firm	(1996)	Revenues
WPP Group	(UK)	3 420	Andersen Consulting		3 115
Omnicom Group	(US)	3 036	McKinsey & Co		2 100
Interpublic Group of Cies	(US)	2 751	Ernst & Young		2 100
Dentsu	(JPN)	1 930	Coopers & Lybrand Consulting		1 918
Young & Rubicam	(US)	1 198	Arthur Andersen		1 380
Cordiant	(UK)	1 169	KPMG Peat Marwick		1 380
Grey Publicité	(US)	988	Deloitte & Touche		1 303
Havas Publicité	(F)	974	Mercer Consulting Group		1 159
Hakuhodo	(JPN)	898	Towers Perrin		903
True North Communications		890	A.T. Kearney		870

Note: Information services are predominant. Included in this category are professional computerized services, databases and networks processing services, and electronic information services: professional computerized services constitute the most important sub-sector as they represent 58% of total revenues.
Source: US Industry and Trade Outlook 1998, and Goldman Sachs Investment Research for data relative to software firms (OECD, p.112).

Two remarks can be made. On the one hand, knowledge producers offer their services in the framework of multinational firms and among the biggest world firms. The dominance of US firms can be emphasized. On the other hand, these figures explain the astonishing weakness of the TP/BERD ratio in the USA: 5% in 1996. The buying and selling of knowledge take place mainly on the domestic market.

The Coombs and Battaglia study reveals the significance of an estimation of the outsourcing supply for the year 1996. The procedure they use[9] enables the part of outsourcing services rendered by 77 firms to be evaluated. The table 8 does not reproduce individual data of firms, but the global figures for the 4 retained sectors.

Table 8.   Outsourcing Market Value: selected industries (4 KIBS)
             ($ million –year: 1996)

	Total Revenue (A)	Outsourcing Services Revenue (B)	Outsourcing Services % Share (A) / (B)
Logistics Services	41. 425	1. 262	44,1
Business Services	10. 755	6. 918	64,3
IT Services	269. 005	78. 402	29,1
Telecommunications Value-added Services	459. 393	55. 413	12,1
Grand total	780. 578	158. 995	20,3

Source: Coombs and Battaglia, pp. 8-9-10

Globally, outsourcing services represent 20% of global revenues of the 4 considered sectors. Nevertheless, this 'indirect' measure of outsourcing market remains, according to the authors, subject to serious limitations. The heterogeneity of outsourcing activities does not enable the frontiers of practices that interest us to be defined precisely. Besides, statistics only concern large firms. But, as we have said, knowledge providers are often of modest size in some sectors.

In a more restrictive perspective, statistics have been established concerning only the strategic services to enterprises, which include the following categories: software information processing services, R&D and technical services, marketing services, firm organization services and human resources added value services (OECD, 1999). Tables 9 and 10 include the data for the UK and France.

Table 9. Selection of business services, United-Kingdom 1996

	Employment	Number of firms 1996	Sales GBP million	Added value GBP million
Computerized and connected services	**282 000**			
Software and information processing	**240 000**	**54 979**	**15 749**	**8 275**
Equipment Consulting	13 000	2 959	463	223
Consulting and software supply	184 000	50 544	13 057	7 367
Data processing	35 000	1 277	1 934	546
Databases services	8 000	199	295	139
R & D and technical services	**116 000**	**3 445**	**5 162**	**2 707**
Experimental R & D	91 000	2 085	3 996	2 017
Analysis and technical tests	25 000	1 360	1 166	690
Marketing services	**107 000**	**11 369**	**14 606**	**3 493**
Market studies and opinion surveys	30 000	1 341	1 257	602
Advertising	77 000	10 028	13 349	2 891
Firm organization services	**549 000**	**41 604**	**18 140**	**11 004**
Management Consulting	142 000	33 438	8 432	4 065
Recruitment / personnel disposal	407 000	8 166	9 708	6 939
Human resources added value services	**170 000***	**4 994****	**3 628****	**1 389****
Adults teaching and other forms of professional teaching				
Workers training and professional reinsertion				

Note: * include the public sector; ** exclude the public sector
Source: ONS, UK, OECD, p.233

Table 10. Selection of business services, France, 1995

	Employment	Number of firms	Sales FRF million	Added value FRF million
Computerized and connected services				
Software and information processing	**176 907**	**20 493**	**114 191**	**61 587**
Information technology consulting	61 202	8 366	36 873	21 019
Software consulting and software production	60 052	7 183	37 376	21 162
Data processing	52 363	4 220	37 512	18 318
Databases services	3 291	724	2 430	1 088
R-D services and technical services	**51 508**	**3 977**	**31 251**	**16 804**
Experimental R-D	20 444	784	18 586	8 872
Trials and technical analysis	31 064	3 193	12 665	7 932
Marketing services	**111 261**	**16 936**	**107 185**	**32 265**
Market studies and surveys	17 886	2 107	8 992	4 475
Advertising	93 375	14 829	98 193	27 790
Firms organization services	**487 117**	**40 520**	**190 908**	**104 330**
Management Consulting	136 589	38 351	124 475	42 846
Selection and staff supply	350 528	2 169	66 433	61 484
Human resources added value services	**26 895**	**5 037**	**11 964**	**6 236**
Adults teaching and other forms of professional teaching				
Workers training and professional reinsertion				

Source: INSEE/Services' account, OECD, p.147

In the two countries, enterprise organization services represent the most important revenues. The labor force used in firms supplying this type of services is greatest and the average size of these firms is low and very similar in the two countries: 12 persons in France for 13,2 in the U.K. Next come software services and information processing emanating from very small size enterprises, close to 9 persons on average in France and a little more than 4 persons in the U.K. We note the relative weakness of R&D services and of technical services, compensated in the UK by external knowledge acquisitions (cf. ratios TP/BERD). French firms present, on consideration of statistical data, a more integrated diagram of R&D and design activities. Despite this data fragility, we observe that employment in strategic services to enterprises is much more developed in the U.K. than in France (around 1,467,000 persons for 853,000 persons). Firms there are also more numerous: around 115,000 for 86,000. Knowledge markets are more developed in the U.K. than in France.

4. CONCLUSION

Firms' knowledge acquisition strategies have been deeply modified during the last twenty years. Integrated organization of knowledge production activities inside the firm is modified to the benefit of other complementarities notably supplied by the market. On the one hand, firms seek to control production costs of certain types of knowledge and to adjust the knowledge flows to their needs (Ratchford). On the other hand, firms seek to enter new networks to be in phase with scientific and technological advances.

It is this aspect which appears to be the most important. Actors-prescribers of the new organization of knowledge production are no longer solely internal to the firm. They include specialized firms (KIBSF) that hold part of scientific and technologic knowledge and that intervene to guide the absorptive capacity of some industrial firms. Knowledge markets facilitate the diffusion of *new norms of management* that influence at the same time the composition of knowledge bases and the re-organization of firms' portfolio products. Insofar as competition intensifies by the decompartmentalization of national markets and technological change becomes the norm in many industries, knowledge markets represent a necessary but not sufficient condition of competitiveness on internal and external markets.

A new cognitive regime is being set up the running of which demands possibility conditions (information technologies favor the transfer and coordination processes among firms) *and 'profit-sharing' conditions* (the problem of property rights is crucial here). More fundamentally, we have outlined the idea that knowledge markets do not constitute an atypical and transitory phenomenon, but that they come within the framework of a global coherence with respect to the underlying institutional architecture of the different national economies and the technological specialization forms of which they were the center.

NOTES

[1] 'Electronic communication also provides partners with access to internal data banks and software. Partners can participate in co-design processes in cases of complex innovation requiring a variety of new components. Opportunistic behavior can be effectively sanctioned by excluding members from the data communication systems' (Antonelli, 1999, pp 157-158).

[2] A very clear difference is drawn between physical products and intellectual assets. When a user buys a product, he does not have access to know-how and skills used to manufacture this product. 'A production process reaches the stage of yielding a saleable product when downstream users can work with, or can consume, the 'product' without themselves being knowledgeable about its production' (Demsetz, 1991, p.173).

[3] Let us remember that ownership theories (Grossman and Hart, 1986) emphasize that tangible assets ownership is a key element of the integration definition.

[4] The extreme form of specialization is called 'virtual company', a set of firms principally connected by data networks and that cooperates to realize many functions. Coordination becomes crucial: 'the exchange of information and knowledge is a basic essential... a virtual company relies on exchange through intensive use of information technology' (Probst, Raub and Romhardt, 1999, p.167).

[5] Innovation orientation linked to cumulative knowledge is equally observable in high-tech activities. 'Research in therapeutics is characterized by almost permanent shifts in technology, often involving radical changes in the entire research department. Moreover, the difficulties in testing, the long-term nature of drug approval and the high R&D costs, make financial risk extremely high in this segment. As a result, the deregulated institutional arrangements in the labor and capital markets that characterize the liberal market economies are the most appropriate for this business line 'bio-tech'.

By comparison, platform technologies -e.g. the development of tools for therapeutics research- rely considerably more on cumulative knowledge, almost always a result of long tenure within firms. Since total debacles are almost excluded, regulatory hurdles small and commercialization possibilities high, the financial risk is much lower' (p.3).

[6] This remark concerns US firms in general. Nevertheless it is important to understand that US firms can employ intermittent persons to accomplish R&D tasks. 'Outsourcing takes place for people doing R&D as well as R&D itself' (Ratchford, 1997, p.215).

[7] After correction of their sample to make possible significant comparisons between the Yale Survey and the Carnegie Mellon Survey (33 industries), Cohen, Nelson and Walsh (2000, p.129) do acknowledge that couples secret / lead time for products and secret / manufacturing capability for processes register the highest scores among appropriation mechanisms.

[8] More precisely, the notion of complexity degree or decomposability of a product is useful to differentiate technologies and industries, system-based industries vs material-based industries (Kusunoki, Nonaka and Nagata, 1998). Complex products represent a great number of sub-systems, i.e. elements that could be patented separately (electronic, automobile, machinery-tools). In material-based industries (chemistry, pharmaceuticals, oil, textiles), the products decomposition is less elaborated and the endured transaction costs to constitute a patent portfolio are fewer. In complex products industries, conditions of mutual dependence are created between technologies' holders that encourage cross licensing. In simple products industries, patents could be used to negotiate cross-licensing agreements, but equally sales of licenses procuring revenues (Cohen, Nelson and Walsh, pp.19 and 20).

[9] 'The approach adopted here is to infer the overall dimension of outsourcing by collecting data from the Income Statements of these outsourcing supplier companies. Specifically, we aggregated the revenues from those business units within these companies that provide the sort of services listed above. These revenues measure the upper limit to the supply of services, which have most likely been outsourced. We then estimate the proportion of those revenues

which might be derived from the conduct of outsourcing contracts with clients. Thus, we obtain a proxy for the annual outsourcing supply. This exercise is repeated for a number of firms in 4 different representative sectors, chosen both for their relatively high knowledge content, and because they account for a major share of the overall KIBS supply' (logistics services, business services, IT services, telecommunications added value services) p.8.

REFERENCES

Amable, Bruno, Barré, Rémi, Boyer, Robert, *Les systèmes d'innovation à l'ère de la globalisation.* Paris: Economica, 1997.

Antonelli, Cristiano, *The Microdynamics of Technical Knowledge.* Routledge, London, 1999.

Antonelli, Cristiano, *The Microdynamics of Technological Systems.* Forthcoming.

Argyres NS. The impact of information technology on coordination : evidence from the B-2 "stealth" bomber. Organization Science 1999; 10:162-80.

Argyris, Chris, Schön, Donald, *Organizational Learning.* Reading: MA : Addison-Wesley, 1978.

Arrow, Kenneth, *The Limits of Organisation. New* York: N.W. Norton and Co, 1974.

Arundel A, Kabla I. What percentage of innovations are patented ? Empirical estimates for european firms. Research Policy 1998; 27:127-41.

Azoulay N, Weinstein O. Les compétences de la firme. Programme TSER de la Commission Européenne, contract n° SOE 1–CT 97–1078, Revue d'Economie Industrielle, forthcoming.

Brousseau, Eric, *L'Economie des contrats. Technologies de l'Information et Coordination Interentreprises.* Paris : Presses Universitaires de France, 1993.

Caby, Laurence, Greenan, Nathalie, Gueissaz, Albert, Rallet, Alain. "Quelques Propositions pour une Modélisation." In *Innovations et Performances,* sous la direction de D. Foray et J. Mairesse, Editions de l'Ecole des Hautes Etudes en Sciences Sociales : Paris, 1999.

Cohen WM, Klepper S. Firm size and the nature of innovation within industries: the case of process and product R&D. The Review of Economics and Statistics 1996; 78:232-43.

Cohen WM, Nelson RR, Walsh JP. Protecting their intellectual assets: appropriabilty conditions and why US manufacturing firms patent (or not). Working Paper n°7552, NBER, 2000.

Cohendet P, Kern F, Mehmanpazir B, Munier F. Knowledge coordination, competence creation and integrated networks in globalised firms. Cambridge Journal of Economics 1999; 23:225-41.

Demsetz, Harold. "The Theory of the Firm Revisited." In *The Nature of the Firm, Origins, Evolution and Development,* Oliver E. Williamson and Sydney G. Winter eds, New-York, Oxford: Oxford University Press, 1991.

Gambardella A, Torrisi S. Does technological convergence imply convergence in markets ? Evidence from the electronic industry. Research Policy 1998; 27:445-63.

Grant RM. Prospering in dynamically-competitive environments : organization capability as knowledge integration. Organization Science 1996 b; 7:375-87.

Grindley PC, Teece DJ. Managing intellectual capital: licensing and cross-licensing in semiconductors and electronics. California Management Review 1997; 39:8-41.

Guellec D. A la recherche du temps perdu. Revue Française d'Economie 1999; 1:117-69.

Hancké B. Varieties of capitalism revisited: globalisation and comparative institutional advantage. La lettre de la régulation 1999; 30:1-4.

INPI, *Statistiques des Echanges Techniques entre la France et l'Etranger.* Paris, 1998.

Kogut B. The network as knowledge :generative rules and the emergence of structure. Strategic Management Journal 2000; 21:405-25.

Kusunoki K, Nonaka I, Nagata A. Organizational capabilities in product development of japanese firms: a conceptual framework and empirical findings. Organization Science 1998; 9:699-718.

Langlois, Richard N, Robertson, Paul L, *Firms, Markets and Economic Change. A Dynamic Theory of Business Institutions.* London and New-York, Routledge, 1995.

Levin R, Klevorick A, Nelson RR, Winter SG. Appropriating the returns from industrial R&D. Brookings Papers on Economic Activity 1987; 2:783-820.

Lewin AY, Long CP, Carroll T₁J. The coevolution of new organizational forms. Organization Science 1999; 10:535-550.

Maskus KE. The international regulation of intellectual property. Weltwirt-Schaftliches Archiv 1998; 134:187-208.

Monteverde K. Technical dialog as an incentive for vertical integration in the semiconductor industry. Management Science 1995; 41:1624-38.

OCDE, *Les Services Stratégiques aux Entreprises.* Paris, 1999.

Orsi F, Moatti JP, Eisenger F, Chabannon C. Les relations recherche publique / industrie génomique: américanisation ou voie européenne ? Médecine / Science 2000; 16:21-32.

Patel P, Pavitt K. The technological competencies of the world's largest firms: complex and path dependent, but not much variety. Research ˜Policy 1997; 26:141-56.

Patel, Pari, Pavitt, Keith. "Patterns of Technological Activity: their Measurement and Interpretation." In *Handbook of the the Economics of Innovation and Technical Change*, P. Stoneman, ed. Basic Blackwell, Oxford, 1995.

Paulré, Bernard. "L'Economie de l'information." Séminaire *Economie de l'information*, Commissariat Général du Plan, Juin 18, 1996, Paris.

Pavitt K. Technologies, products and organisation in the innovative firm : what Adam Smith tells us and Joseph Schumpeter doesn't. Industrial and Corporate Change 1998 ; 7 : 433-51.

Pisano, Gary P, *The Development Factory. Unlocking the Potential of Process Innovation.* Havard Business School Press: Boston, Massachusetts, 1997.

Probst, Gilbert, Raub, Stephen, Romhardt, Kaï, *Managing Knowledge Building Blocks for Success.* John Wiley & Sons, LTD, 1999.

Ratchford JT. Science and technology in government and industry: whence and whither ? Technology in Society 1997; 19:211-36.

Spender JC. Making knowledge the basis of a dynamic theory of the firm. Strategic Management Journal 1996; 17 (Winter Special Issue) : 45-62.

Steinmuller E. The Knowledge infrastructure in IT industries. Working Paper n°95-2, MERIT, 1995.

Teece DJ. Capturing value from knowledge assets: the new economy, markets for know-how, and intangible assets. California Management Review 1998; 40:55-79.

The Outsourcing Institute. *The Outsourcing Index.* http : //www.outsourcing.com /news/dnb/1997.

Van Den Bosch FAJ, Volberda HW, de Boer M. Coevolution of firm absorptive capacity and knowledge environment : organizational forms and combinative capabilities. Organization Science 1999; 10:551-68.

West J. Institutions, information-processing and organization structure in R&D: evidence from the semiconductor industry. Research Policy 2000; 29:349-73.

Whittington R, Pettigrew A, Peck S, Fenton E, Gonyon M. Change and complementarities in the new competitive landscape : a European panel study, 1992-1996. Organization Science 1999; 10:583-600.

PART II

SECTORAL APPLICATIONS

The second part includes four chapters devoted to sectoral applications: the chemistry (chapter 5), the bio-pharmaceuticals (chapter 6), the semiconductors (chapter 7), and the software (chapter 8). These studies reveal the existence of markets for knowledge which differ according to their extent and their working.

Chapter 4

THE MARKET FOR KNOWLEDGE IN THE CHEMICAL SECTOR

Fabrizio Cesaroni
Scuola Superiore "Sant'Anna", Pisa (Italy)

Myriam Mariani
University of Camerino (Italy), and MERIT, University of Maastricht, Maastricht (The Nederlands)

1. INTRODUCTION

Few industries epitomize the market for knowledge as the chemical industry. Large and small companies, universities, and research laboratories are heterogeneous sources of scientific and technological knowledge. Market and non-market interactions are the means through which knowledge diffuses among them, and enhance the potential complementarities.

As far as market transactions are concerned, markets for product technologies, markets for process technologies, and market for engineering services are the means through which knowledge transactions take place in this sector. In pharmaceuticals, for instance, trade in knowledge coincides with trade in product technologies. Differently, knowledge transfer is embedded in engineering services when chemical plants have to be built up. By providing empirical evidence on the existence and extent of knowledge transactions, this chapter explores the characteristics and functioning of markets for knowledge in the chemical industry. In so doing it will also concentrate on technology strategies of large companies.

The large size of the industry, its strong science base and its long history allow a comprehensive study of the determinants and effects of such markets. Compared to younger industries where markets for knowledge have also developed, not only can the chemical industry better illustrate the evolution of the markets for knowledge, but one can also draw the implications that come with them. However, a lot has been written on the chemical industry (see, for example, Arora, Landau and Rosenberg, 1998), and also on markets for technology in it (Arora, Fosfuri and Gambardella,

2000a). As a result, it is difficult to invent anything new in this area. This contribution will then use existing studies to build up an original framework for understanding the markets for knowledge in this sector, and provide new empirical evidence on the extent of these markets. Differences among countries and firms' strategies will be also highlighted.

In order to explore the characteristics of the market for knowledge in the chemical industry this chapter uses two databases. *Securities Data Company* (1998), provides data on about 52,000 inter-firm agreements during 1990-1997. This is a comprehensive source of information on transactions for product technologies and cooperation agreements. *Chem-Intell* (1998) collects data on about 36,000 chemical plants built world-wide since the early 1980s, and provides detailed data on licenses for process technologies and engineering services.

The chapter is organized as follows. Section 2 describes the basic characteristics of the chemical sector. Section 3 illustrates the innovative tradition of the sector, and the historical conditions that allowed the markets for knowledge to emerge. Section 4 explores the limitations to the rise of these markets. Sections 5 and 6 provide empirical evidence on knowledge trading in the sector, and licensing strategies implemented by large chemical companies. Section 7 concludes.

2. SOME BASIC CHARACTERISTICS OF THE SECTOR: INDUSTRY STRUCTURE AND CORPORATE STRATEGIES

The chemical sector is a large and heterogeneous sector (Cook and Sharp, 1992). The heterogeneity, the size of the industry, its scientific tradition, and the linkages with many other industries and products are important characteristics of the sector. They strongly influence industry structure and firms' technology strategies.

As for heterogeneity, chemical products range from bulk chemicals – or basic or commodity chemicals – to speciality chemicals. Basic chemicals are high quantity and low value-added products characterized by low differentiation. By contrast, speciality products such as dyes and paints, food additives and photography are more differentiated and sophisticated products. They are also produced in low volumes, and they are sold for high prices. This heterogeneity mirrors completely different technological, scientific and R&D strategies by individual sub-sectors and firms.

As far as size is concerned, the chemical sector is today the largest manufacturing industry in the United States, and the second largest in Europe. It produces about 1.9% of the US gross domestic product and about 11.3% of US manufacturing value-added (Arora, Landau and Rosenberg, 1998). The order of magnitude of these percentages is similar for Europe and

Japan. From a global perspective, in 1996 the US chemical industry had about 24% of the global market. Japan was second with 14%. The market share of Germany and Britain was 8% and 4%, respectively. The rest of chemical production is spread across the rest of Western Europe and Asia. Twelve of the largest chemical multinational companies are European (Cook and Sharp, 1992).

Another important characteristic of the chemical sector is its long tradition in innovation and R&D activities. Since its origins in the second half of the XIX century with the British and German dyestuff manufacturers, the chemical sector is a science-based sector. Innovation in this industry derives from the interaction between the academic world, individual firms, government economic policies, and historical events. Empirical work has shown the importance of the linkages between internal R&D capabilities and external sources of scientific knowledge for successful innovation (among others, see Freeman *et al.*, 1963). Universities and small firms are key for carrying out basic research and developing product innovations. Firms' in-house R&D is the essential complement to exploiting external linkages.

Private firms were also the major source of R&D funding and the locus of technological applications. Today, the firm average R&D intensity in the chemical sector is about 5%, which is higher than the average R&D intensity in other sectors. In fields like pharmaceuticals and biotechnology, firms' R&D intensity may exceed 20%. All the major technological innovations in the 1920s and 1930s – such as polystyrene, perspex, PVC, polyethylene, synthetic rubbers, nylon and other artificial fibers – were developed in the laboratories of large chemical companies, most of which still exist today (e.g. DuPont, Bayer, BASF, Hoechst, and ICI, among the most influential).

Another important feature of the chemical industry is that more than 50% of chemical products are intermediate goods used by a wide range of industrial sectors (Albach *et al.*, 1996). More than 70,000 products like paints and coatings, fertilizers, pesticides, solvents, plastics, synthetic fibers and rubber, explosives and many others are building blocks at every level of production and consumption in agriculture, construction, manufacturing, and in the service sectors. Put differently, the chemical sector is the upstream sector providing intermediates for several downstream users. Moreover, since successful innovations have positive effects in many downstream industries, the chemical sector is also an important source of knowledge spillovers and technology diffusion.

The strategies and the innovative decisions of chemical firms are dependent upon the characteristics of the branch of the industry in which they operate. For example, products heterogeneity leads chemical firms to follow strategies of cost leadership or specialization depending upon the products being produced (Porter, 1985). Firms adopt a cost leadership strategy in areas characterized by price competition. This is the case of basic chemicals. By using information drawn from the Community Innovation

Survey, Albach *et al.* (1996) show that during the past few years, European firms in the commodity chemicals focussed on cost leadership strategies. In so doing they increasingly concentrated in their core areas, and engaged in strategic alliances with other companies. By contrast, firms in the specialty sectors tended to pursue specialization strategies characterized by great product differentiation and customization, and higher profit margins.

In turn, the decision to follow cost leadership or specialization strategies influences firms' innovative behavior. Cost leadership leads companies to promote process innovations in order to reduce the cost of production. By contrast, specialization strategies require companies to focus on product innovations, in order to better respond to customers' needs, and to set higher prices. Albach *et al.* (1996) show that in agrochemicals, paints and varnishes –i.e. speciality products– more than 60% of firms allocate at least 75% of their R&D budgets to product innovations. The share of companies devoting 75% of total R&D expenditure to product innovation falls to about 30% in basic chemicals. However, firms producing basic chemicals spend about 75% of their R&D budget on process innovations. This survey also suggests that companies are increasingly entering into strategic alliances in the area of R&D, both with other firms, and with academic and research institutions. Again, however, the use of cooperative arrangements varies according to the sector. Companies from the agrochemical sector have the highest propensity to R&D collaboration. The opposite holds for firms in soap and detergents. Cooperation with universities, government laboratories, and other research institutions is frequent for companies from basic chemicals and man-made fibers.

3. THE CHEMICAL INDUSTRY: A SCIENCE-BASED INDUSTRY

This section describes how discoveries and innovations are developed in the chemical sector. It explores the characteristics of the scientific base from which innovations are born, the organization of the innovative process and its evolution over time. It also examines how the "upstream" features of the industry affect firms' strategies and industry structure.

The modern chemical industry started in Great Britain in the first half of the XIX century, when the first inorganic chemical firms emerged. However, although the industry started by producing inorganic products – such as soda, soda ash and blench – the engine of growth was organic chemistry, particularly dyestuff. Due to the rapid pace of technological change in organic chemistry, firms changed their approach to innovation. They started to adopt innovative strategies based on the methodical application of scientific discoveries to chemical manufacture.

The *synthetic-dyestuff model* is a meaningful example of the new approach to innovation. Its main feature is the use of scientific knowledge for developing new products and processes. Advances in the scientific principles governing organic chemistry provided a good understanding of how carbon atoms were linked to hydrogen and to other atoms to form complex molecules. This knowledge was the beginning of the development of a "general purpose technology" (Bresnahan and Trajtenberg, 1995) according to which different chemical composites could be designed by using the scientific background on the properties of the atoms.

The direct implication of the rise of the synthetic-dyestuff model was the possibility of exploiting economies of scope in knowledge. A common scientific base was used to develop different organic products. Firms that could master this knowledge had a strong incentive to diversify their product portfolio in sectors that share the common scientific base, like pharmaceuticals, explosives, and photographic materials.

A second implication of the application of the synthetic-dyestuff model was the resurge of the role of universities and other scientific research institutions. Being the synthetic-dyestuff model a science-based model in which the invention of new products was strictly dependent upon advances in the scientific understanding of the chemical structure of new molecules, the largest and most innovative firms established strong links with the academia. Chemical companies began to recruit researchers in the universities, and promoted research collaborations aimed at inventing new products. They also applied for joint patents. This was the case of Hoechst and the University of Erlangen (and its researcher Ludwig Knorr), whose joint venture produced the Hoechst's first drug Antipyrin (Murmann and Landau, 1998). In other cases, German dyes firms tried to promote alliances with German universities to set up special research institutes. During the period between 1911 and 1914, three new chemical research institutes were formed –such as the Kaiser Wilhelm Institutes for Chemistry and Physical Chemistry in Berlin– largely financed by private and corporate founds (Johnson, 1990).

However, the synthetic-dyestuff model was only the beginning of the science-based approach to innovation in chemicals. The "evolution" of the synthetic-dyestuff model was *polymer chemistry*. Initiated by Herman Staudinger and other German scientists in the 1920s, polymer chemistry is based upon the idea that any material consists of long chains of molecules – i.e. polymers– linked together by chemical bounds. The scientific understanding of the existence and configuration of these long chemical macromolecules led to the principle of "materials by design" (Arora and Gambardella, 1998).

According to this principle, the proprieties of materials are directly linked with the characteristics of the macromolecular structures. This means that the scientific understanding of chemical composites is the base for different product applications. A wide range of products can be developed by "simply" using different building block molecules, and changing the way in which these molecules are pulled together. Of course, long experimentation was still needed before obtaining the desired material. However, the scientific base made the search for new products more productive. The use of catalysts represented a fundamental tool in this process. By controlling the rate and the manner in which monomers were connected, they made it possible to obtain the desired length and physical structure of the polymers, leading to new and differentiated materials.

Like in the case of the dyestuff model, the rise of polymer chemistry strongly influenced the evolution of the chemical sector in the post-war era. The reasons are twofold. First, polymer chemistry provided a common technological base for developing applications and product differentiation in five distinct and otherwise unconnected product markets – i.e. plastics, fibers, rubbers and elastomers, surface coatings and paintings, and adhesives. This lowered the amount of time and research needed for product innovation in the sector. However, while the process of producing new products was comparatively easier for any chemical firm, competition among firms shifted to the correct anticipation of the users' requirements, and to the development of the most suitable applications. This meant that, to innovate successfully, firms had to become knowledgeable about the characteristics of different market segments. To do so, they developed extensive linkages with the downstream markets. This interaction allowed the producers to collect information about the users' characteristics. It also helped train the users in how to use the new products.

Second, entry in the sector was much easier. The opportunities created by polymer chemistry were exploited by a large number of companies world-wide which had the required size, scope, and in-house expertise to exploit them (Freeman,1982). Many chemical companies and some oil producers found themselves competing in very similar markets. The increased competition in almost every market segment led to a renewed attention to product differentiation and commercialization strategies as important sources of competitive advantages. This encouraged extensive investments in R&D to develop new product variants, and to tailor them for specific applications. Again, the development of systematic linkages with the users appeared to be key for understanding the desired proprieties of the new materials.

To conclude on polymer chemistry, it is worth noting that the success of polymer chemistry owes a great deal to the shift from coal to petroleum hydrocarbons. This shift began in the years before the Second World War in the US, which had abundant reserves of oil and natural gas. By 1950 petrochemicals covered half of the US organic chemical production. Ten years later this proportion was 88% (Chapman, 1991). But the development of a world market in oil and the international diffusion of the petrochemical technologies led to the early decline of the American leadership in petrochemicals, and to the catching up of Western Europe. This was strongly due to the upsurge of chemical engineering. By developing and diffusing chemical processing technologies, they determined a steep drop in the cost of basic petrochemicals that were the basic inputs for synthetic polymers. The rise of chemical engineering is described below as the third example of how technological advances occur in chemicals.

The concept of *unit operation* presented by Arthur D. Little to the Corporate of MIT (Massachusetts Institute for Technology) in 1915 was key to the development of chemical engineering. The idea of unit operation consists in the breaking down of chemical processes into a limited number of basic components or distinctive processes that are common to many product lines. According to this principle, any complex chemical process can be broken down in a series of basic components such as evaporation, filtration, grinding, crushing, etc., which are common to many different chemical contexts (Wright, 1998). This abstract and general concept became a "general purpose technology" of the chemical sector, and provided the unifying base for more contextualised and problem-solving innovations at the plant level (Rosenberg, 1998). It also allowed the separation of product innovation from process innovation, and led to important changes in the structure of the sector.

First, by making process technology into a commodity that could be traded, a large market for process technology developed. This allowed chemical technologies to diffuse rapidly. By supplying the necessary process technologies, the design and the engineering know-how, the *Specialised Engineering Firms* (SEFs) facilitated entry of new firms into the chemical industry after the Second World War, and allowed other countries such as Germany to catch up quickly in petrochemicals.

Second, strong economies of specialization were achieved at the industry-level, and a large number of vertical linkages were developed between chemical companies and the SEFs. These vertical ties often resolved into partnering relationships of two types: i) between the SEFs and a number of chemical firms developing new technologies; and ii) between the SEFs and an even larger number of firms buying these new technologies. As Freeman (1968, p.30) points out, in the period 1960-1966 '(N)early three quarters of the major new plants were 'engineered', procured and constructed by specialist plant contractors', and the SEFs were the source of about 30% of all licenses of chemical processes.

Third, the rise of chemical engineering led to a renewal importance of university research for developing innovations. In the first decades of the 20th century, many American universities established departments of chemical engineering. The link with the industry, and its partial dependence upon private industry funding, assured the focus on industrial needs. Moreover, in order to develop many processing technologies, and to achieve meaningful results, chemical engineers needed the large scale operations of the chemical firms, that the university alone could not supply. An important example of university-industry relationship in this period is that between the New Jersey Standard and the MIT at the research facility in Baton Rouge, Louisiana (Landau and Rosenberg, 1992).

This interaction between profit-seeking institutions and independent or semi-independent professional scientists influenced the evolution of the technology in the engineering discipline. DuPont, for example, which interacted extensively with the academic world, experienced the inadequacy of the level of rigor in chemical engineering, and pushed toward a higher scientific and mathematical base. Interestingly, despite the influence of large research-oriented companies, scientists maintained their independence and their professional status (Wise, 1980). Threatened by the possibility of going back to the academy, firms often had to adapt their employment conditions to match those typically found at the university. In so doing they allowed a certain degree of freedom and flexibility to chemical scientists and engineers, and gave the possibility to publish their research achievements. In the US, this might have limited the corporations' ability to appropriate knowledge, and to channel new technologies. Germany resisted chemical engineering as an autonomous discipline until the 1960s, and drew a clear demarcation line between subjects to be studied at the university, and those of more immediate usefulness of the industry.

To sum up, the three examples of synthetic-dyestuff, polymer chemistry and unit operation along with chemical engineering illustrate how the organization of innovative activities in chemicals has relied on the application of general scientific knowledge to the discovering of new products and processes. This approach to innovation led to major changes in firms' strategies and market structures, and allowed a market for knowledge to arise in the chemical industry.

4. CONDITIONS FOR THE RISE OF A MARKET FOR KNOWLEDGE IN THE CHEMICAL INDUSTRY

This section discusses the limitations and factors that allowed a market for knowledge to arise in the chemical industry. As Arora, Fosfuri and Gambardella (2000a) point out, there are three broad limitations and determinants for the emergence and functioning of markets for technology: *Transactional* limits; *Cognitive* limits; and limits that depend on *Market Size and Composition*. The chemical sector is a good example of how these limitations have been overcome allowing a market for knowledge to develop.

The *transactional* limitation arises from incomplete contracts. As Arrow (1962) pointed out, the difficulty of appropriating returns from an innovation limits the trade in intangible goods. This is because the property rights for intangible goods can be difficult to define and enforce. When this is the case, either the potential buyer of knowledge can appropriate and use it without having to pay a market price, or the seller might decide not to reveal the content of that piece of knowledge in order to avoid others to use it for free. The net result is that such transactions may not take place. There are means, however, that can solve the appropriability problem. Patents and contracts, for example, can facilitate the purchase and sale of technology. Arora (1995) shows that as long as patent protection is sufficiently broad, simple contracts can be written to transfer technologies and tacit know-how. More precisely, while contracts regulate the economic setting for transferring know-how, patent protection – that pertains to the part of the innovation that is codified – prevents the acquirer to behave opportunistically by "inventing around" the technology of the licensor. Greater patent protection increases the efficiency of knowledge exchange. As far as the chemical industry is concerned, patents and licensing contracts have been extensively used, and allowed firms and individuals to profit from their innovations (see also Anand and Khanna, 1997).

Cognitive limits arise from the context-dependent nature of knowledge. Indeed, knowledge often includes a tacit – or "inarticulable" – component. The more general and abstract is a piece of knowledge, not linked to the people and organizations that develop it, the easier it is to transfer that knowledge to other people and organizations that might use it for different purposes. By contrast, as the tacit nature, context-dependence and firm-specificity of knowledge increases, the more it is difficult and costly to transfer that knowledge. In turn, the possibility of transferring general and abstract knowledge allows for a division of labor in innovation, with some firms or institutions developing more general technologies and others using them for specific applications. This opens up different alternative modes for organizing the innovative process, and allows firms to pursue different strategies in order to get access to new technologies, from in-house development to technology "outsourcing". Related to the characteristics of knowledge is the fact that it can be difficult to partition the innovative process into independent and self-contained tasks (Kline and Rosenberg, 1986; von Hippel, 1990), and assign them to different agents located in different organizations and places. In the case of the chemical industry, however, the characteristics of the knowledge base can lower *cognitive* problems, both for reducing context-dependence and enhancing task-partitioning.

Third, the *size and composition of the demand* can also limit the rise of a market for knowledge. It is well known that the demand for a good is a necessary condition for the rise of any market. This applies also to the case of markets for knowledge. They are unlikely to arise if the demand for a "piece" of knowledge is low. With high demand, increasing returns to the production of a certain good as well as the benefits to specialized technology producers arise. Together with the size, also demand variety can create strong incentives to specialize and trade in technological knowledge. Bresnahan and Gambardella (1998) show that not only is the absolute size of a market important for fostering the rise of a market for technology, but also the breadth of its potential applications contributes to make the market arising. This also means that the more a technology is "general-purpose", the better it can be used for different applications and contexts, and the larger is the potential demand. This increases the payoff to specialization in producing and selling (general-purpose) technologies.

The chemical industry has specific features that reduce the impact of these three limitations, and favor the rise of markets for knowledge. As far as transactional limitations are concerned, contracts and patents helped create a market for technology in the chemical industry after World War II. Before World War II, patents were used to protect innovations from competitors. They were not a means for trading in technology. Large firms tended to control entirely a new technology by exploiting it alone or with other firms (cartels) in order to avoid the entry by competitors.

Only after World War II patents and licensing contracts started to be used to profit out of innovations. A market for technology developed due to the effectiveness of patent protection in chemicals. In turn, the effectiveness of patent protection depended upon the cost and effectiveness with which new knowledge could be written down and described in terms of general categories. The possibility to generalize a piece of chemical knowledge and express it in a formula derived from the possibility of understanding the scientific principles governing the underlying structures. The same applies for chemical processes that the chemical engineering discipline (and polymer chemistry) conceived in terms of the combination of their elementary units. Hence, advances in the scientific understanding of chemical sciences allowed innovators to precisely describe the content of their discoveries. Moreover, patents work well because it is relatively easy to relate the structure of a chemical compound to its functions. This clear relationship protects the inventors for sets of related compounds without the need to test and list the entire set, and clearly defines their property rights.

As far as cognitive factors are concerned, the knowledge base from which innovations are developed in chemicals help reduce the cognitive limitations. The three examples shown in Section 3 on the characteristics of the innovation processes in the chemical industry suggest that knowledge in chemicals can abstract from specific contexts and is generic to several applications. This increases the probability of contracting for knowledge.

For example, the concept of the unit operation and the emergence of chemical engineering as an academic discipline created the possibility to separate process design – which is based on the very general concept of the unit operation – from the details of the compound being produced. Due to its general-purpose nature, process technology became a commodity that could be traded. This generality also allowed specialized companies to focus on the development of process technologies without interacting extensively with the acquiring firms, and without having to accumulate expertise on the production of chemical products. This led to a vertical division of labor in the chemical-processing sector, and to the rise of a market for technological knowledge operated by a large number of specialized and technology-based SEFs. These companies rarely developed radically new processes. More frequently they acted as independent licensors on behalf of other firms' technology. In so doing they allowed the rapid diffusion of process technologies invented by large oil and chemical companies. Section 6 will provide evidence on the existence of this market for technological knowledge.

The story of SEFs also suggests that the size of the market has been a crucial factor for their rise. By the end of World War II, the demand for chemical products grew rapidly – especially for petrochemicals. This led companies to raise the scale of production. The large scale increased the size and complexity of plants, so that companies often faced a technological capability constraint, and demanded the intervention of external engineering specialists. The size and variety of applications allowed the technology producers to reach economies of specialization. This explains why the SEFs started as an American phenomenon. The American market had the characteristics needed for the development of a market for knowledge. According to Freeman (1968), 50% of the total value of engineering contracts world-wide in 1960-66 were done by American SEFs.

Finally, it is worth noting that the market for knowledge in the chemical industry is a self-enforcing phenomenon. The existence of SEFs, whose business is to sell process technologies and to appropriate rents from innovations, encouraged other chemical and oil firms to license their own technologies for making profits. Traditional managerial literature argues that companies can gain value from their innovations mainly by exploiting them in-house (among others, see Teece, 1988). As suggested by Arora and Fosfuri (1999), there are several reasons why technology licensing might be an undesirable strategy. Licensing can facilitate entry of new competitors in downstream product markets, thus reducing incumbents' profits and dissipating their rents (*rent dissipation effect*). However, licensing can generate revenues from the sale of technologies (*revenue effect*), in the form of licensing payments. Hence, the question is: what are the conditions that make the revenue effect be greater than the rent dissipation effect? Arora and Fosfuri (1999) show that when the technology holder is a monopolist, she will not have enough incentives to license. However, as is typically the case, a substantial fraction of innovations do not provide the innovator a monopoly in the product market. When another (or more) incumbent exists, the losses due to increased competition are shared with the other incumbent in the product market. The licensor does not fully internalize the rent dissipation effect, while she alone gets the revenues. In this case, if the latter are greater than the residual of the former, the company will both supply products and technologies. This reasoning perfectly fits to the chemical sector.

Technology licensors (SEFs) that lack the downstream complementary assets in production and commercialization, license more. Arora, Fosfuri and Gambardella (2000a) find that in the sub-sectors in which firms without downstream assets license, also large chemical producers tend to license more. In this case, the rent dissipation effect is zero. In the chemical industry, SEFs' licensing creates new competitors, and reduces profits in the product market. This behavior induces downstream chemical companies to supply technologies as well. As a consequence, the mechanism initiated by the SEFs tends to strengthen over time.

5. EVIDENCE ON THE EXISTENCE OF MARKETS FOR KNOWLEDGE IN THE CHEMICAL INDUSTRY

This section provides empirical evidence on the existence and extent of a market for chemical knowledge, and on the role of SEFs in giving rise to this market. We will compare different sub-sectors of the chemical industry and different countries in their propensity to engage in knowledge transfer agreements. In so doing we differentiate between knowledge trading embedded in engineering services – i.e. through SEFs – and knowledge transfer through "pure" market mechanisms – i.e. product and process licenses.

Data on technology trading in the chemical sector are drawn from two data sources: the SDC database (*Securities Data Company*, 1998) and *Chem-Intell* (1998). The SDC database typically reports product licenses. The database is constructed from SEC filings (10-Qs), financial journals, news wire services, proxies and quarterly reports. There are information on about 52,000 inter-firm agreements world-wide in all sectors. For each transaction there are information on the type of agreement (i.e. license, joint R&D, joint manufacturing, etc.), whether the agreement involves a technology transfer, the number of partners involved, the sector, the country and the region of the transaction. Data are available from 1990 to 1997.

The *Chem-Intell* database collects information on about 36,000 chemical plants built world-wide since 1980. For each plant, it reports information on the products been produced, the production capacity, the technology used, the owner, the contractor that provided the engineering services, the licensor, and the year of construction. *Chem-Intell* is a good source of data for process licenses and technology transactions embedded in engineering services.

As a first look at the data, Table 1 shows the most frequently licensed products and processes worldwide. While process licenses mainly refer to commodity chemicals – such as ammonia, sulphuric acid, urea and polyethylene – product licenses involve special compounds, such as biological products. This distinction is reflected in the two databases. *Chem-Intell* focuses on the largest chemical plants built worldwide. Plants for the production of bulk chemicals are widely diffused, and many of them have been set-up by using process technologies licensed by external suppliers. This is very common in less developed countries. By contrast, product licenses reported in SDC are usually the result of agreements among (large) chemical or pharmaceutical companies aiming at developing and producing specific products. Therefore, the number of licenses of biological and pharmaceutical products is very high.

Table 1. Most frequently licensed product and process technologies (1980-1997).

Rank	Process technologies	Nr. Licenses (1980-1997)	Product technologies (SIC)	Nr. Licenses (1990-1997)
1	Ammonia	574	Biological products (2836)	950
2	Sulphuric acid	539	Diagnostic substances (2835)	369
3	Urea	387	Organic fibers (2834)	262
4	Polyethylene	359	Medicinal chemicals (2833)	134
5	Chlorine	353	Plastics materials (2820)	95
6	Sodium hydroxide	348	Synthetic resins (2821)	77
7	Sulphur	318	Ind. Organic chemicals (2869)	54
8	Nitric acid	292	Ind. Inorganic chemicals (2819)	42
9	Ethylene	276	Other chemical products (2899)	29
10	Phosphoric acid	271	Plastics products (3089)	28
11	Hydrogen	262	Adhesives (2891)	26
12	Polyvinyl chloride PVC	236	Perfumes & cosmetics (2844)	26
13	Polystyrene	234	Petroleum refining (2911)	14
14	Polypropylene	214	Paints & varnishes (2851)	12
15	Polyester fibres & PET	210	Cyclic crudes (2865)	11

Source: Chem-Intell (1998) and SDC (1998).

Table 2 shows the distribution of 14,818 inter-firm agreements in the chemical industry since 1988. These data are drawn from SDC.
Joint manufacturing (22.0%), joint marketing (15.6%), joint-R&D (14.5%), and licensing agreements (14.4%) are the most frequent form of collaboration. Joint-venture agreements, which involve production, marketing and technological collaboration together, cover the 19.9% of the agreements.

Table 2. Inter-firm agreements: 1990-1997 (Shares of Total Number of Agreements by Chemical Sector).

Type of inter-firm agreement	General Chemicals	Pharma.	Soaps & Cosmetics	Rubber & Plastics	Petroleum Refining	Total
Joint Manufacturing Agreement	11.4	6.1	1.0	2.3	1.2	22.0
Joint Venture	10.8	3.8	1.0	2.3	2.0	19.9
Joint Marketing Agreement	3.9	9.8	0.6	0.8	0.4	15.5
Licensing Agreement	2.2	11.6	0.2	0.4	0.1	14.5
Joint R&D	2.2	11.8	0.1	0.3	0.1	14.5
Royalties	0.2	4.2	0.0	0.0	0.0	4.4
Equity Purchase	0.5	2.5	0.1	0.1	0.1	3.3
Funding Agreement	0.1	1.9	0.0	0.0	0.0	2.0
Supply Agreement	0.4	0.7	0.0	0.1	0.1	1.3
Joint Natural Resource Exploration	0.1	0.0	0.0	0.0	0.1	0.2
Original Equip. Manuf. Agreement	0.0	0.1	0.0	0.0	0.0	0.1
Privatizations	0.1	0.0	0.0	0.0	0.0	0.1
Spinout	0.0	0.0	0.0	0.0	0.0	0.0
Other	0.5	1.1	0.0	0.1	0.5	2.2
Total	32.4	53.6	3.0	6.4	4.6	100.0

Source: SDC, 1998.

The diffusion of different forms of agreements is different across sectors. Joint-venture agreements and joint-manufacturing operations are more frequent in the general chemical products (10.8% and 11.4%), a relatively more mature branch of the industry. As the sector becomes more research intensive, the share of R&D agreements and licenses increases. The share of joint-R&D operations is 11.8% in pharmaceuticals. Also licensing agreements are relatively more common in pharmaceuticals where they reach 11.6% of total inter-firm agreements, and about 80% of total licensing agreements in chemicals.

Among the different types of agreements, licenses are the more market oriented. As expected, Table 2 suggests that markets for knowledge are more developed in research-intensive sectors. For example, the pharmaceutical sector, which is the most R&D intensive sector, shows the highest share of product licenses.

Tables 3 to 8 focus on licensing agreements for the exchange of product or process technologies. Table 3 compares the chemical and electronic-software sectors in their propensity to develop licensing agreements. Notoriously, markets for knowledge in these two sectors are more developed compared to the average. Table 3 shows inter-sectoral differences in the "value" of licensing agreements during the period 1990-1997.

In order to calculate the values in Table 3 we proceeded as follows. We first considered the whole SDC database (52,000 transactions), and selected the licensing agreements that disclosed the unit value. We then attributed each license to one of the 8 industrial sectors shown in Table 3. For each of these 8 sectors we computed the average value of a license (first column on the left). We then calculated the number of licenses by sector and, based on the estimated mean value per license, we computed the total amount of money involved in the exchange of knowledge in the 8 sectors (first column on the right).

Table 3. Licenses: value and number by sector: 1990-1997 (Millions of dollars)

	Estimated Value per License	Nr. of Licenses	Total Value per Sector
Chemical sector			
General Chemicals	104.2	248	25,835.4
Pharmaceuticals	117.4	1,394	163,606.7
Soaps & Cosmetics	3.0	29	87.0
Rubber & Plastics	3.0	41	123.0
Petroleum Refining	6.2	33	203.2
Average	46.7	349	16,298.3
Electronic-software sector			
Electronics	8.1	598	4,827.5
Telecommunications	183.2	102	18,680.8
Software	5.5	1,785	9,757.5
Average	65.6	828.3	61,131.0
Total Average	73.8	4,230	312,126.7

Source: SDC, 1998.

Among the 8 sectors shown in Table 3, the pharmaceutical sector moves the largest amount of money. It is also the sector with the second highest number of licensing agreements after software (1,394 licenses vs. 1,785 licenses in 1990-1997). As far as the unit value of alliance is concerned, pharmaceuticals is second to the telecommunication sector (117.4 vs. 183.2 millions of dollars). This suggests that in the pharmaceutical sector firms tend to develop a high number of alliances of high unit value compared to the other sectors shown in Table 3. By contrast, in the general chemical sector, licensing agreements tend to be less numerous, although the unit value is high. The market for knowledge seems to be less developed in soaps and cosmetics, rubber and plastics and petroleum refining, where both the number and the unit value of agreements are low compared to the other sectors in Table 3.

As far as the pharmaceutical sector is concerned, SmithKline Beecham, Schering-Plough, Roche, Eli Lilly and Johnson & Johnson are the most active firms in the market for knowledge. SmithKline Beecham is the first licensor of biological products different from diagnostic substances, followed by Eli Lilly and Schering-Plough. In the case of general chemicals, the most active licensors of products technologies are Union Carbide, British Petroleum, Phillips Petroleum, Hoechst and Elf Aquitaine. In particular,

Union Carbide and Phillips actively supply plastics and synthetic resins' technologies.

Table 4 compares different regions in the propensity to engage in licensing agreements. It shows the country share of licensing agreements in the chemical and electronic-software sectors over the period 1990-1997.

Table 4. Shares of total number of licenses: 1990-1997

	Regions				
	Europe	**Japan**	**North America**	**Rest of the World**	**Total**
Chemical sector					
General chemicals	1,58%	1,16%	7,67%	4,18%	14,59%
Pharmaceuticals	7,47%	5,14%	59,59%	7,40%	79,59%
Soaps & Cosmetics	0,14%	0,00%	1,23%	0,34%	1,71%
Rubber & Plastics	0,41%	0,34%	1,03%	0,27%	2,05%
Petroleum Refining	0,14%	0,07%	0,89%	0,96%	2,05%
Total	9,73%	6,71%	70,41%	13,15%	100,00%
Electronic-software sector					
Electronics	1,29%	2,80%	16,68%	2,11%	22,89%
Telecommunications	0,18%	0,14%	3,26%	0,83%	4,41%
Software	3,31%	2,85%	62,96%	3,58%	72,70%
Total	4,78%	5,79%	82,90%	6,53%	100,00%

Source: SDC, 1998.

The "superiority" of the US as the locus where a market for knowledge developed both in chemicals and in the electronic sector is apparent. About 70% of total licenses in chemicals and 83% of total licenses in the electronic-software sector are signed in the US. Europe is second in chemicals, while Japan is second in electronics and software.

However, when one looks at the comparative advantages of countries in different chemical sub-sectors, a market for knowledge in Europe is comparatively more developed in general chemicals – about 11% of total licenses in general chemicals – and in rubber and plastics – 21% of total licenses in rubber and plastics.

By using information drawn from *Chem-Intell*, Table 5 looks at the country distribution of the licensors of 5,442 licensing agreements, which have been signed in Germany, UK, Japan or the US over the years 1980-1997. The information in *Chem-Intell* allowed us to distinguish between different kind of licensors. We distinguished between the SEFs, the Top Chemical Companies – those ranking in the top 50 positions in terms of number of plants owned and reported in the database – and other chemical companies. We could also isolate the cases in which firms developed in-house their process technologies – i.e. the *staff*.

Table 5. Licensing agreements: 1980-1997 (Shares of Total Licenses by Type of Licensor and Region).

| Licensor | Receiving country | | | | |
	Germany	UK	Japan	US	Total
Top Chemical Companies*	1.7	1.4	2.7	3.7	9.5
Other Chemical Companies*	0.1	0.2	0.2	0.3	0.8
SEFs	8.9	8.3	10.4	23.3	50.9
Staff	7.4	5.6	9.5	16.3	38.8
Total	18.1	15.5	22.8	43.6	100.0

Top Chemical Companies: Companies in the top 50 positions in terms of number of plants; *Other Chemical Companies*: Companies with more than 5 plants, excluded the top 50 companies. Source: Chem-Intell, 1998.

Table 5 shows that the SEFs are the most important source of chemical processes technologies in all the developed countries. They own 50.9% of the total market for technology. Half of the transactions are in the US (23.3%), followed by in-house technology development (16.3%). However, when one considers the frequencies of SEFs transactions and in-house technology development conditional upon each receiving country, these shares are very similar. In all the four countries, about 50% of technologies are supplied by the SEFs, and 40% by the companies' staff. This suggests that, apart from using its own technology expertise, chemical companies often rely on the specialised suppliers of process technologies. In order to analyse the phenomenon in greater detail, Table 6 looks at the type of companies involved in the vertical networks for 36,343 licensing agreements world-wide since 1980.

Table 6. Licensing agreements: 1980-1997 (Shares of Total Licenses by Type of Licensor and Licensee).

| Licensor | Receiving Company | | | |
	Top Chemical Companies*	Other Chemical Companies*	"Non" Chemical Companies*	Total
Other Chemical Companies*	0.2	0.9	0.4	1.5
SEFs	9.3	39.8	19.1	68.2
Staff	8.6	8.8	1.7	19.1
Top Chemical Companies*	1.6	6.9	2.7	11.2
Total	19.7	56.4	23.9	100.00

Top Chemical Companies: Companies in the top 50 positions in terms of number of plants; *Other Chemical Companies*: Companies with more than 5 plants, excluded the top 50 companies; *"Non" Chemical Companies*: Companies with 5 or less than 5 plants. Source: Chem-Intell, 1998.

Table 6 confirms that SEFs are the principal suppliers of technologies in the chemical sector for all types of companies with at least one chemical plant. They cover 68.2% of total licensing agreements. The SEFs license almost 50% of technologies used by top chemical firms, 70% of the know-how used by companies with at least 5 chemical plants, and 80% of technologies used by companies with less than 5 plants. The top chemical companies have the lowest share of technology received from the SEFs, probably due to their higher in-house technological capabilities. This is confirmed by Table 5. Not only do the top chemical companies develop by themselves almost half of their technological know-how, but they also sell these technologies to other chemical companies.

This is suggestive of the role of the SEFs, which was also pointed out by Arora and Fosfuri (1999). The existence of the SEFs, whose business is to sell process technologies to appropriate rents from innovations, encouraged other chemical and oil firms to license their own technologies for making profits out of them. This also increased the amount of intra-industry linkages among producers and users of technologies. Table 7 shows the market for chemical process technologies embedded in engineering services during the period 1980-1990. By looking at the nationality of the seller and acquirer of the technology, it highlights the international nature of linkages among technology suppliers and acquirers.

Table 7. Market share of SEFs – Engineering Services: 1980-1990 (Shares of Total Number of Plants by Region).

Nationality of SEFs	Regions				
	USA	West Europe	Japan	Rest of the World	Share of Total World Market
USA	58.8	19.8	3.7	18.9	26.0
West Germany	1.9	18.5	4.6	12.7	11.7
UK	6.9	12.2	2.0	7.3	8.1
Italy	0.3	8.2	0.0	5.8	5.1
France	0.2	2.3	0.3	4.6	3.2
Japan	0.2	0.2	34.0	5.1	4.0

Source: Chemical Age Profile (Arora and Gambardella, 1998).

Although the SEFs started as an American phenomenon, Table 7 shows that other countries are now successfully competing with the US, particularly in Europe and in the third-world markets. Between 1980-1990, Germany, the UK, Italy, France and Japan had 11.7%, 8.1%, 5.1%, 3.2% and 4% of the total market of SEFs' services, compared to 26% of plants engineered by American SEFs. These vertical networks fostered by the SEFs are also very regional in nature. Most of the plants in the US are engineered by US SEFs, those in Europe are done by European SEFs, and the plants in Japan are built by Japanese SEFs. Moreover, when the licensee and the licensor are of different nationality, Table 7 shows that the probability of an American SEF serving a foreign chemical company is higher than the probability of an European or Japanese SEF selling technology to the US. In particular, while the US SEFs have a sizeable share of the European market, the European SEFs have only a small share of the US market. This might be due to the establishment of many American SEFs' subsidiaries in Europe after the Second World War, which have then become full-fledged "national" companies.

Table 8. Market share of SEFs – Licenses: 1980-1990 (Shares of Total Number of Plants by Region).

	Regions				
Nationality of SEFs	USA	West Europe	Japan	Rest of the World	Share of Total World Market
USA	18.0	10.3	6.5	16.9	15.1
West Germany	3.1	11.3	1.0	10.2	8.8
UK	1.2	3.0	2.7	1.4	2.4
Italy	0.1	1.4	0.0	2.2	1.6
France	0.1	0.6	0.0	0.9	0.7
Japan	0.1	0.1	1.5	1.1	0.7

Source: Chemical Age Profile (Arora and Gambardella, 1998).

Table 8 reports the country shares of SEFs for licensing. The US market share is 15% for licensing, which, compared to her competitors, is larger than that for engineering (ref. Table 7) – with the only exception of Germany. The comparative advantage of US SEFs in licensing is even more apparent if one looks at the share of US licenses in Europe and Japan with respect to the shares of her competitors. This suggests that, in the case of licensing, vertical networks typically involve American or German SEFs that license technology to European, Japanese or third-world firms.

6. LARGE COMPANIES' TECHNOLOGY STRATEGIES: IN-HOUSE EXPLOITATION VS. LICENSING

Traditional managerial contributions consider in-house technology exploitation as the most efficient means to capture value from firms' internal R&D activity (Teece, 1986 and 1988). Over the past decades, however, greater attention has been paid to different strategies for making profits out of internal R&D investments, such as technology trading. Technology licensing and the rise of markets for technology suggest that firms may choose to exploit their technologies "externally".

In the chemical industry, technology trading has long historical origins. Its development is due to the raise of chemical engineering and to the emergence of the SEFs. Also the willingness of chemical companies to license their technologies affects the functioning of markets for technology. The decision to license some proprietary technology is a strategic decision, which is influenced by incentive mechanisms.

There are quite a few examples in the chemical industry that show that firms increasingly choose to license their technologies. Companies such as Union Carbide, Amoco, Montedison, Phillips, Exxon and British Petroleum have been important technology suppliers. Also some leading chemical producers such as Dow Chemical, DuPont, Monsanto and Hoechst, traditionally reluctant to license, recently started to sell proprietary technologies. This section analyses the technology strategies of the 40 largest corporations from Western Europe, North America and Japan. We selected from *Chem-Intell* all the plants in which these 40 companies appeared as technology licensors. Figure 1 shows the name of the companies, and the share of technologies that they exploit in-house (*Staff*) or license out to other firms (*License*).

Figure 1 shows that large corporations license a large amount of their proprietary processing technologies. On average, 52.5% of internally developed technologies are sold to other firms. However, differences emerge among companies. Firms such as Air Liquide, Mitsubishi and Texaco license more than 80% of their proprietary technologies. On the other extreme, Nestle sells only a small share of its technologies, and Grupo Torras and Enterprises des Recherches exploit their technologies only internally.

This suggests that firms adopt different technological strategies. For example, Exxon and Union Carbide have the same number of technologies, but show different strategies toward licensing. Union Carbide licenses about 70% of process technologies, while Exxon uses the same share of technologies for internal production purposes.

Interestingly, Figure 1 also shows that there is a high share of technologies (20.4%) that firms both exploit in-house and license out to other firms. In so doing they license process technologies to potential competitors, thus reducing expected profits in the product market. Also in this case, there are differences among firms. For example, companies like Allied Signal, Enterprises de Recherches and Nestle do not have technologies that are both licensed and used internally. Others, such as BOC and Solvay, use for both internal and external purposes about 50% of their technologies.

The question is then: why should (chemical) companies license their technologies to other companies in the same market? The choice between licensing and in-house exploitation depends on three major factors (Arora, Fosfuri and Gambardella, 2000b). First, if a firm has distinctive complementary assets in production and marketing activities, it might be efficient to exploit technologies in-house.

By contrast, if firms lack downstream assets, licensing might be a better strategy in order to profit from innovations. This is the case of the SEFs.

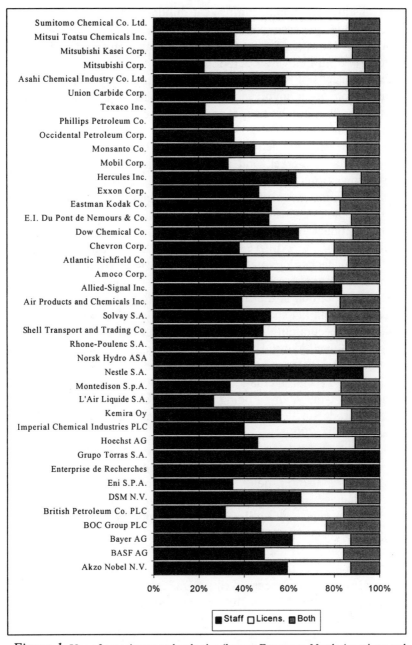

Figure 1. Use of proprietary technologies (largest European, North American and
Japanese companies).
Source: *Chem-Intell*, 1998.

Compared to large chemical companies, the SEFs have a competitive
disadvantage in production and marketing activities. This leads them to
concentrate on technology licensing. Similarly, many small chemical firms

without distinctive manufacturing capabilities may focus on technology trading. Also in this case, compared to the risks and to the expected returns of production activities, licensing may be a viable and profitable strategy in order to gain from innovative activities.

Second, licensing strategies depend also on the nature and importance of the transaction costs involved in the exchange of complementary assets, compared to the importance of transaction costs involved in selling or licensing technologies. If the latter are greater than the former, a company without the needed complementary assets may choose to acquire those assets in the specialized market, and then exploit the technology in-house. This strategy allows firms to save resources, compared to licensing.

Finally, firms may choose to license their proprietary technologies instead of exploiting them in-house, because of the extent of competition in the final product markets. The degree of competition influences the capability of firms to extract rents from innovations. Firms choose to operate in the market – technology vs. product market – with lower competition.

For example, BP decision to license out technologies depends on the degree of competition in the final product markets. In the case of acetic acid, BP has a large market share and faces a weak competition. Therefore, acetic acid licensing occurs only for selected cases and limited regional markets. In the case of polyethylene, BP has a smaller market share, faces a stronger competition, and there are many different technologies for producing the same product in the international arena. Polyethylene technology is then licensed more widely. In so doing BP competes with Union Carbide that is the market leader in licensing polyethylene technology. (See Arora, Fosfuri and Gambardella, 2000b.)

Firms' licensing decisions is also influenced by a "residual" factor. The managerial literature has shown that firms are increasingly diversifying technologically, also in fields and sectors not directly related with their primary business (Granstrand, Patel and Pavit, 1997). As a result, many technologies remain under-utilized. Licensing may represent a further option for capturing value from those innovations. Examples from DuPont and Monsanto confirm this pattern.

Traditionally, DuPont has exploited her proprietary technologies in-house. However, in recent years, DuPont realized that most of the technologies developed internally were under-utilized. In 1998, about 12,000 out of 18,000 active patents were not used to run the enterprise. Hence, starting from 1994, the company decided to promote an aggressive licensing program. In order to purse this goal, a specialized corporate division engaged in technology transfer. The company has also created an on-line technology market called "yet2.com". The same happened in Monsanto (Chemical Week, 1997) that, in 1997, started licensing technologies like acrylonitrile and acrylic fiber that were not used in any internal business.

The examples explored in this section show that trade in technology is becoming an appealing strategy. The development and functioning of a market for technological knowledge has been a relevant switching factor in this direction. However, firms' actual decision responds to internal incentive mechanisms and external factors. This is shown by the fact that firms take advantage of this option differently.

7. CONCLUSION

This chapter discussed the origin, development and functioning of markets for technological knowledge in the chemical industry.

The process through which innovations are developed in this industry help explain the rise of markets for knowledge. For example, the rise of chemical engineering as an academic discipline, and the development of the concept of the unit operation provided the codified and general-purpose technology independent of specific applications and contexts. This reduced the *cognitive* limits to technology trading, and allowed contracts for technology exchange to be written. Furthermore, it led to strong economies of specialization at the industry-level, with the development of a large number of vertical linkages between chemical companies and technology suppliers – i.e., the SEFs.

Other limits to the rise of markets for knowledge – i.e. *transactional* limits and the *size and compositions of the market* – are less pronounced in the chemical sector compared to other sectors. As far as transactional limitations are concerned, the low cost and the effectiveness with which new knowledge could be written down and described in terms of general categories allowed for great patent protection. As for the size and composition of the demand for chemical products, by the end of World War II, the large size of the US market led companies to raise the scale of production. To achieve economies of scale, the services supplied by *Specialised Engineering Firms* (SEFs) were needed. Moreover, the size and variety of the applications demanded allowed the technology producers to reach economies of specialization at the industry level.

Moreover, once markets for knowledge emerged, they continued to develop and diffuse because of self-reinforcing mechanisms. The existence of the SEFs, whose business is to sell process technologies and to appropriate rents from innovations, reduced market entry and encouraged other chemical and oil firms to license their own technologies.

To conclude on the development of markets for knowledge in the chemical industry, recent contributions noted that chemical companies license their proprietary technology not only as a reaction to the activity of the SEFs. Technology licensing is becoming an important strategy by itself. Companies may lack the needed downstream complementary assets, or face a strong competition in the final market. Or they can have technologies that are under-utilized, and that can provide rents if traded. In all these cases, licensing may represent a profitable option. The chemical industry is a meaningful example of the conditions, existence and functioning of markets for knowledge.

NOTES

This was the case of Hoechst, that in 1883 produced the pain-relieving Antipyrin, and Bayer, that in 1899 patented the pain-relieving, fever-reducing, anti-inflammatory Aspirin. AGFA used the technological convergence of some organic intermediates to diversify in photochemicals in 1887.

For instance, Union Carbide, Goodrich, General Electric, IG Farben, and ICI were all doing research in PVC and producing the polymer. Dow, IG Farben, and Monsanto were all involved in the polystyrene business. DuPont, ICI, Union Carbide, Monsanto, Kodak, and many other firms invested in other types of polyamides, acrylics and polyesters (Spitz, 1988; Aftalion, 1989).

See Rosenberg (1998) for the discussion of the "unit operation", and the role of MIT in the development of the chemical engineering discipline.

During the restructuring phase that the chemical industry faced in the 1980s, the cut down of R&D meant that many companies became unable to reach economies of scale in R&D. Inter-firm agreements in R&D, university-industry partnerships and industry-wide research projects represented a solution to the problem, particularly in the more intensive R&D branches of the chemical industry.

In two cases – i.e. soap and cosmetics, and rubber and plastics – we had to few observations (less than 5 licenses). Instead of calculating the mean value, we considered the median value of the whole sample of alliances.

In this analysis we considered all the observations in *Chem-Intell* (36,343) in all countries.

Firm size is measured by the total number of plants as reported by *Chem-Intell*.

One should take into account the geographical localisation of the licensee, and the possibility that the markets of the licensor and the licensee are geographically different. In this case, the companies would not compete in the same market.

See the Internet web site www.dupont.com.

The "yet2.com" market is a virtual technology market which makes use of the business-to-business possibilities offered by Internet. See www.yet2.com.

REFERENCES:

Aftalion, François, *History of the International Chemical Industry*. Philadelphia, PA: University of Pennsylvania Press, 1989.

Albach H., Audretsch D.B., Fleischer M., Greb R., Hofs E., Roller L. and Schulz I. Innovation in the European Chemical Industry. Research Unit Market Processes and Corporate Development. International Conference on Innovation Measurement and Policies; 1996 20-21 May; Luxembourg.

Ananad B.N., Khanna T. Intellectual Property Rights and Contract Structure. Working Paper, 97-016. Harvard Business School. 1997.

Arora A. Licensing Tacit Knowledge: Intellectual Property Rights and the Market for Know-how. Economics of Innovation and New Technology 1995; 4:41-59.

Arora A., Fosfuri A. Licensing the Market for Technology. CEPR Discussion Paper Series 1999; 2284.

Arora A., Fosfuri A., Gambardella A. Markets for Technology (Why do we see them, why don't we see more of them, and why we should care). Unpublished manuscript. 2000a.

Arora A., Fosfuri A., Gambardella A. Markets for Technology and their Implications for Corporate Strategies. Working Paper. University "Carlos III", Madrid. 2000b.

Arora, Ashish, Gambardella, Alfonso "Evolution of industry Structure in the Chemical Industry." In *Chemicals and Long-term Economic Growth: Insights from the Chemical Industry*, Ashish Arora, Ralph Landau, Nathan Rosenberg, eds. New York: John Wiley & Sons, 1998.

Arora, Ashish, Landau, Ralph, Rosenberg, Nathan, *Chemicals and Long-term Economic Growth: Insights from the Chemical Industry*. New York: John Wiley & Sons, 1998.

Arrow, Kenneth. "Economic Welfare and the Allocation of Resources for Invention." In *The Rate and Direction of Inventive Activity*, National Bureau of Economic Research, Princeton, NJ: University Press, 1962.

Bresnahan T.F., Trajtenberg M. General Purpose Technologies 'Engines of Growth'?. Journal of Econometrics 1995; 65:83-108

Bresnahan, Timothy, Gambardella, Alfonso. "The Division of Inventive Labor and the Extent of the Market." In *General Purpose Technologies and Economic Growth*, Elhanan Helpman, ed. Cambridge, MASS: MIT Press, 1998.

Chapman, Keith, *The International Petrochemical Industry*. Oxford: Basil Blackwell, 1991.

Chemical Week, "Turning Process Know-how into Profits." 1997 July 23; p. 45.

Chem-Intell, Reed Elsevier Ltd. London, 1998.

Cook, P.Lesley., Sharp, Margaret. "The Chemical Industry." In *Technology and the Future of Europe*, Chris Freeman, Margaret Sharp, William Walfer, eds. London: Pinter Publishers, 1992.

Freeman C, Young A, Fulker J. The Plastics Industry: A Comparative Study of Research and Innovation. National Institute Economic Review 1963; 26, 22-62.

Freeman C. Chemical Process Plant: Innovation and the World Market. National Institute Economic Review 1968; 45:29-51

Freeman, Chris, *The Economics of Industrial Innovation*. London: Francis Pinter, 1982.

Granstrand O., Patel P., Pavit K. Multi-Technology Corporations: Why They Have 'Distributed' rather than 'Distinctive Core' Competencies. California Management Review 1997; 39:8-25.

Johnson, James A., *The Kaiser's Chemists*. Chapel Hill, NC: University of North Carolina Press, 1990.

Kline, Stephen, Rosenberg, Nathan. "An Overview of Innovation." In *The Positive Sum Strategy*, R Landau, Nathan Rosenberg, eds. Washington DC: National Academy Press, 1986.

Landau, Ralph, Rosenberg, Nathan. "Successful Commercialisation in the Chemical Process Industries." In *Technology and the Wealth of Nations*. R Landau, David C. Mowery, Nathan Rosenberg, eds. Stanford, CA: Stanford University Press, 1992.

Murmann, Johann Peter, Landau, Ralph. "On the Making of Competitive Advantage: The Development of the Chemical Industries in Britain and Germany Since 1850." In *Chemicals and Long-term Economic Growth: Insights from the Chemical Industry*. Ashish Arora, Ralph Landau, Nathan Rosenberg, eds. New York: John Wiley & Sons, 1998.

Porter, Michael, *Competitive Strategy*. New York: The Free Press, 1985.

Rosenberg, Nathan. "Technological Change in the Chemicals: The Role of university-industry Relationships." In *Chemicals and Long-term Economic Growth: Insights from the Chemical Industry*. Ashish Arora, Ralph Landau, Nathan Rosenberg, eds. New York: John Wiley & Sons, 1998.

Spitz Peter H., *Petrochemicals: The Rise of an Industry*. New York, NY: Wiley, 1988.

Teece D.J. Profiting from Technological Innovation: Implication for Integration, Collaboration, Licensing and Public Policy. Research Policy 1986; 15:285-305.

Teece, David J. "Technological Change and the Nature of the Firm." In *Technical Change and Economic Theory*. Giovanni Dosi, Richard Nelson, Gerald Silverberg, Luc Soete, eds. London: Francis Pinter, 1988.

Von Hippel E. Task Partitioning: An Innovation Process Variable. Research Policy 1990;19:407-418.

Wise G. A New Role for Professional Scientists in Industry. Technology and Culture 1980; 21:408-429.

Wright Gavin. "Can a Nation Learn? American Technology as a Network Phenomenon." In *Learning by Doing in Firms, Markets and Countries*. Raff D. Lamoreaux, Peter Temin, eds. Chicago: NBER, 1998.

Chapter 5

THE MARKET FOR KNOWLEDGE IN BIO-PHARMACEUTICALS

Daisy Rhuguet, Christophe Silvy
CEFI-CNRS, Aix-en-Provence, Université de la Méditerranée, France

1. INTRODUCTION TO BIO-PHARMACEUTICALS

1.1 Bio-Pharmaceutical Market Structure

The pharmaceutical industry can be simply defined as a gathering of all pharmaceutical product manufacturers. But in a wider sense, it encompasses large areas including the health care sector, whose objective is the development of 'products of chemical or biological origin which are intended or purported to have a medicinal effect on man or animals and which are used especially for detection, prevention or treatment of diseases, injuries or disabilities' (Roche, 1998).

1.1.1 The International Bio-pharmaceutical Market

More then 80% of the estimated market of $293.4 billion[1] is shared between North America at 34.8%, Europe at 29.3% and Japan at 18.5%; these three zones representing the pharmaceutical industry's growth areas. Emerging countries have not yet recorded growth in this field with the exception of a few nations such as Brazil.

The demand for medicines is weakly influenced by the economic cycle. Products are dominated by structural evolution. The pharmaceutical industry relies on fundamental, accepted growth factors such as:
- demographic evolution, in particular the aging of populations in industrial countries[2];
- an expected consumer growth in some parts of the world (southern nations of the EEC and Eastern Europe) and in the longer run, an expected

emergence of new markets where developing nations improve their standard of living;
-    the continued development of new drugs for untreated or little treated illnesses, in the context of constant research into high level health care.
However, economic constraints have recently counterbalanced the pharmaceutical market growth. The importance of governmental measures controlling health expenditure in Europe and the United States has modified market evolution within a short space of time[3].

1.1.2   Concentration and Competition in Pharmaceuticals

Several characteristics dominate this market:
-    an increasing number of firms: the market is broken down into individual groups. Compared to the automotive industry (Table 1), the market is weakly concentrated. In 1996, the leading world group only possessed 4.4% of the global market. In 1998, the ten leading pharmaceutical companies only represented 36.1% of the global market, and the top twenty 57.3% (Table 1).

Table 1. Market share and net profit ratio in pharmaceuticals and in automotive in 1996

Pharmaceutical firms	Market shares %	Automotive firms	Market shares %
Novartis	4,4	General Motors	16,2
Glaxo Wellcome	4,4	Ford	12,8
Merck	3,9	Toyota Motors	9,2
Net profit %			Net profit %
Novartis	6,1	General Motors	3
Glaxo Wellcome	24,3	Ford	3
Merck	19,6	Toyota Motors	2,4

Source: Weinmann (1997)

-    high returns: net profit ratios on turnover are higher than the automotive market. There are strong financial and technological entry barriers for creating new molecules: $370 million to create a molecule in an international level. 15.5% of turnover is absorbed by the R&D budget which is constantly increasing[4] (Table 2).

1.2 Market Dynamics

1.2.1   Product Specificity

In order to catch the sector dynamic, the OECD (1985) adopted a typology, dividing it according to the specificity of the product dealt with. The pharmaceutical industry produces complex, non-durable goods, which are classified according to prescription or non-prescription and degree of innovation (Table 3).

Table 2. Market Share of Top Ten in Pharmaceuticals (1998)

Rank	Firms	Sales 1998 en U.S $B	Market shares %
1	Novartis	10,6	4,2
2	Merck & Co	10,6	4,2
3	Glaxo Wellcome	10,5	4,2
4	Pfizer	9,9	3,9
5	Bristol-Myers Squibb	9,8	3,9
6	Johnson & Johnson	9	3,6
7	American Home	7,8	3,1
8	Roche	7,6	3
9	Lilly	7,4	2,9
10	Smithkline Beecham	7,3	2,9
	Top ten	**90,7**	**36,1**

Source: Pharmaceutiques-Pharmaactualités, 2000

Table 3. Classification of pharmaceutical products

Products on medical prescription	• **patented or ethical** pharmaceutical products; pharmaceutical products on which the patent has expired: **generic** drugs
Non-prescription products	• Freely available or brand products: **OTCs**; over the counter or self-medication products

Source: OECD (1985)

The aim of this classification is to order pharmaceutical products by category according to their technological intensity. This typology has the advantage of distinguishing three sub-markets with different characteristics. In the case of freely available products, the drugs choice, purchase and consumption are left to the discretion of the patient. With respect to ethical or generic products, the choice is made by agent type while the purchase and the use depend on one or several other agent types in the market place[5]. These characteristics widely influence the behavior of the various actors in the health sector and especially in the pharmaceutical industry, by changing the nature of competition within the market.

1.2.2   Segmentation of Markets and Competition

The OECD classification allows us to examine competition in the different market segments.
-    ethical products are manufactured by large scientific-based companies and sold on a highly selective market. Competitive advantage lies in innovation. It cannot be exploited without close, permanent links to medical practitioners. High R&D and marketing expenditure must be recovered by means of high profit margins. These companies generally operate throughout the globalized market;
-    Generic product are close to that of basic product. Small and medium size firms are coupling with price competition. R&D and advertising play a

minor role though cost savings are more than offset by low prices leaving a small profit margin. Here, activities are limited to the national level and its border areas;
-   self-medication products still only represent a small part of the drug market but their share is growing .

Companies which form these different market segments enter into competition when patents expire. Then occurs a transitory period during which innovative firms benefit from factors such as reputation and established commercial practices. The latter are potentially counterbalanced by price competitive imitative firms. According to Caves et al. (1991), these differences never last and, in the long term, the rules of price competition dominate for generic products.

1.2.3   Regulations

Though the different competitive contexts shape the evolution of the pharmaceutical industry, they are themselves influenced by regulatory authorities. A peculiar characteristic of this sector lies in the impact of different regulations on innovative activities and the main path followed by pharmaceutical companies toward globalization.
The case of the United States is illustrative: the F.D.A's[6] regulatory controls are more stringent than before on test procedures[7] whilst covering a wider range of drug types. Consequently, this has lengthened the time between the patent filing and its effective approval. In 1984, the Waxman-Hatch law prohibiting repeated tests by imitators seems to have promoted the development of generic products sales of these imitated drugs now match those for the original within one year whereas it previously took five years. These measures lengthen the drug approval process and strengthen competition once patents become publicly available. Accordingly, the quasi-monopoly period of innovative firms is reduced driving them to look for new markets in order to make up for the shortened product life cycle.
Regulatory systems such as those adopted in other geographic areas with high pharmaceutical consumption, allow an increase in the domination period of the ethical drug but reduce profit opportunities (with slight recourse to generic drug and a sound tendency toward price control).

1.2.4   Success Conditions in Bio-Pharmaceuticals

The survival and success of firms in this highly regulated and competitive market relies mainly on successful research (Weinmann, 1998). The patent's 20 year protection period encourages leading firms to maintain an efficient R&D department. Groups with research programs that have not come up with any successful innovation are compelled to merge with

companies having a more efficient R&D. To limit the financial risks there are choices to be made:
- focusing projects toward profitable research areas;
- follow-up research on blockbusters to extend the product life through wider therapeutic applications;
- acquisition of research-dedicated firms, *i.e.* start-ups on biotechnology;
- multiplication of research projects with other companies (agreements and alliances).

A firms' success relies largely on ownership of blockbusters. These are medicines for which turnover exceeds $500 million per year. They allow business to jump ahead and can represent more than 50% company turnover (table 4). Thus, research is made profitable.

Table 4. Blockbusters sales of top 10 pharmaceutical firms (1996)

Firms	Number of blockbusters	blockbusters sales (millions of US $)	blockbusters sales on total sales (%)
Novartis	2	1,96	19,8
Glaxo Wellcome	4	4,9	49,2
Merck	4	5,1	57,3
Hoesch Marion Rousselt	1	0,76	10,4
Bristol Mayer Squibb	2	1,41	19,8
Johnson & Johnson	1	0,73	10,4
American Home	1	0,71	10,1
Pfizer	4	4,01	58,4
Smithkline Beecham	2	2	33
Roche	1	0,74	12,5

Source: IMS

The pharmaceutical industry is strategic with respect to both its market value and its social character. Pharmaceutical firms are faced with a highly competitive environment and their survival depends on their ability to deal with various problems; i.e. the regulatory decisions, the generic drug entry, the globalized market. This study focuses on another crucial factor: the need for innovative drugs.

We aim to study the role of knowledge in the industrial organization of bio-pharmaceuticals in order to understand how, and to what extent, knowledge markets can emerge.

Let us consider, over the last century, the role of science in the pharmaceutical industry. Then we can examine the current trend of drug innovation and trace the conditions that lead to the emergence of biotechnological knowledge markets. Finally, we can quantitatively analyze the use of market agreements compared to other knowledge exchange methods.

2. THE ROLE OF SCIENCE IN THE NEW DRUGS DISCOVERY

2.1   From the 'Chance' Discovery of New Medicines...

2.1.1   Pharmaceutical Discovery and Empiricism

Drug research goes back a long way. Over the centuries, discovering drugs has been largely based on empirical research, driven mainly by religious belief and superstition. Empirical research has been based on the practices of witches, herbalists and healers. From the 19th century, accumulated experience and cumulative knowledge, along with the growth of science, allowed a better understanding of the effects of drugs on the human metabolism. The development of modern drug research closely followed that of natural sciences.

Chemistry was the first and most important factor in the development of new drugs. As Jürgen Drews underlined (1996), the mode of thought in the field of chemistry encouraged research into new medicines in two ways: on the one hand, by systematic follow-up of the therapeutic objective based on empirical knowledge, and on the other hand, by the serendipity of the suitable molecule. The author here underlines the highly unpredictable character of the chemistry introduction into the new medicines discovery. In 1856, William Perkin attempted to synthesize quinine and in its place obtained mauveine, the first synthetic dye. In 1871, a young student named Paul Ehrlich wanted to color parasites. He found during this work that certain dyes selectively stained tissues and cells and inhibited their life cycle. Thus, he opened the way of anti-infectious chemotherapy. Numerous examples illustrate the importance that chance played in discovery and the budding drug industry. Chance, rather than scientists' perspicacity, had often been at the beginning of medicinal development. However, we must not neglect the role of scientific progress: advances in chemistry have led to the isolation and characterization of active ingredients in medicinal plants; for example long established drugs such as opium and morphine.

2.1.2   Scientific Progress and the First Pharmaceutical Laboratories

Until the end of the 19th century, drugs had been produced in a craft-industry environment, i.e. the pharmacy. Between 1870 and 1890 medicines became industrial goods being manufactured within well structured laboratories.

Advances in extractive chemistry between 1820 and 1860 led to the isolation of numerous active vegetable origin substances. At the same time, the first steps in organic synthesis led to the design of chemical drugs such as local anesthetics and barbiturates and to the appearance of the first large laboratories.

The pharmaceutical industry thus developed around two lines of research:
- the first derives from medicinal plants and their extractions as active substances . Thus, activity shifted from the apothecary's craft production to industrial pharmaceutical production (Merck, Schering and Smith Kline);
- the second, initially based on diversification in the dyeing industry, progressively moved toward the pharmaceutical industry (Sandoz, Ciba and Hoechst).

The pharmaceutical industry was thus founded on two distinct types of competence. Firstly, the pharmacist's know-how based on cumulative experience in the use of medicines and secondly, the chemist's know-how centered on the mastery and understanding of the process of chemical synthesis and extraction.

2.1.3   The Role of Science in Industrial Development

Drug research based on organic synthesis and not on empirical use of plants has faced difficult obstacles. Not only must their therapeutic value be validated but their toxicity must also be mastered. Pharmaceutical laboratories were founded from the beginning of the 20th century, but pharmacology as a scientific discipline did not actually take off until the 1920s. The latter was thus developed around a chemical paradigm, consisting of 'discovering the interactions existing between exogenous substances, medicines and poisons and biological systems that are living organisms' (Roche, 1998). The first scientific development stage consisted in describing the chemical composition of active substances in order to analyze, at the second stage, their side effects during experimental and clinical trials. The final stage concerned the full-scale production of active substances. At this stage of development, mastery of the chemical production process was essential.

Advances in pharmacology, coupled with those in physiology led to the discovery of neurotransmitters and the existence of enzymes. The enzymes ensuring the synthesis of the neurotransmitters thus became the basis of numerous medicines; e.g. the first neuromuscular blockers in modern anesthetics. All these molecules developed and examined in the large industrial research laboratories were used as fundamental instruments in the understanding of physiological functions and pathological mechanisms.

Later, microbiology and fermentation techniques became core disciplines in the process of the new substance production. The rise of biochemistry in the first decades of the last century only had an impact on results and targets of pharmaceutical research in the 1940's and 1950's. Scientific advances opened up new perspectives for industrial pharmaceutical research but with lead time. We can quote the accidental discovery of antibiotics, which was the result of experiments and scientific concepts developed in the past. Later, microbiology and fermentation techniques became core disciplines in the process of the new substance production. Scientists had to wait for 63 years and for the penicillin purification by Florey's before they could exploit antibiotics in therapeutic application.

These examples highlight the dependence of drug research on scientific advances. Researchers must wait until fundamental research defines a theoretical context for the invention of new active substances. Therefore, therapeutic needs, do not determine major research orientation but rather scientific opportunity. The same goes for the discovery of genetic engineering. Initially used to produce known proteins, genetic engineering together with molecular biology[9] allowed the production of new proteins and the discovery of monoclonal antibodies were discovered without any pre-defined therapeutic target.

2.1.4   Conclusion: The Chemical Paradigm

Two conclusions can be drawn here:
-    pharmaceutical research often developed independently of basic research through modes of thought and techniques linked to an experimental approach. Accidental discoveries were numerous. Many promising patents were applied for though their therapeutic applications were still uncertain;
-    under the successive influences of pharmacology, physiology, biochemistry and molecular biology, pharmaceutical research followed investigation procedures grounded on the chemical interpretation of disease. Diseases were supposed to reflect chemical imbalances that were recognizable from chemical parameters and could therefore be corrected by chemical intervention.(Drews, 1996)

The pharmaceutical industry was thus developed around a chemical paradigm. The scientific paradigm defines *a scientific theory, shaping the scientists' path within specific thought and experimentation field.* Until the 1970s, pharmaceuticals had built its knowledge base from the chemistry and experimentation sciences; this led to an organization of this industry characterized by large integrated firms having their own R&D laboratories. Two distinct paths may be identified. The first which guided Merck, is based on the experimental competence of the pharmacist. The second which guided Hoechst, is based on a high level of competence in chemistry. Before the 'biotechnological revolution', the industrial landscape was structured around mastery of the chemical processes.

2.2 ...Toward Finalized Research

2.2.1 Advances in Molecular Biology

The rise of molecular biology interrupted the link between scientific discovery, empirical observation and chance. Basic research is now motivated by other goals. While we were looking for the discovery and implementation of new therapeutic solutions, we now focus on the understanding of natural phenomena.

Molecular biology had first to test its theoretical principles and methodological catalogue on simple organisms: phages, bacteria, viruses and mammalian cells. Now, in its mature phase, it is able to develop and use the human genome, which creates a new situation for research. Whatever we learn within projects dealing with the genome, it is very quickly applicable in a medical context. Moreover, apart from anti-microbial drug therapy, pharmaceutical treatments are often symptomatic and do not eliminate the causes of disease. The human genome project will allow to understand the structure of the human organism and will lead to the study of the causes of diseases rather than the symptoms. Böhme (1978) describes this phenomenon as the "finalization of science. Molecular biology is really oriented toward applied sciences such as medicine, nutrition or agronomy. Nevertheless, it remains a science that continues to evolve and to give itself new questions to answer.

2.2.2 The Development of Biotechnology

The successive advances in bio-sciences; molecular biology, biochemistry, enzymology and genetics, have largely contributed to the emergence of new production techniques of active substances; i.e. biotechnology. The OECD defines them as *'the application of scientific and engineering principles to the treatment of biological matter and agents with the aim of producing goods and services* (OECD, 1982). Their implementation is made possible due to two breakthroughs at the scientific level: the first gene transfer in 1973 by Boyer and Cohen and the discovery of monoclonal antibodies in 1975, by Köhler and Milstein.

Since 1978 recombinant DNA technology, or genetic engineering, has been used for natural proteins mass production with the first genetically manufactured bacteria producing insulin being marketed. Since then, several drugs have been introduced by genetic engineering methods. Lymphokines and growth factors come from genetically produced bacteria and are used today in the treatment of cancer. Many vaccines have also been discovered, e.g. hepatitis B. Research is currently concentrating on the AIDS specific genes to discover an efficient vaccine.

Technology based on monoclonal anti-bodies at the origin of the first hybridoma allowed scientists to generate anti-bodies by combining a leukocyte-producing anti-body with cancerous cells. Such a technology led to the anti-bodies mass production and the production of diagnostic tests for the detection of hepatitis, venereal disease and, more recently, AIDS. These antibodies contained a certain degree of radioactivity and were used in combination with medical imaging technology in order to localize and study diseased tissue *in vivo*.

During the two last decades, other types of biotechnology have emerged, notably recombinant chemistry. This appeared during the 1980s through the work by a research team from Affimax, a San Diego start-up. The team used this technique as a method of generating the collection of simple protein-like molecules[10]. This new technique links knowledge and skills, not only in chemistry and biology but also in the material sciences, instrumentation, applied mathematics, statistics and computer sciences (Ronchi, 1999).

Biotechnology emerged outside the pharmaceutical industry within academic laboratories and inside dynamic research teams with small biotechnological start-ups resulting from scientific progress in various fields. This entailed an increase in collaborative research between industry and academic science. In the United States, 45% of biomedical published papers were in fact co-publications between industry and universities, i.e. an increase of 50% between 1981 and 1994 (Stephan, 1996). Biotechnology has modified the pharmaceutical research process and was at the origin of the birth of new companies and the reshaping of the cognitive industrial organization.

2.2.3   Toward a New Paradigm?

The described advances in pharmaceutical science seem to correspond to a paradigmatic change[11] expressed by Kuhn. Drug research for a long time guided by chemistry has been progressively shifting since 1970s toward a new thought pattern; 'informational paradigm' according to Drews terminology. He argues the idea that the genome determines the phenotype, the chemical composition and all the other functions of the organism. Then, disease is explained by an information deficit, defect or redundancy or as a cybernetic disorder at the genetic level. 'An informational paradigm in medicine makes information the central point of consideration and thereby establishes itself as the principal all-encompassing attempt at interpretation of biological processes and the diagnostic and therapeutic measures derived from this understanding' (Drews, 1998, p 86) In this model, medical diagnostics should be oriented to the description of information states. The aim of the therapy is to offset to an information defect. To do so, we have the options of both chemical drugs or gene therapy.

The fast-growing number of genetic databases, the increasing use of bio-information technology and the growing interest in decoding the human genome and biotechnology consolidate the integration by pharmaceuticals of new and old methods of research.

The pharmaceutical industry has been developed through chance and science for many centuries. Advances in pharmaceuticals usually stem from scientific rather than industrial fields, firstly through chemistry then molecular biology. Scientific paradigms are easily demonstrated but therein exists the problem of superimposition and coexistence of two scientific paradigms within the same industry; the chemical and the informational paradigm. How, in terms of industrial organization, do we interpret the confrontation between two knowledge blocks based on different knowledge bases?

2.2.4 Paradigms and technological trajectories.

Dosi proposed the concept of the 'technological paradigm'. This approach conceptually defines the problems to be met and requirements to be satisfied, the scientific principles on which to rely and the specific technology to be used practically (Dosi, 1982). A technological paradigm is a model of solutions to selected problems deriving from accumulated knowledge and experience.

In a given industry, 'company innovative activities are thus highly selective, finalized in altogether specific directions, cumulative in the acquisition of abilities for the resolution of problems' (Dosi, 1988, p 1128). A company will thus follow a technological path resulting from the tradeoff between economic constraints on the one hand and technological constraints on the other. Explorations are limited here by the paradigm, and dependent on the company[12] knowledge base. A paradigm change will lead to a modification of trajectories. Biotechnology enables the synthesis of new chemical and biological molecules in great number, and is thus opposed to traditional chemical synthesis technology. In this way it constitutes a technological opportunity for pharmaceutical production but rests on a knowledge base not mastered by pharmaceutical companies. Which way, in such a cognitive context, should the industry go? Two propositions may be considered:

The first, in Shumpeterian tradition, predicts the substitution of pharmaceutical companies by small biotechnology companies. This scenario would consider that large firms have not been able to modify and adapt their technological path and knowledge base. The biotechnological skills would thus destroy existing competence (Tushman and Anderson, 1987). The second, more moderate proposition leans toward the emergence of a bio-pharmaceutical industry where biotechnological skills would reinforce the competence of existing LDFs (Large Drug Firms). McKelvey considers that both scenarios may take place. Companies react differently to technological change, three differentiation factors are recognized by the author: 'expenditure orientation in internal R&D, external contacts and the capability to integrate multiple technologies'. The LDFs will look to integrate new biotechnological advances and thus modernize their method of research, while DBFs (Dedicated Biotechnology Firms) will attempt to bring their new molecules to the market place and will for this reason have to acquire mastery of the development, production and distribution process. The co-existence of the two scientific and technological paradigms, is characterized by the use of complementary knowledge bases. The survival of established or new firms and their development of new paths will depend on their ability to exploit this complementarity. The following section will show that the implementation of strategies is complex and requires time, high costs and the reorganization of the innovation process.

3. CONDITIONS FOR THE EMERGENCE OF THE MARKET FOR KNOWLEDGE IN PHARMACEUTICALS

The preceding analysis has allowed us to underline the essential role of science in the discovery of new medicines and in the conquest of new markets. The appearance of a new 'informational' paradigm has profoundly modified the traditional pharmaceutical knowledge base and has led to cognitive industry reshaping. Let us consider evidence that the nature of knowledge needed for innovation has changed and that this difference advanced the organization of new drugs research. Pharmaceuticals is thus characterized by a new division of innovative labor, which favors the emergence of a knowledge market.

3.1 Characteristics of the Innovation Process

3.1.1   A long, costly and uncertain process

Pharmaceutical research appears as a key factor in the success and survival of companies faced with more intensive international competition. The advent of biotechnology coupled with progress in the instrumentation and bio-information technologies, has certainly shaken the scientific and technological panorama of the industry, but above all, has forced it to integrate new knowledge. This integration has not been achieved at low cost. Whether by means of in-house or external research, the use and exploitation of new biotechnological knowledge has necessitated high investments, notably in R&D expenditure. In the United States, the pharmaceutical industry invested nearly $24 billion in research and development in 1999, representing 20.8% of total industry turnover whereas in 1980, it represented only 11.9%. (Phrma, 1999). R&D expenditure for ethical drugs thus doubled over the period R&D expenditure for ethical drugs thus doubled over the period (figure 1). Investment is essentially home-based with only 16% of funds going abroad. An indicative international comparison places the United States at the top of the list for R&D expenditure.

Research budgets increase world-wide while the rate of new products launched tends to decrease. According to Andersen Consulting, 'the number of new molecules in the development phase per 1,000 researchers should increase from 4 to 5 per year (in 1997), to 14 per year (in the year 2000), by means of an increase of 19% in the workforce and 40% in the budget'.

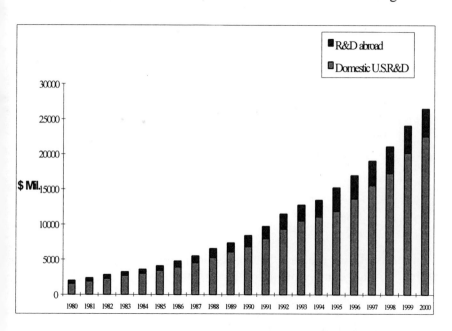

Figure 1: Growth in U.S Domestic R&D and abroad, 1980-2000.
Source : Pharmaceutical research and manufacturers of America, PhRMA annual survey 2000, P113

Moreover, laboratories wishing to maintain an annual growth rate of 10% will have to market 5 to 6 molecules per year, considering that the top twenty world-wide pharmaceutical groups have only introduced on average 0.45 molecules over the period 1990-1994.

According to Grabowski (1990), the United States provide on average, for the period 1961-1987, 23.3% of new molecules, Europe 55.9% and Japan 13.9%. Taking into account consensual products[13] for the period 1970-1985 tends to put these conclusions into perspective. Where the United States marketed 43.5% of consensual products, Japan sold only 4% of the same type of products. Recent studies (EFPIA, 1999) report on a European advance in terms of new chemical or biological entities (NCBE) discovered, but this advance disappears when we take into account the small number of NCBEs launched in the world market place. So the United states is ahead of Europe and Japan. The pharmaceutical market is characterized by competition for new active molecules, but in spite of growing R&D expenditure, the annual rate of new products accepted has decreased considerably over the last few years (Figure 2).

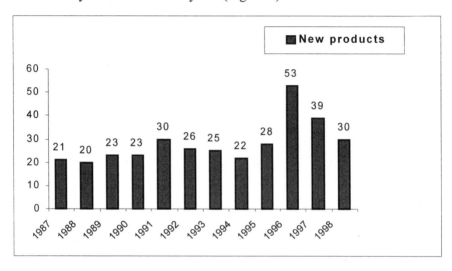

Figure 2: New products approved in USA from 1987 to 1998.
Source: U.S. Food and Drug Administration, 1999

In terms of new products launched, the discovery of an active molecule thus requires huge investment for lower and lower return. What are the reasons for this?

3.1.2   From Molecule to Drug

In enabling the identification of target cells, the biotechnological revolution has led to the reshaping of the research process. Industrial laboratories have partially[14] substituted the hazardous chemical synthesis process of new molecules with 'biochemical screening'. Biotechnology allows the synthesis and mass manufacturing of molecules within shorter time (Figure 3). A molecule requires, on average, 12 to 15 years and $300 to $500 million before its launch on the drug market. Since the innovation process can be linearly split, we can examine it beginning with biochemical screening: a pharmaceutical firm conducts studies using various systems designed to explore the pharmacological activity of compounds. These may involve the use of whole animals, isolated cell cultures and tissues, enzymes and cloned receptor sites, as well as computer models. This leads to a selection of the more promising molecules by in vitro testing. The active molecule is then developed using pre-clinical animal testing followed by human clinical trials (Figure 4).

It is common practice to divide the innovation process into two main steps; discovery and development. The first encompasses all pre-clinical trials and is included in basic research[15]. In 1997, this represented 40% of the American pharmaceutical companies' budget (PHRMA, 1999). The second stage is considered as applied research and requires 42% of the overall budget for industrial research.

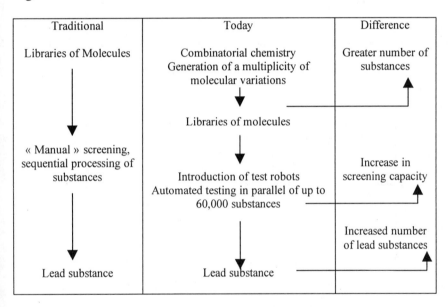

Figure 3: Improvement in Research Methodology.
Source : *In quest of tomorrow's medecines* ;Jürgen Drews, 1997, p 123

In the last few years, the growth in R&D expenditure can be partially explained by an increasing product development time. The rise of biotechnology and its use in the drug research process requires the mastery of new biotechnological skills and new expertise in the instrumentation and bio-computing fields. The product becomes more and more complex and requires increasing development time and costs (Figure 5). Regulatory authorities are also responsible for increased development time and costs due to the imposition of progressively stricter tests and trials for candidate substances. In 1995, the average number of clinical trials per new medicine reached 66, compared to only 30 in 1980.

Pharmaceutical R&D results are analyzed from different perspectives: the first consists of measuring their profitability in terms of new medicines launched in the market place. The second allows the assessment of their scientific and technological return on investment by considering the number of new chemical and biological entities patents (NCBEs). These variables do not evolve in the same direction. The number of NCBEs is increasing but paradoxically, this does not systematically lead to the market launch of new drugs. Therefore, the discovery of an active molecule is a necessary stage in the production process of a new medicine.

	Early Research /Preclinical Testing	Clinical Trials						Phase IV
		Phase I	Phase II	Phase III	FDA			
Years	6.5	1.5	2	3.5	1.5	15 Total		
Test Popula-tion	Laboratory and animal studies	20 to 80 healthy volunteers	100 to 300 patient volunteers	1000 to 3000 patient volunteers				
Purpose	Assess Safety and biological activity	Determine safety and dosage	Evaluate effectiveness, look for side effects	Confirm effectiveness, monitor adverse reactions from long-term use	Review process/ approval			Additio-nal post-marketing testing required by FDA
Success Rate	5,000 -10000 compounds evaluated	5 enter trials			1 approved			

In the USA it takes an average of 15 years for an experimental drug to travel from the laboratory to the patient. Only five in 5,000 compounds that enter pre-clinical testing make it to human testing and only one of these five is finally approved.

Figure 4:The Drug Development and Approval Process in the '90s.
Source: PhRMA, 2000

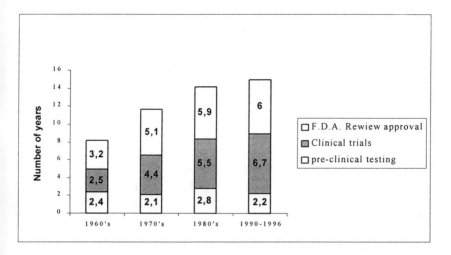

Figure 5: Total development time from synthesis to approval.
Source: PhRMA, 1999

Indeed, molecular discovery is either a *scientific input* when it enables the understanding of disease causes and mechanisms, or a *technological input* when the molecule is an instrument in the synthesis of new active substances.

The use of biotechnology does not seem to have had a major impact on the number of new medicines discovered. On the contrary, data tends to show that R&D expenditure has increased. However, we should not draw too hastily any conclusions from this trend. The biotechnological paradigm is still in its development stage and continues to open up new opportunities for companies with more than 300 potential molecules in the pipeline. Analysts predict that such new companies will be responsible for around half of all new products during the next 10 years (Pharmaceutiques, 2000).

The main contribution of this biotechnological revolution has been in widening the set of opportunities. The race is on to discover NCBEs that will potentially enrich the future of drugs research. Biotechnology, and more specifically the human genome project, constitute an enormous source of new knowledge and information which have advanced the frontiers of science.

3.2 Fragmentation of Knowledge and Division of Innovative Labor in Pharmaceuticals

3.2.1 Information Paradigm and Generalization of Knowledge

The emergence of biotechnology and the development of associated scientific disciplines constitute for Arora and Gambardella (1994) 'The

Changing Technology of Technological Change'. When innovation depended principally upon trial and error procedures in physical experimentation, knowledge bases relied principally on tacit knowledge and experience. The information generated was local and context-dependent and so it was preferable for the innovator to own the specific complementary assets for development and marketing. In such a context, the innovation process had to be vertically integrated.

Conversely, if concrete information can be associated with a general phenomenon, it becomes less context-dependent and can be codified for use by other firms. The use of general and abstract knowledge makes it possible to reach a higher degree of information access than before. Moreover, developments in the fields of information technologies and computerization reduce even further the inter-firm communication costs.

This reflects the fact that 'the changing technology of technological change' makes the new technology production process more divisible. All things considered, the body of knowledge and information required to innovate can be separated into distinct pieces of knowledge, expertise and information, within different organizations, and gathered at a later stage. The emergence of many firms providing biological databases is widespread where the knowledge can be codified giving rise to formulae, blueprints and designs. As early as the 1980s, the American National Library of Medicine developed the concept of a 'matrix of biological knowledge'. This concept reflects the idea of interconnectedness and underlines the unity of such knowledge related to all species and at all levels from molecular biology to populations and ecosystems (Cantley and Dibner, 1998).

As we have outlined, the growth of scientific knowledge in the fields of molecular biology and genetic engineering has clarified important aspects of the human metabolism as well as the biological and chemical action of certain substances. At the same time, new high-performance instruments have enabled the study of the behavior and structure of proteins and molecules. Pharmaceutical knowledge has become more abstract, though scientific advances have supported the development of biotechnology. We can thus partially justify the division of innovative labor which has taken place between the large pharmaceutical companies and the small biotechnology-based firms.

It is nonetheless necessary to distinguish two phases in the pharmaceutical knowledge generalization process. The first phase began with the first generation of biotechnology. This latter principally emerged within scientific spheres and was then transferred via *star scientists* (Zucker and Darby, 1996 and 1997) toward biotechnological start-ups. The transfer from university to this bio-industry was made at a lower cost, since academic research teams incorporated scientific and technical knowledge, and mastered research theories and methodologies associated with the biotechnological product. Knowledge was thus abstract and generally applicable within this large scientific community. Progressively, knowledge became fragmentable and embedded in different research teams as a foundation for the biotechnological industry composed of a myriad of small firms. During the first phase knowledge transfers occurred between university and industry. Different reasoning supports the ongoing second phase where both the receptors/emitters and the content of this knowledge transfer are being modified. The different DBFs specialize and acquire expertise in biotechnological R&D. They work on screening, biological synthesis, genetic engineering or genome decoding. The knowledge and expertise produced now become dependent on the production context and are not easily transferable from one organization to another. Only the result of research activity; i.e. the molecule, can be transferred. The development of an active ingredient requires research procedures and a good deal of intuition, but its structure and effects are easily communicable in formulae and blueprints. Thus, the research results become subject to market transactions. Accordingly, a distinction must be made between the R&D process and the R&D results since they entail differences in the knowledge exchange modes.

We assume that the division of innovative labor in this second phase is carried out among DBFs, but also between DBFs and LDFs, in order to better exploit biotechnological advances.

3.2.2 Chemical Paradigm and Localized Knowledge

As many authors have underlined, there is a DBF specialization in the area of bio-pharmaceutical research and development. (Arora and Gambardella, 1994; Pisano, 1997; Teece, 1998; Saviotti, 1998 and Senker, 1998). There is a functional specialization (Pisano, 1991) between DBFs and LDFs. The DBFs act as R&D laboratories, while the LDFs deal with clinical trials, production and marketing of new products. Several factors could explain this industrial configuration. The first is that DBFs have in their possession a huge potential of new active molecules to exploit. They possess the technological knowledge that the LDFs do not have since the latter are only concerned with chemical trajectory. Their technological knowledge base is therefore complementary to that of the LDF.

Very few biotechnological firms achieve complete vertical integration. Several reasons can be put forward: high development costs, weak distribution networks, uncertainty associated with the innovation process. Small firms lack the competence that is required in order to bring a product to market, which Teece (1986) calls complementary assets. They are not able to master the approval procedures for a new pharmaceutical product. Pharmaceutical companies derived from the chemical paradigm have clinical test experience. Commonly a molecule that reaches phase III and does not obtain approval will lead to a drop of 40% in the DBF's securities value. The authorization phase is highly risky and is very costly for a start-up. Conversely, a large firm has enough financial resources to offset losses due to a molecule that is not finally approved, by relying on molecules belonging to other therapeutic fields. Moreover, they generally possess the distribution networks necessary for the new products sale. These networks are crucial when the molecule discovered only constitutes a minor innovation. This is the case for all molecules approved under different dosages, for the recombination of several existing molecules, or for active ingredients that only marginally improve the therapeutic effects of existing drugs.

Thus, large firms have the knowledge associated with product development, production and marketing. This tacit knowledge cannot be easily transferred to DBFs, and therefore cannot easily become the subject of market transaction, due to its roots in the organization and its component individuals. However, this does not prevent the exchange of production services or clinical trials. If we consider the product or service markets, we observe that knowledge, belonging to the product or the service traded, is not purchased as an input but as an output, whereas the biotechnological knowledge is an input of the innovation process. To synthesize a biotechnological molecule is just a step in the innovation process. Discoveries must be developed, validated and marketed before being sold in the new drugs final market place(figure 6).

Many knowledge exchanges are expected between DBFs and LDFs, taking into account that their respective knowledge bases are complementary.

3.2.3   Transfer Modes of Biotechnological Knowledge

At the stage of the analysis, we can study the knowledge transfer modes. New knowledge has long been acquired in-house, according to a linear model of innovation, from the invention to the marketing of the new product. Pharmaceuticals has developed in this way within the chemical paradigm. The sources of knowledge creation were in-house R&D and production process learning. The advent of biotechnology has allowed the development of another innovation model exploiting both the internal sources of knowledge, to maintain a sufficient absorptive capacity (Cohen and Levinthal, 1990), and external sources, by means of different institutional arrangements. Arora, Fosfuri and Gambardella (1999) highlighted the rise of 'markets for technology' in the fields of chemistry and pharmaceuticals. Howells names them 'contracts, research and technology markets (CRTMs)'. One can think of the chemical and pharmaceutical components either as technological inputs or as scientific and technological knowledge. We suggest using the generic term of *biotechnological market for knowledge*, which offers the advantage of integrating both the scientific and technological dimension.

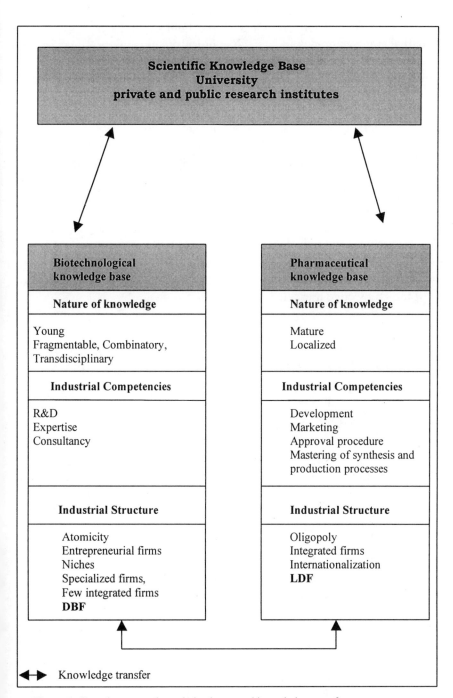

Figure 6: Complementary knowledge bases and knowledge transfer.

Outsourcing is being developed in the forms of joint ventures, partnerships, licenses or R&D contracts (Howells, 1997), thus promoting the emergence of specialized providers in the field of biotechnology. Several alternative transfer modes of biotechnological knowledge are then possible between these specialized suppliers and firms wishing to acquire this knowledge. The existence of a scientific and technological input market protected by an efficient system of property rights allows the different biopharmaceutical competitors to trade knowledge (Teece 1998). However, there are alternatives to the market mediation that many authors have underlined and analyzed, especially the growing collaboration in the bio-pharmaceutical industry (Shan, Walker and Kogut, 1994; Sapienza, 1989; Tapon and Thong,). Such exchange can be implemented via joint ventures, co-development of new molecules or R&D collaboration contracts.

Here, the purpose is twofold. On the one hand, we empirically underline the importance of biotechnological knowledge flow between different companies within the industry. On the other hand, we specify the exchange modes selected by the different agents. This will enable us to analyze the relationship between the evolution of the cognitive industrial context and the rise of the knowledge market.

4.   THE EMERGENCE OF THE BIOTECHNOLOGICAL MARKET FOR KNOWLEDGE; QUANTITATIVE ANALYSIS

4.1   Data and Methodology

The co-evolution of pharmaceuticals and biotechnology has been widely studied. Various works have focused on the empirical analysis of knowledge transfer between the academic sphere and biopharmaceutical industry.(Zucher and Darby, 1997; Stephan, 1996) However, these studies do not give us enough information about the privileged modes of knowledge transfer.

The purpose of the following study is to determine which are the privileged knowledge transfer patterns, and to observe their evolution over the past fifteen years, with reference to exchange partners and their knowledge base.

4.1.1   Data

Empirical information comes from the Recap database[16]. It is built on three types of public information: articles in the business and financial press, US Securities and Exchange Commission files and presentations made by firms during conferences and public meetings. It covers 7,900 alliances in the field of biological sciences since 1978. Several types of agreement are included: between pharmaceutical and biotechnological firms, between biotechnological firms and between pharmaceutical ones. In alliances involving a pharmaceutical and a biotechnological firm, the former is most often the customer which buys assets, sponsors the component development or research or contracts a license. The latter is regarded as the R&D-dedicated firm selling financial and technological assets, research and/or development services and licenses. For the period 1982-1999[17], there were only 4,350 agreements of this type recorded.

4.1.2 Multiplicity of Agreements and Patterns of Knowledge Exchange

Several types of inter-firms relationship coexist in bio-pharmaceuticals: 31 types of agreement are met in biotechnology covering acquisition, marketing, R&D contracts, joint-ventures, collaboration, etc.

Data analysis is complicated due to the great variety and complexity of agreements. Alliances involving only simple contracts (development, research, or the granting of licenses) are unusual and often coupled with financial exchange and/or acquisition of equity. Up to six different agreements can be found in the same alliance. The difficulty consists in the selection of a main contract, i.e. which is at the bargaining core. Order of priority must be imposed Four categories of agreement will be analyzed and classified according to the exchange modes.

Market exchange
If the object of a contract is research and/or development and/or the granting of a license and implies a payment from the customer, it is considered as a *market transaction on biotechnological knowledge*, which may or may not be coupled with an acquisition of equity. Three categories will thus be analyzed. The first encompasses all research and/or development contracts initiated between the companies involved in a given R&D (R/D) project. The terms of the contract define the different stages of research, the delivery deadlines for the molecule, the total expenditure depending often on the speed of advances and results, and property rights of each part. The second category (L+D/R) groups together the granting of license contracts which may or may not be accompanied by research and/or development. Obviously, the substance, which is the object of the license, is already patented and its content is less uncertain than in the case of a pure R&D contract. These two categories form the market for knowledge . The object of exchange is the knowledge embedded in the targeted molecules.

Acting on this principle, Genentech and Lilly signed as early as 1978 a development agreement, coupled with a license for the recombined insulin patented by Genentech. Lilly assumed the development costs of the insulin and then obtained the right to market it, but the technology remained the ownership of Genentech.

If the contract concerns research and/or development (R/D) and/or the granting of a license (L) and if it is coupled with the acquisition of equity (E), it is qualified as a *sponsored market*. The customer partially funds the supplier's R&D activities through the acquisition of equity. This has the effect of reducing opportunism and thus provides opportunities for further negotiation. It represents a double financial transfer which includes payments associated with the R&D contract or the license transfer on the one hand, and the acquisition of equity on the other. Similarly, Bayer (LDF) invested $96.6 billion per equity in Millennium (DBF) in 1998 and initiated a research contract at the same time for a 'target discovery program' using 'the gene expressing and sequencing technology' (Recap) owned by Millenium.

Co-operation

If an agreement supposes some kind of collaboration, joint venture (JV), co-development (Co-D), co-marketing (Co-M)[18] or co-promotion (Co-P)[19], it will not be noted as an element of a market for knowledge, but rather as a more or less formal *co-operation agreement*. Different co-operation agreements are possible and are classified according to the contract with which they are associated. Three categories are considered: the first encompasses collaboration on research and/or development (Col + R/D), the second regroups various collaboration agreements with the granting of a license (Col + L + R/D). By collaboration we understand the definition of a common project by two companies aiming to extend scientific and technological knowledge in a specific field. Any additional information must be communicated to the partners. Property rights are not fixed ex ante and are negotiated between two parties once research has been completed. This can lead to patenting or co-patenting and therefore to licensing. In 1993 Human Genome Sciences (HGS) and SmithKline (SB) collaborated 'to obtain useful EST (expressed sequence tag) sequence data on all expressed human genes and, by themselves or with third parties, to develop practical applications therefore. Such data shall consist principally of HGS technology, HGS patents, SB technology and SB patents' (Recap, 2000).

Joint ventures and co-development, co-marketing, co-promotion agreements form the last category. A very early example of successful co-marketing was the co-operation between Roche and Wellcome with trimethoprim, under the names Bactrim and Septrin, respectively (Financial Times Pharmaceuticals, Dec. 1999).

Financial Operations
We classify exchanges of a purely financial nature under the same heading. Merger-acquisition agreements (Acq), the purchase of assets (Ast), acquisition of holdings (E) and diverse financial operations such as swaps and options (option)[20] are placed together under the heading *financial operations*. We place less importance on their impact if they are coupled with development or research contracts, collaboration, joint ventures or licenses.

4.2 Predominance of Market Transfer of Biotechnological Knowledge

4.2.1 Exchange Partners (Table 5)

The number of agreements involving biotechnological knowledge increased considerably, growing from 177 agreements for the period 1982-1985 to 2,131 agreements over the period 1996-1999. This increase in number of agreements underlines and confirms the rising interest in these new technologies (Figure 7).

Exchange of biotechnological knowledge was first made between small biotechnological firms and large pharmaceutical companies covering 94.4% of exchanges over the period 1982-1985. Transfers between start-ups did not take off until the 1990s, to finally represent 44% of the exchanges between 1996 and 1999; while transfers between the biotechnological and pharmaceutical firms represent only 45.5% of the exchanges. (Table 5) Agreements between large firms are less frequent since they represent at most 14.8% of the total exchanges.

Here, we could put forward two arguments. On the one hand, the volume of exchangeable knowledge is lower for large firms recently entered, in an in-house manner, into the field of biotechnological research. On the other hand, their development and marketing capabilities lead them toward strategies of in-house new molecules development.

Table 5. Evolution of exchange partners from 1982 to 1999 (%)

Years	1982-1985	1986-1990	1991-1995	1996-1999	Total
Drug/Drug	3.4	5.0	14.8	11.7	11.5
Drug/Biotech	94.4	83.4	56.5	45.5	56.8
Biotech/Biotech	2.2	11.6	28.7	42.8	31.7

Source: Recap Database 2000

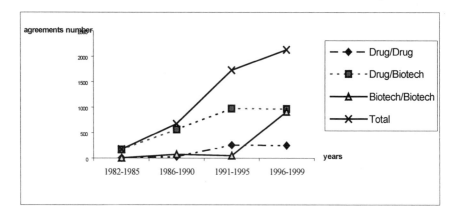

Figure 7: Evolution of biotechnological agreements with reference to different types of partnerships for the period between 1982 and 1999.
Source: Recap Database, 2000

Knowledge transfers between biotechnological and pharmaceutical firms represented almost all exchanges during the 1980s, this phase corresponds to the development of the first biotechnological drugs. Large firms need then to integrate new competence through biotechnology start-ups. During this period, start-ups act as intermediaries, ensuring the transformation of generic knowledge originating from the academic sphere, toward specific knowledge applications (Autio, 1997). These exchanges between large and small firms increased during the early 1990s, but their relative share has since fallen to the benefit of inter-DBF transfers. Growth of these exchanges can be explained by a higher maturity of DBF which leads them to integrate other activities, e.g. development test, manufacturing, marketing, and thus to become larger. An analysis of exchange modes will enable us to obtain a more complete understanding.

4.2.2   Biotechnological Knowledge Transfer Modes between Different Partners

DBF/LDF (table 6a)

Over the period studied[21], 2,508 agreements transfers of biotechnological knowledge occurred between biotechnological and pharmaceutical firms. A great number of these exchanges (65% of the agreements) were carried out through market channels. We may note the emergence of a market for knowledge between DBFs and LDFs. Two main features may be underlined:

The first is the importance of the licenses share among total exchanges, it is evaluated at 63.5% of the market exchanges (table 6a; 1,035/1,631).

Licensing appears then as a privileged instrument for knowledge exchanges where there is no uncertainty with respect to molecular discovery since it is already patented. Only the length and cost of the development phase are not precisely known. License is more often associated with a development or a research agreement (55%). Indeed, the small firm undertakes the pre-clinical development phase of the molecule, which is licensed to the large firm. The latter will then ensure the costs of clinical development, those associated with manufacturing and marketing and the drug approval procedures. In France, in 1999, licensed drugs represented 30% of laboratory revenues as opposed to 24% in 1992[22]. This trend can also be observed in table 7a, where the number of licenses is seen to increase by 30% between 1986 and 1999.

The second characteristic reflects moderate use of R&D contracts. In this case, contractual uncertainty is very high which explains the relatively low statistical significance of this type of agreement, representing only 11.56% of agreed contracts. The traded knowledge is hardly observable at the early stage of the contract and thus can lead to opportunist behavior. The biotechnological firm might not provide all the information and knowledge associated with the molecule, and the large pharmaceutical firm can renegotiate the terms of the contract once the molecule is delivered.

The technological input market is thus more developed than the innovation market. As for sponsored markets, acquisition of equity is less frequently used: only 19.7% of agreements. This means that the large pharmaceutical firms are sometimes attempting either to influence the orientation of the knowledge suppliers' research goals, or to help them in a difficult financial context. The funding of a DBF may represent opportunities for a future research collaboration.

Exchange modes have evolved over the period studied. Transfers carried out at the end of the 1980s were principally made via the market; co-operation represented only 2 to 10% of exchanges. This tendency was reversed during the 1990s, when collaboration between LDFs and DBFs intensified, reaching 28.1% of agreements in 1995. This result, associated with the growing number of mergers and acquisitions, can be explained by the strongly localized knowledge in second generation biotechnology (Pisano, 1991). Consequently, transfer requires informal relations and higher transaction costs, and the exchange of formulae and reports no longer suffices. The purpose of the exchange is to access to each firm's specific expertise; the knowledge is then more tacit and cannot be exchanged on the market This is particularly the case for new biotechnological production processes (Pisano, 1997).

This evolution may reflect mature technological trajectories, the cognitive and other costs involved in the technological transfer will thus lessen the competitive advantage of biotechnological knowledge specialized firms. The market for knowledge involving the LDFs and the DBFs is dwindling due to increasing R&D internalization by the knowledge purchasers.

LDF/LDF: (Table 6b)

The small number of agreements registered before the beginning of the 1990s means that, due to lack of information, we cannot draw conclusions from the biotechnological knowledge exchange modes. Market transactions represented between 30% and 50% of the biotechnological knowledge exchanges for the period 1992-1999, and were essentially composed of licenses accompanied (or not) by R&D contracts (86% of market transactions). The mid-1990s were characterized by an increasing proportion of financial operations. In fact, the share of merger-acquisitions out of the total number of agreements oscillated between 13 and 20%. Intensified competition and growing R&D costs led firms to merger in order to reach a critical size, enabling them to hold an optimal molecules portfolio. This allowed them to anticipate the availability of key molecules in the public domain and to guarantee a portfolio of profitable ethical drugs. Knowledge transfer via co-operation has diminished over the last four years, representing only 12% of exchanges in 1999 against 25% in 1995.

DBF/DBF: (Table 6c)

Over the period studied, the knowledge market preponderance weakened while financial co-operation transactions grew. There was only one acquisition in 1988 against 44 in 1999. Most small firms were created in the 1980s. Some of these have reached a degree of maturity, which allows them to release the necessary funds for their external growth. In the long run, the growing number of R&D co-operations reflects their wish to extend their biotechnological knowledge base. Co-operation allows them to do so while limiting risks associated with wider R&D programs, which a small structure cannot support.

A market for knowledge has emerged between small firms. On the average it represents 50% of the agreements studied, and is essentially composed of license agreements. Thus, LDFs and DBFs try to extend their product portfolio in order to support their R&D investments. The continuous increase in the number of agreements between DBFs, whether or not market agreements, shows a more advanced stage of paradigmatic development. Some small firms are in a position to develop their own products and launch them on the market without any support from large firms. Indeed, they have integrated and developed the necessary competencies for the new drugs development.

This is a result of learning by doing in the biotechnological production process, but also of learning through successive interactions during collaboration with LDFs.

4.2.3   Emergence of a market for Knowledge.

Whoever the partners involved in the agreements, we noticed a market predominance in the transfer of biotechnological knowledge. 59.7% of agreements consist in licenses, R&D or sponsored markets. Even though co-operation agreements represent only 18% of exchanges we should be prudent when interpreting this figure. Many agreements evolve in time, for instance a license can be later transformed into a closer co-operation between two or more firms. Likewise, a co-operation agreement can favor future market relationships between the current partners in other therapeutic areas.

These results demonstrate the existence of a biotechnological knowledge market between LDFs and DBFs (60% of agreements) and thus empirically confirm the existence of an innovative labor division in bio-pharmaceuticals. But above all, they allow us to complete the preceding theoretical analyses by highlighting the recourse to market channels for inter-DBF and inter-LDF knowledge exchanges. This reflects a change in the technological paths within the industry. A convergence is taking place between the biotechnological and the chemical knowledge base. Certain small firms are integrating and manufacturing their own products, while large ones are developing biotechnological skills in-house, occasionally becoming specialized providers (42.6% of agreements between LDFs in 1999) (Figure 8).

Conclusion

The great recourse to market in order to purchase the required biotechnological knowledge brings us to formulate some comments:
-    it confirms the idea developed by Arora and Gambardella according to which there is a generalization of abstract knowledge in pharmaceuticals which, by allowing fragmentation of knowledge, has led to a division of innovative labor;
-    the importance of market agreements between DBFs and LDFs rather expresses a *vertical division* of innovative labor while inter-LDF or inter-DBF market transactions point out evidence of a *horizontal division* of innovative labor;
-    the property rights system for biotechnological knowledge favors an efficient functioning of a market for knowledge However the system is not perfect, with many firms having to resort to court cases in the aim of defending their IPRs[23];

-      the growing exchanges of biotechnological knowledge show yet another proof of the increasing role played by knowledge and information in a globalized economy.

Table 6a. Biotechnological knowledge exchanges between DBFs and LDFs

	1986	1987	1988	1989	1990	1991	1992	1993	1994	1995	1996	1997	1998	1999	Total
1. Market exchange	**57**	**85**	**81**	**101**	**144**	**124**	**125**	**136**	**127**	**105**	**136**	**127**	**151**	**132**	**1631**
License	13	12	26	20	24	32	30	51	45	35	44	41	48	40	461
L+D/R	17	25	23	32	48	39	42	44	34	32	55	57	65	61	574
Total license	**30**	**37**	**49**	**52**	**72**	**71**	**72**	**95**	**79**	**67**	**99**	**98**	**113**	**101**	**1035**
R/D	18	36	22	31	43	27	24	22	15	10	5	6	16	15	290
Market for knowledge	**48**	**73**	**71**	**83**	**115**	**98**	**96**	**117**	**94**	**77**	**104**	**104**	**129**	**116**	**1325**
E+L+R/D	8	5	8	15	25	20	25	15	31	27	31	20	20	16	266
E+D/R	1	7	2	3	4	6	4	4	2	1	1	3	2	0	40
Sponsored market	**9**	**12**	**10**	**18**	**29**	**26**	**29**	**19**	**33**	**28**	**32**	**23**	**22**	**16**	**306**
2.Coopération	**5**	**11**	**7**	**3**	**15**	**20**	**20**	**35**	**58**	**61**	**56**	**69**	**47**	**44**	**451**
CoI+R/D	1	5	2		2	5	5	8	21	18	18	25	19	21	150
CoI+L+D/R		3		1	2	4	9	13	21	32	24	36	15	7	167
Collaboration	**1**	**8**	**2**	**1**	**4**	**9**	**14**	**21**	**42**	**50**	**42**	**61**	**34**	**28**	**317**
Joint-Venture	4	3	5	1	9	9	6	6	10	3	6	5	6	10	83
Co-D/Co-P/Co-M				1	2	2	0	8	6	8	8	3	7	6	51
3. Financial Operations	**3**	**6**	**9**	**18**	**19**	**32**	**21**	**27**	**33**	**51**	**52**	**63**	**48**	**44**	**426**
Acq	1			2	3	5	3	5	16	23	22	24	27	31	162
Ast	1	2	1	7	10	16	12	11	2	13	26	33	18	11	163
option		1		1	2	2	3	2	3	9	2	2	2	1	30
Equity(E)	1	3	8	8	4	9	3	9	12	6	2	4	1	1	71
Total agreements	65	102	97	122	178	176	166	198	218	217	244	259	246	220	2508

Source: Adapted from Recap Database 2000

Table 6b. Biotechnological knowledge exchange between LDF

Years	1986	1987	1988	1989	1990	1991	1992	1993	1994	1995	1996	1997	1998	1999	Total
1.Market exchange	5	2	3	6	4	0	9	35	30	25	32	27	25	20	223
License	5	1	1	3	1	0	3	19	16	12	26	11	9	16	123
L + D/R	0	1	1	1	3	0	4	11	9	7	6	13	11	2	69
Total license	5	2	2	4	4	0	7	30	25	19	32	24	20	18	192
R/D	0	0	1	2	0	0	2	5	5	5	0	2	4	2	28
Market for knowledge	5	2	3	6	4	0	9	35	30	24	32	26	24	20	220
E + L + R/D										1		1	1		3
E + D/R															
Sponsored market	0	0	0	0	0	0	0	0	0	1	0	1	1	0	3
2.Cooperation	0	1	3	1	0	2	10	25	25	20	31	12	9	5	144
Col + R/D								1	2	2	8	3	1	1	18
Col + L + D/R								1	2	1					4
Collaborations	0	0	0	0	0	0	0	2	4	3	8	3	1	1	22
Joint Venture	0	1	3	1	0	2	3	11	12	8	14	3		1	59
Co-D/Co-P/Co-M							7	12	9	9	9	6	8	3	63
3.Financial operations	0	0	0	6	3	0	1	10	29	34	27	23	21	17	171
Acq				5	3			7	18	17	12	11	11	10	94
Ast				1				3	10	16	10	12	9	7	68
Option											1				1
Equity							1		1	1	4		1		8
Total agreements	5	3	6	13	7	2	20	70	84	79	90	62	55	42	538

Source: Adapted from Recap Database 2000

Table 6c. Biotechnological knowledge exchange between DBF

Years	1986	1987	1988	1989	1990	1991	1992	1993	1994	1995	1996	1997	1998	1999	Total
1.Market exchange	7	10	11	8	23	32	56	47	62	64	104	96	99	111	730
License	6	2	7	4	17	11	25	19	20	26	48	41	54	50	
L + D/R	1	4	2	3		6	12	12	17	13	26	25	18	43	
Total license	7	6	9	7	17	17	37	31	37	39	74	66	72	93	
R/D		3	1	1	2	8	9	3	10	16	10	11	12	14	
Market for knowledge	7	9	10	8	19	25	46	34	47	55	84	77	84	107	612
E + L + R/D		1	1		3	6	10	12	13	9	19	19	15	3	
E + D/R					1	1		1	2		1			1	
Sponsored market	0	1	1	0	4	7	10	13	15	9	20	19	15	4	
2.Coopération	1	0	0	0	2	6	19	17	20	35	53	77	61	56	347
Col + R/D					2	2	7	13	9	12	24	45	38	45	
Col + L + D/R						3	9	3	8	14	22	27	19	8	
Collaborations	0	0	0	0	2	5	16	16	17	26	46	72	57	53	
Joint Venture	1					1	3	1	3	7	6	3	2	2	
Co-D/Co-P/Co-M										2	1	2	2	1	
3.Financial operations	0	0	3	9	4	10	11	18	43	56	69	53	59	75	410
Acq			1	4	3	8	8	12	35	34	55	36	40	44	
Ast			2	5		1	1	6	5	15	9	12	14	28	
Option										5	1			1	
Equity					1	1	2		3	2	4	5	5	2	
Total agreements	8	10	14	17	29	48	86	82	125	155	226	226	219	242	1487

Source: Adapted from Recap Database 2000

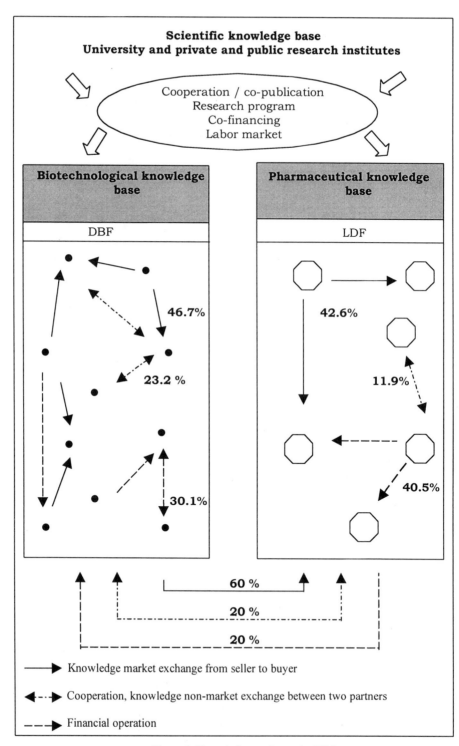

Figure 8: Knowledge exchange in 1999.

NOTES

[1]Source:IMS,1996

[2]According to some surveys, people over 65 years of age consume three times as many medicines as their juniors. In thirty seven years, French domestic expenditure on medicines has increased tenfold. This trend can be observed in all developed countries.

[3]One observes a high increase in production between 1987 and 1991, slowing in 1992 to reach a critical point in 1993 (sales fell by 15% in Germany and 7% in Italy) then picking up again in 94 (except in Italy).

[4]8% in the 1990s

[5]A specificity of this market resides in the fact that pharmaceutical products are certainly neither chosen (this is done by the practitioner) nor totally paid for the consumer (in many countries the cost is partially born by the state).

[6]Food and Drug Administration

[7]Amendments Kefauver-Harris 1962

[8]Especially Japan and Europe

[9]Scientific field that studies molecular processes and seeks in particular to characterize and isolate genetic heritage

[10]Recombinant chemistry uses the principle of natural selection to study and explain a wide range of biotechnological phenomena. Evaluated molecules are considered to be analogous to variants or mutants present in nature. The parallel evaluation of different groups of molecules is considered as a kind of artificial biological selection that leads to the emergence of an acceptable product or the identification of components to be used in later refining.

[11]In his work '*The Structure of Scientific Revolution*', Thomas Kuhn analyses the concept in relation to physics and shows that when a predominant theory is no longer sufficient to explain contradictory observations and discoveries, one shifts to a new paradigm with greater exploratory potential. This move often gives rise to the birth of a new generation of scientists in the field in question.

[12]Nelson and Winter (1982) define the knowledge base as the sum of information and past experimentation and codified knowledge, but it also requires the use of inventors' specific non-codified ability.

[13] In Grabowski's study, consensual products are newly discovered chemical and biological entities, patented and rapidly distributed in a number of countries. In this way he links the degree of importance of a discovery to the speed with which it is distributed internationally.

[14]Firms have not totally abandoned the chemical process of molecular production. Some substances are still made by chemical synthesis.

[15]It is fundamental in the sense that its aim is to create and develop a general knowledge of the human metabolism, in reaction to different substances tested. It is nonetheless applied since it is carried out in an industrial context and therefore from a production point of view.

[16]Recombinant Capital: http/www.recap.com/

[17]One can refer to the works of Zucker and Darby for information relating to modes of transfer of knowledge between these different entities.

[18]Co-development assumes the sharing of development expenditure, co-promotion and co-marketing entail distribution of costs and marketing revenue.

[19]Co-promotion consists of marketing a product under the same label and brand whereas co-marketing markets this same product under a different name.

[20]Different financial agreements such as swaps or options are rarely the object of specific transaction, they more often than not accompany licence agreements or collaboration.

[21]The analysis of modes of transfer of knowledge was made here over a shorter period due to the small number of agreements recorded for the period 1982-1985.

[22]Source: Pharmaceutiques (1999): http/www.pharmaceutiques.com/

[23]Intellectual property right

REFERENCES

Antonelli C. The Evolution of the Industrial Organisation of the Production of Knowledge, 1998; S14S, Topical Paper STEP Group.

Arora A, Gambardella A. The changing technology of technological change: general and abstract knowledge and the division of innovative labour. Research Policy; 1994, 23:523-47.

Arora A, Gambardella A. Complementary and external linkages: the strategies of the large firms in biotechnology. Journal of Industrial Economics, 1990, 4: 361-79.

Arora A, Gambardella A,Fosfuri A.: Markets for Technology (why do we see them, why don't we see more of them and why we should care), Business Economics Series, Working Paper, 1999,17, 523-33.

Autio E. New technology-based firms in innovation networks synpletic and generative impacts. Research Policy, 1997; 26: 263-81.

Athreye S.: On Markets in Knowledge, ESRC, Working Paper, 1998, 83, Cambridge University.

Böhme G, van der Daele W,. Die Geselschaftliche Orientierung des wissenchaftlichen Fortschrittes . in Starnberger Studien, 1978; 339-75.

Cantley Mark, Dibner Mark. ' The Impact of Modern Biotechnology on R&D in the Life Sciences, and on Organisational Structure end the Management of Research in the Biopharmaceutical Industry: Concepts and measurements.' In *Part II: Biotechnology, Medical Innovation and the Economy: The Key Relationships.* OECD (DSTI/STP/BIO(98)8/Final), 1998 .

Caves R, Whinston M, Hurwitz M. Patent Expiration , Entry, and Competition in the U.S. Pharmaceutical Industry: An Exploratory Analysis. Brooking Papers: Microeconomics, 1991,Mars.

Cohen W.M, Levinthal O.A. Absorptive Capacity: a New Perspective on Learning and Innovation, Administrative Science Quarterly, 1990; 35: 128-152.

Darby M, Zucker L.G. Present at Biotechnological Revolution: Transformation of technological Identity For a Large Incumbent Pharmaceutical Firm, Research Policy,1997; 26: 429-447.

Dosi Giovanni. *Technical Change and Economic Theory.* London: Pinter Publishers, 1988.

Dosi G. Technological Paradigms and Technological Trajectories: A suggested Interpretation of the Determinants and Directions of Technical Change. Research Policy, 11: 147-162.

Drews Jürgen. *Intent and Coincidence in Drug Research: The Impact of Biotechnology.* Basel: Editiones Roche, 1996.

Drews Jürgen . *In Quest of Tomorrow's Medecines*, New York: Springer-Verlag, 1998.

European Federation of Pharmaceutical Industries and Associations. *The Pharmaceutical Industry in Figures.* EFPIA: 1999.

Finch S. Building the Compagny's Portfolio. Financial Times Pharmaceuticals.1999, décember.

Grabowski H. An Analysis of US International Competitivness in Pharmaceuticals, Managerial and Decision Economics; 1989, spring, 27-33.

Howells J. Research and Technology Outsourcing, CRIC Discussion Paper, 1997,6.

Kühn Thomas. *The Structure of Scientific Revolution*. Chicago: Second ed. University Press, 1970.

Mc.Kelvey. Discontinuities in Genetic Engineering for Pharmaceuticals? Firm Jumps and Lock-in Systems of innovation. Technology Analysis and strategic management,1996; 8, 2: 107-16.

Nelson Richard, Winter Sidney. *An Evolutionary Theory of Economic Change* . Cambridge MA: Harvard University Press, 1982.

OECD. Biotechnology: International Trends and Perspectives 1982

Pharmaceutiques OnLine. www.pharmaceutiques.com.

Pharmaceutical Research & Manufacturers of America. Pharmaceuticals Industry Profile. PhRMA reports: 1999 and 2000 available on www.phrma.org..

Pisano Gary. -*The Development Factory. Unlocking the Potential of Innovation Process*, Boston : Harvard Business School Press, 1997.

Pisano G. The Governance of Innovation: Vertical Integration and Collaborative Arrangements in The Biotechnology Industry, Research Policy; 1991,20: 237-251.

Roche. *The Pocket Roche*. Basel: F.Hoffmann-La Roche, 1998.

Ronchi E. 'The Cycle of Innovation'. *In Part II: Biotechnology, Medical Innovation and the Economy: The Key Relationships* OECD (DSTI/STP/BIO(98)8/Final), 1998 .

Ronchi E. Biotechnology and the Revolution in Health Care and Pharmaceuticals: The Science and the Technology. STI Review, 1996, 19.

Sapienza A. R&D Collaboration as a Global Competitive Tactic: Biotechnology and the Ethical Pharmaceutical Industry. R&D Management; 1989, 19, 4: 285-295.

Saviotti P.P. ' Industrial Structure and the Dynamics of Knowledge Generation in Biotechnology.' In *Biotechnology and Comparative Advantage. Europe's Firms and the Challenge,* Senker J, ed. Cheltenham: Edward Elgar Publishing, 1998.

Senker J. *Biotechnology and Comparative Advantage. Europe's Firms and the Challenge.* Cheltenham: Edward Elgar Publishing, 1998.

Shan W, Walker G, Kogut B. Interfirm Cooperation and Startup Innovation in the Biotechnology Industry. Strategic Management Journal; 1994, 15: 387-394.

Sharp M. The Science of Nations: Multinationals and American Biotechnology, STEEP discussion paper, SPRU,1996,28.

Stephan P. The Economics of Science. Journal of Economic Litterature; 1996,34, 3, September, 1199-235.

Tapon F, Thong M. Are Research Collaborations an Effective Strategy for Pharmaceutical Firms? An Empirical Study: 1988-1995, Working Paper, University of Guelph: june 1999.

Teece D.J. Capturing Value from Knowledge Assets : The new Economy, Markets for Know-How, and Intangible Assets. California Management Review, 1998, 40, 3, 55-79.

Teece D.J. Profiting from technological innovation, Research Policy, 15, 6: 285-305.

Tushman M.L, Anderson P. Technological Discontinuities and Organizational Environments, Administrative Science Quarterly, 31, 3: 439-465.

Weinman N. *Grands Groupes Pharmaceutiques Mondiaux: Une Nouvelle Approche de la Santé.*, France: Ministère de l'Economie, des Finances et de l'Industrie, décembre 1997.

Chapter 6

INNOVATIVE LABOR AND INTELLECTUAL PROPERTY MARKET IN THE SEMICONDUCTOR INDUSTRY

Rajà Attia, Isabelle Davy & Roland Rizoulières
CEFI-CNRS, Aix-en-Provence, Université de la Méditerranée, France

1. INTRODUCTION

Anyone wishing to outline the strategic characteristics of the semiconductor industry must look for the common point between those industries which currently lead worldwide growth. In fact, semiconductors act as intermediary products in a growing number of applications (automotive, telecommunications, computers, consumer electronics) which represent a significant part of the global worldwide exchanges, as shown in table 1.

Table 1. End uses of semiconductors

1989		1995		1999	
Computer	45%	Computer	53%	Computer	33%
Automotive	6%	Automotive	5%	Automotive	9%
Industrial	14%	Industrial	9%	Industrial	10%
Consumer	19%	Consumer	13%	Consumer	12%
Communications	12%	Communications	19%	Communications	35%
Military	4%	Military	1%	Military	1%

Sources: ICE (1995); Penn (1996b)

Although it emerged at the beginning of the 1950s, the semiconductor industry shows sustained dynamics, through both an increasing variety in final applications and a continual flow of technological innovations. The existence of market cycles, describing periodic gaps between supply and demand, do not however alter the observed long run growth (16% average annual growth over the last thirty years).

Within the semiconductor market[1], we can pinpoint different segments according to the functions fulfilled by the various products (memories, microprocessors, optoelectronics) and technologies used (MOS/bipolar; digital/analog). This market segmentation is illustrated in figure 1.

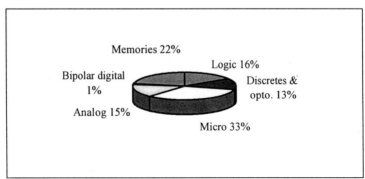

Figure 1: Semiconductor market segments in 1999.
Source: Penn (1999b)

The major issue in this industry is the heterogeneity of both products and agents. Initially dominated by the large vertically integrated American firms, the industry records periods during which the nationality of leaders and their structure are seen to evolve. Japanese firms then dominate during the 1980s, a period during which South Asian firms also enter the market, and later new more specialized ones emerged in the world top ranks (cf. table 2).

Table 2. Top 10 semiconductor manufacturers

	1981	1990	1999
1	Texas Instruments	NEC	Intel
2	Motorola	Toshiba	NEC
3	NEC	Hitachi	Toshiba
4	Philips	Motorola	Samsung
5	Hitachi	Intel	Texas Instruments
6	Toshiba	Fujitsu	Motorola
7	National Semiconductor	Texas Instruments	Hitachi
8	Intel	Mitsubishi	STMicroelectronics
9	Matsushita	Philips	Philips
10	Fairchild	National Semiconductor	Infineon

Sources: ICE (1995); McCall (2000)

The industry has thus witnessed stages of increasing specialization, shifting from a model of integrated organization to a more fragmented model characterized by a division of innovative labor. Henceforth, we observe firms without physical production units, specialized in the production of intangible assets. This chapter aims at analyzing the nature of the relationships between this new type of agent and the firms operating within the semiconductors *filière*. Are these interactions purely co-operative or do they come within the scope of more traditional market relations ? In the following section, we describe the technological evolution in order to underline the progressive reshaping of the organization of industry. The nature of the relationships between agents and the current characteristics of their knowledge base favor the emergence of a market for knowledge. The final part is devoted to the study of this market's working. In order to solve coordination problems, we explain how agents set up a body of social institutions, namely standards and systems of intellectual property protection. On the basis of these institutional arrangements, we examine the business models upon which knowledge vendors rely. Finally, a case study about the leader of the embedded RISC processors market enables us to better understand how the market operates.

2. THE EMERGENCE OF A MARKET FOR KNOWLEDGE IN THE SEMICONDUCTOR INDUSTRY

Within a few decades, the semiconductor industry has undergone the most spectacular development in the whole history of modern industry. This development is a response to rapid technological changes which have had strong repercussions on the organization of the industry. It entails a process of progressive disintegration resulting in new activities and in particular in the emergence during the 1990s of knowledge-based activities without any manufacturing unit.

2.1 The Coupled Evolution of the Industry and the Knowledge Base in Semiconductors

Since the birth of the industry in 1948, technological innovations have radically influenced industrial evolution. The transistor invention in the Bell laboratories in 1947, the integrated circuit by Texas Instruments and Fairchild in 1961 and Intel's microprocessor in 1972, all constitute the main product innovations. Radical process innovations have been oxide masking by Bell laboratories in 1954, the planar process by Fairchild in 1959, and ionic implantation in 1968 by Accelerators Inc. Yet, characterizing these different stages in terms of mere technological regimes (Winter, 1984) is insufficient, since within the semiconductor industry, technologies and associated products can evolve in different directions (Pavitt, 1998; Gambardella and Torrisi, 1998).

Consequently, we will first study industrial evolution, that is to say the succession of phases dominated by a type of product, which strongly influences the structure of firms and competition, thus highlighting the industry dynamics. We will then attempt to characterize the knowledge base specific to each phase identified.

2.1.1 The Three Paradigms of the Industrial Evolution of Semiconductors

Why describe industrial evolution in terms of paradigm? Indeed, each phase distinguishes itself by competitive characteristics (degree of concentration, existence or not of entry barriers) and a peculiar organization of the industry (entry/exit of firms and the interacting structure) punctuated by the appearance of radical innovations as mentioned above. These latter remain important since they constitute the solution defined by firms, linked to a set of issues they cope with. Thus a technological paradigm (Dosi, 1988) enables us to characterize a set of technological problems and the range of the corresponding solutions which satisfy both cost and marketing constraints. With regard to the semiconductor industry, we can highlight three paradigms (cf. figure 2).

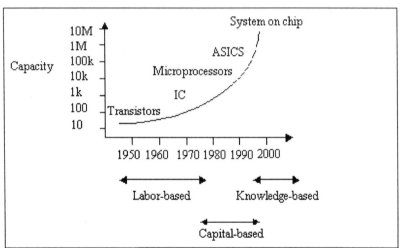

Figure 2: The three paradigms in the semiconductor industry.
Source: Adapted from Martinotti (1998)

Phase 1, labor-based: the paradigm of simple products
Between roughly 1950 and 1975, the semiconductor industry undergoes a labor-based period. The concept of semiconductors is applied to few products within the industry (transistors, diodes, etc.) and still has limited outlets (military, consumer electronics). At this time, firms are large multi-product (in electrical and electronic goods, particularly in Europe). Moreover, some of these firms spin-off from the founding laboratories of the industry, such as Fairchild from Bell. Therefore, the bases of industrial structure are set up due to the researchers and engineers turn-over. Hence, human capital represents the strategic asset at that time.

The invention of the integrated circuit (IC) and its market shipment drive the industry towards mass production favored by the introduction of the planar process. Despite the substitution of transistors by the IC for end use, only few incumbents exit the market. However, we observe an internal consolidation of product lines within leading firms (Langlois and Steinmueller, 1996) such as Motorola, Texas Instruments as well as a few market entries. The differentiation between logic ICs (used in computers) and bipolar ICs (used in consumer and industrial goods), together with a growing demand from the computer industry and the captive production[2], favor a shift towards a new paradigm by modifying the existing competitive strenghts.

Phase 2, capital-based: the paradigm of complex products
From 1975 and up to 1990, a second paradigm emerges due to a combination of three factors (Ibid.). Firstly, the extensive adoption of process innovations upstream consolidates mass production. Hence, competitive advantages are based on economies of scale, the resulting decrease in production costs and the shorter time-to-market. Secondly, the volume of outlets as well as the types of applications grow: this is the pervasiveness phenomenon. Market extension is made possible first by computers, then by consumer electronics (television, electrical domestic appliances, VCRs, etc). Finally, the existence of differentiated ICs (logic/bipolar) and the increasing number of product innovations lead in turn to an increase in the number of market segments within the field of semiconductors. At the same time, these products become generational (memories, microprocessors) and their life cycles progressively shorten. Indeed, the radical innovation dominating this paradigm, the microprocessor, constitutes a complex product both regarding its production and its functionalities (processing, addressing information...) and leads to different generations, i.e. incremental improvements.

All these factors, as well as the rapid succession of product generations and size and reliability requirements (the "yield rate", namely the number of zero-default chips per slice of silicon (Gruber, 1994)), bring about considerable growth in fabrication unit costs (cf. table 3). Technological evolution thus follows a predictable trajectory, the Moore's law, which guides technological requirements: agents know that the density of semiconductors roughly doubles every 18 months.

Table 3. Combined evolution of technical characteristics and investment in DRAMS

Year	Size (in mm)	Capacity (in bits)	Investments (in dollars million)
1975	75	4 K	
1980	100	64 K	100
1985	150	256 K	200
1990	150	4 M	450

Source: Luther and Graml (1996)

At the same time, entry barriers related to design activities are relatively low, favoring the continued spin-off from incumbents (Intel, AMD, National

Semiconductor, then later Cypress and LSI Logic) and the arrival of start-ups managed by independent designers.

This paradigm is thus characterized by a division of innovative labor between design and production which, as we have underlined previously, comes from the surge of more complex products and a higher capital investment level: 'specialization not only took place within market niches but also within the value chain. Some organizations specialized in the production of semiconductors whereas other organizations restricted their attention to the design part' (Duysters, 1996, p.119). Accordingly, two types of firms emerge, namely "fabless" (fabrication-less) companies and foundries, which coexist alongside large vertically integrated firms.

Phase 3, knowledge-based: the "system on chip" paradigm

From the 1990s, the increasing product diversification along with the emergence of specific products (ASICs) increase the complexity of semiconductors which are now integrated into a complex system, the system on chip (SOC) (cf. figure 3). In this system, all functions[3] (storage, transmission, conversion and processing) are integrated on a single chip. The system is also modular so that its architecture can be adapted to the needs of the customer. The SOC includes the microprocessor and the memory as well as other interfaces or more specific components. Finally, the diversity of both products and their corresponding functions are synthesized on the SOC.

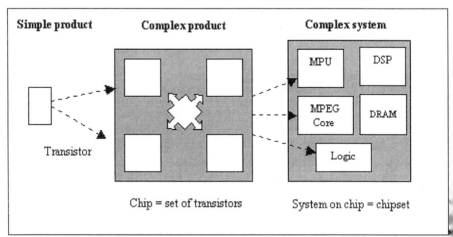

Figure 3: From simple product to complex system.

Henceforth, firms have to deal with the complexity of integrating numerous functions on the chip while meeting shorter market deadlines. As far as the firms' capabilities are concerned, this increasing complexity makes such systems design more difficult for a semiconductor vendor without external resources from their customers and IP vendors. In particular, a SOC requires the development of advanced manufacturing process technologies in the fields of packaging, manufacturing, testing and also the availability of a wide range of knowledge in the form of intellectual properties related to the different functional blocks. As a result, a new type of agent appears, the *knowledge provider*.

Without going so far as to consider this industry as "technology push", one must recognize the major role of technological constraints that contribute to modifying the competitive game and, as a result, the organization of the industry. During the capital-based phase, the strong competition gives way to an oligopoly[4] where large vertically integrated firms coexist with networks based on division of labor. Therefore, some organizational forms related to the first two paradigms subsist despite the fact that the knowledge-based paradigm prevails today.

Together with the evolution of supply and demand and the ensuing competitive and organizational strategies, the scientific and technological knowledge base also evolved.

2.1.2   The Evolution of the Knowledge Base

Table 4 synthesizes for each period the characteristics of the technological paradigm and those of the resulting knowledge base. What are the current features of the knowledge base in semiconductors, which could favor the emergence of markets for knowledge? The main characteristic of today's products and technologies is *complexity*. At the product level, the SOC fulfils simultaneously the functions of numerous existing products. Thus, a *convergence* of products takes place at the industry level. At the same time, technologies become more and more complex due to a twofold purpose: "do better" and "do otherwise". A twofold movement occurs here again (Gambardella and Torrisi, 1998). On the one hand, technological diversification increases within each firm: this latter must master increasingly varied[5] technological fields in order to solve technical problems (integration[6]) and functional problems (compatibility) presented by the system on a chip. On the other hand, a technological convergence occurs among ICTs (Information and Communication Technologies); generic technologies enable increasingly diverse functions integrated on the SOC to be rendered compatible (sound, images, information transmission via Internet, telephone).

The complexity of the required knowledge base cannot be mastered by one firm alone. Meanwhile, as a modular system (integrating variable and interchangeable types of components, linked together by the same architecture) (Langlois, 1992), the SOC allows some specialization on few applications, given the company's initial own capabilities. For example, Philips is specialized in the audio-video field, based on its knowledge cumulated in the field of recording media (compact cassette and compact discs).

Table 4. The evolution of the knowledge base features

Phase	Type of technological problem	Characteristics of the knowledge base
① 1950-1975 Simple Product (transistor); Labor-based	Scientific problems: Transmission of information in the form of electric current. Recourse to solid-state physics (silicon, germanium) and chemistry.	Quasi-public scientific knowledge, with low appropriability. Technological knowledge incorporated in human capital. Development of manufacturing technologies.
② 1975-1990 Complex product (microprocessor); Capital-based	Constraints imposed by performance requirements in terms of density and die size. Solution = integration + planar + silicon	Increase in complexity of the knowledge base due to diversification of products: * microprocessors: production and innovation capabilities; * memories: engineering and production capabilities; * ASICs: link between design and specific applications. Importance of manufacturing process technologies embodied in equipments. Weak role of scientific knowledge. Decreasing uncertainty: Moore's law (exploitation trajectory).
③ 1990... Complex system (SOC); Knowledge-based	Modularity, compatibility, integration, re-use	Intra-firm technological diversification: cross fertilization with other technological fields (nanotechnologies). Inter-industry technological convergence: raise of generic technologies common to several technological fields, related to the growing range of functions carried out by the SOC

Sources: Malerba and Orsenigo (1993), Flaherty (1984), Wright (1996), Duysters (1996),
    Wieder (1996)

Technological complexity has another consequence: production costs are continually increasing (the cost of a new microprocessor plant doubles every three years and currently stands at $3 billion). To prevent yield rate from falling due to the increasing circuit miniaturization, engineers resort more and more often to the CAD in order to delay the manufacturing (defaults are detected earlier during the process): design, simulation, testing, etc.

Finally, the emergence of generic or abstract technologies potentially allows firms to reuse SOC architectures for other applications. The pervasiveness of the semiconductor itself demonstrates the wide range of possible applications. Therefore knowledge appropriability diminishes since it becomes more observable (by reverse engineering). Moreover, the compatibility requirements between different SOC elements limits the tacitness and specificity of knowledge.

To sum up, the knowledge base required today in the semiconductor industry is complex, diverse, and weakly appropriable. Given these conditions, let us state precisely the theoretical conditions of the emergence of markets for knowledge.

2.2 Mutations in the Organization of the Semiconductor Industry

The technological evolution the semiconductor industry has experienced is illustrated by far-reaching modifications of the industrial structure, both quantitative and qualitative. Indeed, from a global point of view, the number of incumbents in the industry has been considerably extended, but this must not hide the ongoing specialization and the *division of productive and innovative labor* (Arora and Gambardella, 1994) leading to new entries. Additionnally, the degree of concentration and the competitive pressure appreciably vary according to each market segment.

2.2.1 Reconstruction of the Production System

In the period from the 1950s till today, we can distinguish three major phases matching with three distinct models of organization of the industry (cf. appendix 2, The Three Models of the Organization of the Semiconductor Industry). During the period between the 1950s and the mid-1970s, the industry is dominated by large vertically integrated firms (Langlois and Steinmueller, 1996). Firms such as IBM, Texas Instruments, etc., carry out internally the entire range of tasks, from product design (transistors, integrated circuits) to marketing through the various stages of development, manufacture and test. With the emergence of minicomputers, non-military applications are being developed, and the semiconductor industry split into two main categories of firms. On the one hand, firms producing standard integrated circuits including incumbents (IBM, TI, etc.) as well as new American entrants such as DEC progressively dominate the minicomputer market, outpacing the incumbents (Malerba et al., 1999; Bresnahan and Malerba, 1996). On the other hand, other firms enter the market by producing specific circuits, ASICs. With Intel's invention of the microprocessor, the microcomputer market is to drive the entire semiconductor industry. During the same period, we notice an upstream disintegration with the arrival of American suppliers of semiconductor production and test equipment.

Beyond the upstream disintegration due for the most part to small equipment tools providers[7], the major reorganization of the industry occurs in the 1980s with the arrival of fabless companies. These are semiconductor vendors which design integrated circuits, sub-contract their production out to pure-play foundries and then recover them to sell or sometimes integrate them in their own specific applications. 'The new start-ups specialized in designing semiconductors but did not have the production capabilities (and hence were fabless). Correspondingly, merchant foundries (...) emerged to fabricate the chips based on the designs being delivered by the design houses' (Arora, Fosfuri and Gambardella, 1999, p.6). Nevertheless, this is not simply a matter of outsourcing or sub-contracting chip manufacturing between fabless companies and foundries[8], since the former often proceed by prior licenses sales of their own designs and architectures to foundries assuming the manufacturing stage (Macher, Mowery and Hodges, 1998). Fabless companies then recover the integrated circuits to be incorporated in applications which are either developed internally, or by downstream customers. Contracts between fabless and foundries often entail arrangements notably in terms of guaranteed minimum volume of production and exclusivity clauses. Finally, we can pinpoint the emergence of specialized firms in engineering and circuit design software supply, namely EDAs such as Cadence Design Systems and Mentor Graphics. At the same time, the stages of assembly and packaging and marginally that of test, are being progressively outsourced towards specialized firms.

During the 1990s, the *fabless model* becomes mature as foundries became relatively inexpensive and low-risk. But more importantly, with the major technological advance of the SOC and the resulting growing complexity of products, chipmakers no longer have the ability nor the necessary resources to produce the entire system design. With the rapid succession of new products generations, they are constrained by anticipation or reaction to time-to-market. Hence, rather than buying and assembling integrated circuits, they buy blocks of IP and integrate them as *virtual components* into one unique system. This demand is satisfied by a profusion of IP vendors specialized in the production of cores, or components of the global architecture of semiconductors (Arora, Fosfuri and Gambardella, 1999; Teece, 1998; Grindley and Teece, 1997). Issues related to the integration and compatibility of these IP blocks led to the emergence of other types of engineering services supplied by design integrators.

During the past decades, the industry thus shifts from a totally integrated model to a highly segmented one with new activities and new types of specialized firms of which an increasing number operate without a manufacturing unit (cf. figure 4).

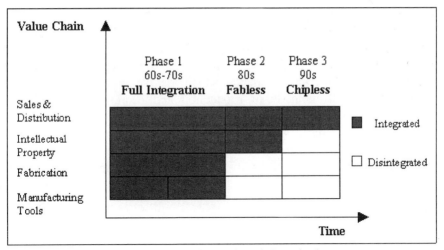

Figure 4: Disintegration of IC production.

In terms of market structure, some IP markets are overpopulated and the fierce competition that prevails leaves room for only brief periods of high mark-up. For some categories of IP, prices go down as much as 90% in just few months. In contrast, foundry and EDA markets are highly concentrated. As regards pure-play foundries, the three market leaders hold 87% of the market in 1997 (TSMC 43%, UMC 29% and Chartered Semiconductor 15%). In the EDA market, the two leaders, Cadence Design Systems and Mentor Graphics, total 90% of the market in 1999. The assemblers' market, coupled with packaging, is less concentrated but one player stands out by its sheer size - Amkor. Although it only owns 25% of the market, it is three times the size of its closest competitor. As for the design integrator market, this has long been dominated by a single agent (VLSI), which was bought out by Philips in 1998.

2.2.2 Division of Labor, Market Expansion and Increasing Returns: A Theoretical Framework for the "System On Chip" Model

The semiconductor industry is characterized by three major elements: a division of labor both vertical and horizontal, market expansion linked to the semiconductor pervasiveness and finally, the role played by increasing returns. The latter is prevalent for knowledge-based industries (Teece, 1998). The analytical bases for increasing returns mechanisms at the source of the observed evolution can be detected in the seminal article by Allyn Young (1928) which has been rediscovered and deeply commented in particular by De Bandt, Ravix and Romani (1990); Ravix (1994); Quéré and Ravix (1998). By emphasizing the division of labor, these authors clarify the concept of organization of the industry and explain the separation between production and trade spheres. The three major elements – division of labor/market expansion/increasing returns – cannot be placed on the same level. Indeed, Young shows that there are endogenous forces which provoke the continuing changes in the industry and which give rise to increasing returns. These forces are to be found in the division of labor and the expansion of the market dimension which are themselves linked (among others) to indirect methods of production and economies of scale and consequently to entrepreneurs' actions (cf. figure 5). 'The winners are the entrepreneurs with the cognitive and managerial skills to discern the shape of the play and then act upon it. Recognizing strategic errors and adjusting accordingly is a critical part of becoming and remaining successful.' (Teece, 1998, p.59) Moreover, once these growing yields are under way, 'thus change becomes progressive and propagates itself in a cumulative way.' (Young, 1928, p.533)

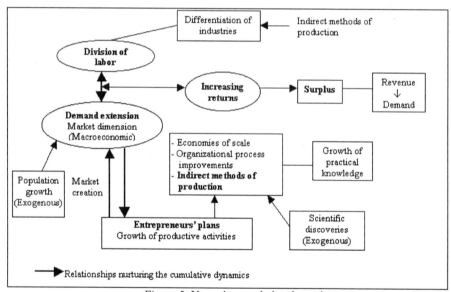

Figure 5: Young's cumulative dynamics.

According to Young, the division of labor leading to the differentiation of industries appears to be a fundamental cause of the cumulative dynamics, but the expansion of demand is a necessary, albeit insufficient, condition for generating increasing returns. If the market dimension does not grow sufficiently, firms cannot see any advantage in specialization within the industry.

In the semiconductor industry, it is the pervasiveness phenomenon that is at the origin of this extraordinary market expansion. Since the 1960s, we actually witness an increase in the use of active electronic components in various applications outside the traditional fields (radio, computers, military). More recently, electronic components find outlets not only within the semiconductor industry itself, but also in other industrial fields such as the automotive industry, telecommunications and in particular mobile telephones and networking. Within the integrated circuit market, the growth of 11% observed between 1993 and 1998 reflects both diversification of outlets and a growth rate exceeding 10% in the three major applications (telecommunications, automotive and computers). Estimates for the period 1998-2003 forecast a growth rate of 17% on the integrated circuit market, principally fuelled by telecommunications and networking (Penn, 1999a).

Within the process of generating increasing returns, Young stressed the feedback effects between the expansion of demand and the division of labor (De Bandt, Ravix and Romani, 1990). As we have seen, market expansion is necessary for the division of labor but this latter, in turn, enables a growth of productive activities and thus of demand. Indeed, increasing returns produce surpluses which convert into revenues and thus demand, giving entrepreneurs the opportunity to create new markets.

Let us now make clear the specific causes of the division of labor in semiconductors. Let us start with the trend observed since the beginning of the 1980s with the arrival of pure-play foundries offering "virtual manufacturing units" to fabless companies, and flexible capacity to IDMs.

The outsourcing of the manufacturing stage started with IDMs which initially only use sub-contractors in response to an urgent excessive demand. Then progressively, some IDMs start outsourcing the least strategic products manufacturing. Today, IDMs only outsource an average of 8% of their production to pure foundries; however, analysts[9] expect this figure to reach 25% or even 28% of worldwide IC production by IDMs. Among those, the most advanced in terms of production outsourcing is Motorola, third in the top 10 semiconductor vendors in 1998. Motorola recently announced its wish to rapidly outsource 50% of its wafer production to pure foundries. As the mutual trust feeling between certain IDMs and foundries gradually develops, the former progressively migrate towards a full outsourcing business model. Let us note, incidentally, that the semiconductor industry lags largely behind compared to its customers, since most firms in the PC, telecommunications and networking industries, such as 3Com and Dell, have already sold their factories in order to reorient their activities and focus on their own value-added expertise (in terms of product design, marketing and planning). In fact, the main reason for this outsourcing trend is the cost of setting up new manufacturing units. For semiconductor vendors, outsourcing allows a reduction in capital costs and their transformation into variable costs, capital costs thus passing from the IDM to the foundry. The latter benefits from higher economies of scale than its customers (IDMs) and, as a result, is able to offer lower prices and greater flexibility. Another incentive to outsourcing comes from the reduction in R&D expenditures for IDMs. In this way, foundries bear the cost of the development process. Concentrated for the most part in Taiwan with TSMC and UMC, the pure-play foundries record a compound annual growth rate of 22% in 1998, which is well above that of the entire IC industry (13%) (Infrastructure, 1998).

Currently, one must moderate the importance of pure-play foundries within the whole chipmaker industry since they only manufacture 10% of all the worldwide silicon chips. However, the wafer foundry market is expected to grow rapidly due to the special relationships between IDMs and pure-play foundries. IDMs now subcontract the production of the most advanced technologies especially because foundries provide complementary manufacturing services.

Beyond the close relationships with IDMs that favor the pure-play foundries business, the development of fabless companies strongly consolidates the position of Taiwanese[10] foundries. The "fabless phenomenon" is typically North American, and the new entrants in the industry since the early 1980s adopt specialization strategies in design, distribution and marketing, eclipsing the manufacturing stage[11]. These new firms experience a rapid development because their supply is devoted to industries with a high growth rate, notably applications in terms of personal computers and telecommunications (Macher, Mowery, Hodges 1998). Here, it is important to note that the fabless companies' profit growth is much higher than that of the semiconductor industry (cf. table 5).

Table 5. Fabless revenue vs semiconductor revenue

	Fabless Companies		Semiconductor industry		Fabless Shares
	$MM	CAGR*	$BB	CAGR*	of Industry Revenue
1987	71.4		32.5		0.2 %
1989	323.8	113 %	48.8	23 %	0.7 %
1991	933.7	90 %	54.6	14 %	1.7 %
1993	2 164.4	77 %	77.3	16 %	2.8 %
1995	5 468.7	72 %	144.4	20 %	3.8 %
1997	6 871.5	58 %	137.2	15 %	5.0 %

*CAGR: Compound Annual Growth, base 1987
Sources: SIA/WSTS, FactSet Research Systems

In the process of labor division within the industry we have also underlined that the assembly, packaging and to some extent test stages are being outsourced. Traditionally, since the 1960s, the American semiconductor industry relies on relocalization of assembly and packaging units towards developing countries because of the non-strategic character of this stage (Geneau de Lamarliere, 1990). It is therefore natural to observe specialized firms emerging in South East Asia. In 1998, 30% of worldwide ICs are assembled by subcontractors. This figure is estimated to reach 50% in the next decade. Yet, test activities require close collaboration with the design stage in order to understand the functioning of the chip, since the knowledge involved is highly strategic. Also, subcontract test only represents about 5% of the worldwide IC market in 1998, and this is essentially concerned with mature products.

Within the current industry organization model, apart from outsourcing manufacture, assembly-packaging and test stages, we observe an increasing recourse to market in order to acquire technological knowledge at design level stage. This concerns the IP market evoked by Arora, Fosfuri and Gambardella (1999); Teece (1998); Grindley and Teece (1997). The reason for this increasingly frequent recourse to market essentially stems from the fact that semiconductor vendors can concentrate their engineering teams efforts and their R&D investments on specific parts of the design stage. This new task sharing within the industry entails new division of costs. In particular, the semiconductor manufacturer only devotes 6% of his profits to R&D for design and 5% for marketing while an IP vendor grants them respectively 38% and 23% (cf. table 6). These specialized IP suppliers then offer more efficient designs because of economies of scale.

Table 6. The economics of independent IP

	IDM	Fabless	IP
Revenue	100%	100%	100%
Wafer Cost	25%	33%	-
Backend cost	17%	20%	-
Other cost	-	-	21%
Support Engineering	12%	5%	-
Marketing	5%	5%	23%
Process R&D	9%	-	-
Design R&D	6%	6%	38%
SG&A	12%	17%	10%
Operating Profit	14%	14%	8%

Source: Adapted from McLeod (1998)

Despite this progressive disintegration process, vertically integrated companies remain the giants which dominate the industry but feel more and more threatened by the efficiency of Taiwanese foundries, IP suppliers and other engineering services firms. Some IDMs react by increasing the number of co-operation agreements, others, such as Intel consider themselves as yet in a sheltered position. Nevertheless, all IDMs now rely on IP suppliers and cannot develop everything internally.

Meanwhile, IDMs are not the only type of agents threatened by the proliferation of IP suppliers. Indeed, some fabless companies producing ASICs are threatened by the fact of their own specialization in specific circuits while the trend is towards system on chip. They respond to these changes in different ways. Some exit the market, others follow the trend and purchase the IP blocks they cannot design internally so as to integrate supplementary functions into the system on chip, while others go even further and conclude partnerships with IP suppliers.

2.3   The Emergence of a Market for Knowledge

For an industry as innovative as the semiconductor industry, the disintegration process of the industry organization leads to an extremely deep division of innovative labor and the emergence of specialized firms in the production of blocks or modules of reusable technological knowledge. The SOC revolution and the extensive demand stemming from increasingly varied applications favor the emergence of a market for knowledge.

2.3.1   From the Division of Labor to the Growth of Knowledge

As far as the concept of division of labor is concerned, *The Principles of Economics* by Menger (1871) and in particular paragraph five 'The causes of progress in human wealth' appears as a complement to the work of Smith (Streissler, 1972). But for Menger, 'the division of labor is not the only, nor even the main, cause of economic progress' (Ravix, 1994, p.158). The fundamental factors are "human knowledge" and "human control" on the production process (Menger, 1871). We are thus close to Young's dynamics of increasing returns which emphasizes indirect methods of production and ensuing advances in knowledge. For Loasby, given that knowledge is dispersed (Hayek, 1937), the genuine issue for economics is therefore the growth of knowledge, since knowledge becomes the "connecting principle" essential in explaining the sources of economic development. Loasby suggests to establish a dialogue between Smith and Menger, which enables to identify their complementarity. 'As Adam Smith saw, specialisation is a condition of progress – though he was wise enough to note that one form of specialisation consisted of 'combining together the powers of the most distant and dissimilar objects' (Smith, quoted by Loasby, 1996, p.9). But if specialisation is to deliver progress, the specialised activities must be integrated, and any close integration requires compatibility between the frameworks that are being used.' (Loasby, 1996, p.9). Thus the division of labor relies not only on the integration of varied specialties within the firm, but also upon the coordination of outside specialties. In fact, the causality observed by Smith is also valid in the other sense, Menger showing in effect that new knowledge also orientates the division of labor. Thus, between Smith and Menger we can outline a circular relationship in the growth of knowledge: 'the causal sequence may be cumulative: ideas for a novel division of labour create the conditions for developing new knowledge, which may inspire a further division of labour.' (Loasby, 1998, p.42)

The division of labor and the division of knowledge are thus the major elements in the generation of increasing returns and economic progress. A progressive shift from a principle of technical division to one of cognitive division of labor is then established in this progressive process of specialization (Moati and Mouhoud, 1995). That is to say, one witnesses a passage from a technical-based division of labor to a division of labor based on the nature of knowledge necessary to carry out different activities in the value chain. The cognitive division of labor responds to a logic of competence and learning. The interpretation of the industry's organization suggested by Loasby (1998) thus enables to perceive it as being an organization of dispersed "capabilities", the latter being only specific forms of knowledge. The coordination of these dispersed capabilities is made possible either within multi-technology corporations endowed with "distributed" competences (Grandstrand, Patel and Pavitt, 1997), or in pure market forms as in the Hayekian tradition, or via some institutional arrangements that Richardson (1960) qualifies as market imperfections.

In this cognitive division of labor framework, we can by extension observe the emergence of firms that break away from physical production to devote their resources to the very production of knowledge. The latter becomes then potentially tradable. This takes us one stage further in the division or growth of knowledge. Indeed, this knowledge corresponds to an indirect method of production in Young's terminology, to improve the increasingly complex products manufacturing, i.e. SOCs. Therefore, a clear separation occurs between the locus of knowledge production and the locus of its use (Antonelli, 1999; Arora, Gambardella and Rullani, 1997). It is therefore important to identify under which organizational form or forms these knowledge production activities are carried out.

As we argued above, firms specialized in the production of knowledge devoted to semiconductor manufacturers appear very early, in particular the appearance of EDA providers in 1980s. Without anticipating their key role in the consolidation of SOCs from reusable designs, it is important to note that the engineering services supplied by EDA providers are costly, often customized, except for the licenses they may sell for software used to carry out the design, test and validation stages. But even, EDAs suffer from a narrow market, which prevents them from off-setting the R&D costs that represent more than 25% of their revenues on average. As a consequence, the EDA market segment undergoes waves of high concentration, since most new entrants are quickly bought out by leaders.

A quasi-identical phenomenon can be quoted as regards to engineering services dealing with equipments for semiconductor fabs. In France, some engineerists[13] were forced to gradually become equipment manufacturers and sell packages (equipment plus engineering services) to survive and grow, while other competitors exit. In effect, the cost of engineering and R&D more often than not exceeds specifications, making it very difficult for small firms to survive, especially when all services are customized and covered by confidentiality clauses, making reuse of knowledge a delicate matter.

Thus, in the two types of engineering quoted, namely EDAs and equipment engineering services, the nature of inter-firm relationships are rather partnership-oriented, whereas things appear to be very different for the IP market. Let us recall that in the 1960s and 70s, the production of integrated circuits was only made by IDMs – i.e. vertically integrated firms. The issue at the time was clearly that of R&D management in these multinational firms. The R&D decentralization can be useful for rapid adaptation and lower costs for specific local markets. Nevertheless, when R&D costs are high, centralization proves vital for the realization of economies of scale. Meanwhile, modularity fundamentally changes the terms of the debate (Arora, Gambardella and Rullani, 1997). In the semiconductor equipment tools market, products and technologies designs clearly appear to be decomposable into basic modules in which reorganization or modularity enables a wide variety of products (Langlois, 1998). This modularity principle has also been applied to less tangible products as in the software sector (Cusumano, 1991) or with regard to scientific and technological knowledge. In particular, the modularity principle around IP blocks appears along with SOCs development. These IP blocks correspond to technological knowledge produced in the form of basic modules which may be combined in many ways. The production of this knowledge in basic modules can be carried out by independent firms, and the innovation process related to IP blocks can thus be subdivided into separate stages and activities. 'As a stylized representation, the innovation process can be divided into two main activities: the *production of modules,* that is the production of basic knowledge components, of "general-purpose" technologies or of basic product designs; and the *combination of modules* to obtain a wide variety of applications that are more finely tailored to the needs of individual groups of users' (Arora, Gambardella and Rullani, 1997, p.5). Apart from SOCs complexity, which obliges design houses to resort to licenses, IDMs find an unbeatable cost advantage in resorting to market in order to limit internal R&D costs (cf. table 6, The Economics of Independent IP). In fact, IP providers, when producing knowledge modules, benefit from economies of scale, and the redeployment toward specific SOCs is carried out at low incremental cost for design houses in comparison to up-front expenditure for the original IP production. The modularity principle thus allows a deeper division of innovative labor, leading to "external economies of scope" (Langlois, 1998). For Arora, Gambardella and Rullani (1997), an important implication in terms of industry organization is that 'the production of modules will be concentrated in a few markets which will be large and most efficient in producing the basic models' (Ibid.). Moreover, the combination of modules takes place in numerous local markets. Let us now see if this proposition is valid for semiconductors.

2.3.2 The Emergence of the Intellectual Property Market

Throughout the 1990s, the SOC market growth was spectacular, going from $2 billion in 1995 to $10 billion in 1999, i.e. an increase of 500%. By purchasing IP blocks related to SOC design, through licenses, system houses enhance their IP portfolio and thereby are able to produce an entire SOC. In fact, the SOC design cannot be carried out without a minimum design reuse. The wide range of electronic products incorporating cores (known commonly as virtual components) and available on the market bears witness. More precisely, a core is a complex pre-designed function, which becomes part of a chip. Ideally, a core should be ready for use in a wide range of silicon-based technologies and designs. When a core is available for sale or license by designers, it becomes an IP, that is to say, a piece or block of marketable intangible knowledge and potentially usable in numerous architectures. There are many categories of IP depending on their function in the system architecture, but more fundamentally, these cores produce distinct market dynamics according to the technology maturity and therefore to its content in terms of property rights.

At this stage of the analysis, we know that the innovative labor division process within the industry has allowed the emergence of providers for IP blocks, physical libraries and engineering services. But the mere existence of such transactions is, in itself, insufficient for the emergence of an IP market; i.e. a market for knowledge.

The surge of such a market is favored by several factors which do not constitute conditions of market existence but simply constitute some incentive factors. Firstly among these there is the technological convergence phenomenon, defined by Athreye (1994) as a 'process by which industries which were once different in terms of their technological and therefore knowledge bases, come to share similar technological and knowledge bases' (p.17). Technological convergence implies intertwining technological bases from different industries in order to integrate new functions in SOCs. Thus, we observe a multiplication of concepts common to several technological fields and favoring the emergence of an intellectual property market. Moreover, the major incentive factor is linked to the growing complexity of SOCs which accordingly means that no firm possesses internally all the knowledge necessary for the complete system design. With the successive technological generations marked by a growing complexity, a wide gap appears between the internal design capabilities and the manufacturing capabilities; a gap which is filled by reusable IPs (cf. figure 6). IP sellers become the focal point of the restructured semiconductor industry. What the original equipment manufacturers[14] are lacking is the practical knowledge necessary for the construction of the chip (know what). On the other hand, even if these firms know which IP blocks are to be integrated in the chip, they sometimes lack the integration capabilities (know how).

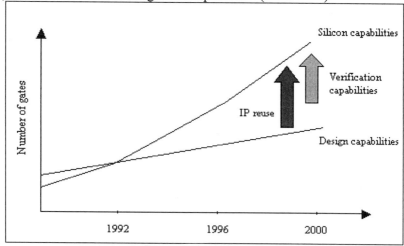

Figure 6: The design gap crisis.

Finally, the incentive factors are not only based on technological criteria (technological convergence and complexity) but also on competitive and financial ones. On the one hand, the market pressure due to both growing competition between system houses and shortening product life cycles are making it more urgent for them to reach the market as quickly as possible, and is forcing them to purchase the required IP from third-party providers. On the other hand, IP production activities present low barriers to entry for new start-ups. Also, such firms are able to attract financial investors, particularly on the stock markets. IP providers are actually considered as operating in activities that do not need as much investment as vertically integrated firms or fabless companies.

Among the conditions of the emergence of a market for knowledge, Athreye (1994), drawing from her study on the chemical industry, insists upon two conditions. Firstly, 'the alienation of knowledge from its context' (p.17). In order to be traded, knowledge must be decontextualized, abstract and "alienable". In other words, the exchange value and the in use value of knowledge are disconnected. We may argue that technological convergence fosters the emergence of new generic technologies (by cross fertilization) and accelerates the decontextualization process of technological knowledge. But the essential issue consists in knowledge reuse. Indeed, analysts from Silicon Strategies claim that in 1991 semiconductor companies redesigned 90% of their integrated circuit architecture while today, the situation is totally reversed and the share of novelty in architecture represents only 10% (cf. figure 7). The remaining 90% consists of IP blocks produced internally or mostly acquired through licenses. These are reusable IP[15], that it to say technological knowledge which has become transmissible – within the same company but above all from IP providers to system houses – by means of a long codification process, costly but vital for the development and rapid market launch for SOCs.

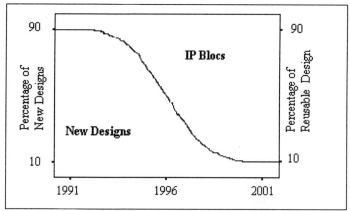

Figure 7: The growing trend of IP reuse.
Source: Adapted from Martinotti (1998)

On the other hand, a minimum volume of trade transactions and minimal frequency are necessary before a market for knowledge emerges. For some categories of IP, prices register a drop of around 90% within just few months, proving that a high number of transactions on the same IP block[16] occurs, even if the price slowdown remains a proxy variable. Moreover, we find another indication on the growing importance of knowledge purchases in a particular category of ICs - the ASICs: in 1996, the sales of ASICs incorporating IPs, although minor compared to more traditional ones, have been increasing and largely dominate in 2000 (cf. figure 8).

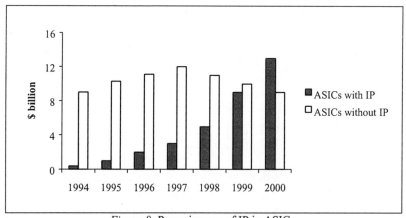

Figure 8: Pervasiveness of IP in ASICs.
Source: Adapted from Gandhi (1998); Integrated Intellectual Property, Inc.

Moreover, while the number of design teams using and buying design libraries – for each new IC fabrication facility – is steadily increasing, those buying design libraries are a growing subset of those using libraries, thus indicating a growing number of teams buying commercial libraries rather than creating libraries of their own (cf. figure 9).

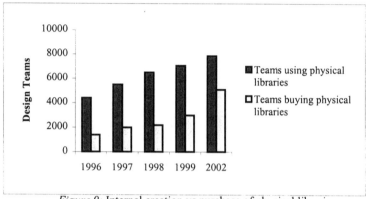

Figure 9: Internal creation vs purchase of physical libraries.
Source: Adapted from McCleod (1998)

The IP market is poised to grow at an astonishing rate of over 55% per year, just over $165 million in 1996 to well over $1.4 billion by the year 2001[17] (cf. figure 10).

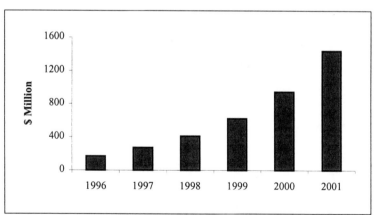

Figure 10: IP market evolution.
Source: Adapted from Lexra Inc.

To sum up, it seems that conditions for the existence of a market for knowledge are fulfilled within the semiconductor industry. Moreover, IPs are sold on globalized markets to customers operating on smaller local markets. Let us now examine how this market works.

3. THE IP MARKET RUNNING

The industry's fast advances into deep sub-micron technology has been fostered by several factors. The increasing availability of virtual components and state-of-the-art design technologies to embedded cores contribute to consolidate the SOC era. Despite this evolution, a definitive business model for IP creation, acquisition, reuse and sales was not yet adopted in 1998.

As we noticed above, a system on chip means that individual ICs (previously discrete chips) are evolving toward virtual IP "building blocks", potentially reusable in a myriad of new single-chip combinations. A SOC is definitely a "modular system" as defined by Langlois (1998), Langlois and Robertson (1995). While these authors apply this concept to physical components in products such as automobiles or stereos, Arora, Gambardella and Rullani (1997), Arora and Gambardella (1994), among others, extend its implementation to intangible components, namely basic scientific and technological "modules" of knowledge. The crucial point in modular system industries is related to coordination issues. How do firms create these building blocks, how do they combine their own blocks with those designed by IP providers, how do they ensure that the resulting SOC operates correctly, and do how IP vendors market and transact the intellectual property contained within these blocks ? All these questions echo throughout the semiconductor industry.

These challenges related to coordination are all the more critical since there is no unique and simple pricing model for IP blocks. Four pricing models are currently used for intangible knowledge assets such as reusable IP blocks. IP vendors may claim high up-front payments and extensive support with a low royalty license fee. Secondly, they may initiate a development contract, with all rights going to the customers and no royalty fee. Alternatively, third-party providers may ask for a low up-front startup fee, with the commercial IP vendors receiving a competitive royalty fee depending on the success of the end product. Finally, the IP price model may correspond to a one-time source license fee with minimal development or integration support (most commonly used for commodity, low-value-added IP). All of these show that the IP market cannot be considered within the traditional microeconomic framework where prices result from the simple confrontation between suppliers and customers on the market place. The price signal is not sufficient to coordinate agents' plans of action. As the market transactions involve reusable technological knowledge modules, the goods exchanged represent, in essence, quasi-public goods. The latter are widely studied in the modern microeconomics drawing on Arrow's seminal works. In order to avoid the incentive defaults to produce and sell knowledge, we must weigh the problem of piracy and thus the institutional frameworks aiming at protecting intellectual property. An efficient system of intellectual property rights is thus a precondition to the successful working of the IP market. In addition, the establishment of standards is crucial in the emergence of modular systems, which call for coordination among the numerous parties involved throughout the value chain. In particular, the emerging IP market has to cope with an extreme proliferation of different technologies, sharpening the quality and compatibility problems. Indeed '[T]he systemic or autonomous nature of innovation is neither entirely exogenous nor driven solely by technology. The structure of organization helps shape the pattern of innovation, which in turn influences the subsequent structure of organization. In short, a theory of organizational structure is properly part of an evolutionary theory of social institutions' (Langlois, 1998, p.2).

Various peculiar types of social institutions influence both innovation and industrial structure. We focus here on systems of intellectual property and standardization. In the absence of such social institutions, a deep division of innovative labor is impossible, connections among the different stages of the value chain then become problematic, autonomous innovation (the IDM model) remains costly but this is the only way to do a SOC. In this case, competitive advantage may go to organizations endowed with significant internal capabilities for systemic innovation.With the emergence of such social institutions, competitive advantage may go to organizations with significant external capabilities for systemic innovation. The aim of the parties involved is to benefit from what Langlois (1998) calls "external economies of scope" which 'are typically economies of knowledge reuse' (Ibid, p.19).

3.1 The Protection of Intellectual Property

In the SOC paradigm, most of the knowledge used lies in externally created IPs. Such IPs are highly abstract and disembodied, which permits trade, but also reuse. For this reason, it becomes very difficult to protect knowledge because it is less tacit. Consequently, there is often a separation between the knowledge design unit and the unit that uses the knowledge. At the time of exchange or transfer of this knowledge, and from the moment it is embedded in the semiconductor, competitors can capture it if not efficiently protected.

The literature often emphasizes two main types[18] of intellectual property: the legal means of disclosing information, and secrecy. The alternative resort to one or the other, determining the propensity to patent, is driven by different motives like companies' size and activities and the type of object (product/process) to protect (Mansfield, 1986; Levin et al., 1987). With regard to this last factor, it seems that in semiconductors, firms maintain secrecy about processes while patenting product innovations (Cohen and Klepper, 1996; Arundel and Kabla, 1998).

As we noted above, the division of innovative labor leads to a separation between the inventor and the user of knowledge and therefore, IP protection must fulfill two conditions. The first consists in enabling the IP exploitation by non-inventors who bought the knowledge. Second, IP protection must maintain the appropriation for the vendor (the inventor) and secure the transaction for the buyer (the user). In this particular context, the disclosure of knowledge and its protection are complementary. They simply intervene at different stages, as shown in figure 11. Summing up then, IP providers have various means of protection at their disposal (Brunsvold, Burgujian and Pratt 1998; Fernandez and Fernandez, 1998): patenting, copyright, trade secrets, maskwork and trademarks.

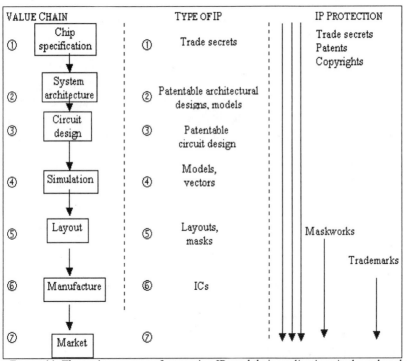

Figure 11: The various means of protecting IPs and their applications in the value chain.
Source: Fernandez and Fernandez (1998)

Patents[19] prevent non-inventors from manufacturing, using, selling or even importing the patented object. With semiconductors, patents protect the concepts (methods, processes, systems, etc.); this is the reason why they seem the most appropriate form of protection for EDA technologies and circuit designs (i.e. as soon as knowledge becomes observable). Moreover, they are costly and time-consuming[20]. Nevertheless, the number of patent applications is increasing worldwide (cf. table 7).

Table 7. Number of patents applied for from national offices (class H01L[21])

	1978	1988	1998
EU	30	387	139
US	261	640	2520
Japan	5246	18313	16325

Source: IBM patents database

Simple or cross-licensing agreements[22] are usually associated with patenting (Grindley and Teece, 1997) and set up the conditions for IPs commercialization. Companies may use this means for various reasons: to draw incomes in order to finance R&D (this is the case of Texas Instruments), to gain greater freedom of design without the threat of involuntary appropriation (IBM) or finally to develop technologies which are likely to become standard (ATT). The latter is particularly important in today's context where standards relative to SOCs have not yet emerged. Some companies do not hesitate in lowering up-front licensing fees in order to favor the adoption of their technology. Indeed, within semiconductors, license transfers often concern patent portfolios or families, since technologies often overlap, making it difficult and costly to isolate an invention. Typically, a cross-license lasts five years, during which time the licensee has access to current and future patents; these licenses are not exclusive and can be renegotiated within the terms of the agreement. The value of licenses is established from a "proud list procedure" (Grindley and Teece, 1997), which selects a representative sample of patents for each company and is based on the rate of royalties, the technological value of knowledge and potential sales of the final product incorporating the knowledge. In summary, protection by patenting and the eventual licensing is desirable when knowledge is embedded in a promising product, in terms of sales and incremental technological development/improvement.

Copyrights are property rights which protect an original work in an tangible form (which also includes software) and which forbid non-holders from reproducing, adapting and distributing it. Contrary to patents, they are fairly easily obtained, free and last for a considerable length of time (50 years after the death of the inventor); however they do not protect from appropriation through reverse engineering[23].

Protection by maskwork is specifically applied to chip layout in its physical form and lasts 10 years. In the United States, the Semiconductor Chip Protection Act (1984) fixes conditions for chip protection and recognizes this means in its statutes. Meanwhile, it does not protect procedures, methods or designs and authorizes reverse engineering.

Trademarks protect the symbols and names of products, services and companies, but not technologies. They are generally used when an IP is about to be marketed.

Finally, the trade secret is used when an inventor would like to protect the potential competitive advantage generated by his innovation, from his competitors. In this case, the efficiency of the protection depends entirely on the company's efforts, particularly on its ability to create and maintain a high tacit degree of knowledge. That is why this means is often used in early stages of design (specification, technical information on chip architecture). Such a means of protection can be used by a company that designs and uses its IPs, or by a simple designer who wishes to secure transactions with customers and as a means of guaranteeing IP exclusivity. Indeed, a competitor can illegally appropriate technology at different stages of design (even within the company via the employees), but also during the transfer of IPs between parties (cf. figure 12).

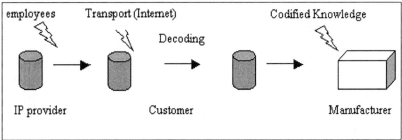

Figure 12: The danger of leaks during the design and transfer of IPs.
Source: Adapted from Hodor (1998)

It is clear that a key element is, in this context, trust within the inventor company and between contracting parties. Moreover, in order to avoid improper appropriation during transfer (notably via the internet when IPs are available in an on-line catalogue), the transmitting company has different means at its disposal: the IP can be conveyed in encrypted form, then decoded by the customer possessing the code (in general a program supplied by an EDA). This method is currently little used since it is costly and complex. Alternatively, the IP can be protected by a digital signature (complex binary code) throughout the process, which identifies and authenticates the inventor.

Broadly speaking, knowledge protection means have evolved significantly through the impetus given by new requirements of the System on Chip paradigm. New technological tools and new, more complex protection strategies have been developed within the companies. At the public level, laws relative to IP protection are now better adapted to the intangible nature of IPs. The stake is here crucial since the basis of competitive advantage is knowledge. Without a legal framework that methodically sets up the rights of inventors, the incentive to innovation and the technological progress are dramatically reduced and can affect the competitiveness of an entire nation.

3.2 Standards as Institutional Arrangements

Recently, SOC technology crossed the quarter-micron threshold, which means that tens of millions of transistors are potentially built on a single die, and every six months, new thresholds are crossed within research laboratories. Also, long before commercialized SOCs introduced new process technologies, companies knew that they had to quickly find engineering techniques to fulfill the potential in order to create designs of incredible densities and lightening-fast speeds while consuming far less power than ever before. In other words, they had to cope with a design productivity crisis (cf. figure 6 above).

To keep up with the growing silicon densities, the only practical method was to reuse internal design as well as previous design work from other teams of engineers. This involved recombining existing building IP blocks several times in distinct designs. The *design revolution* – design for reuse – required a change in the engineer's way of thinking in order to promote IP block portability. Managers had to persuade engineering teams to invent techniques for knowledge transfers both inside and between organizations. More importantly, it was necessary to find a means of ensuring quality for portable reuse designs, since at the moment of market emergence and because of the great number of IP providers, IPs available on the market presented many problems related to integration and quality. The meaning of "reusable designs" varied from company to company. Industrial agents have thus gathered different standardization organizations to agree upon and define basic shared elements. '...[T]he origins of the standards...were, if not exactly "spontaneous", then at least far more grass-roots and collaborative in character.' (Langlois, 1998, p.27) Thus, these organizations have attempted to impose a set of non-product standards on the industry in general (Tassey, 2000).

The issue is that whatever solutions are developed, they have to include continued innovation and improved integration, balanced in several key standardization areas[24]. In spite of the considerable advantages of standardization at SOC development and manufacturing stages, the increasing number of organizations and associations involved did not facilitate this task. Nowadays standards efforts are being mainly governed by several organizations, such as the EDA Industry Council, Open Verilog International (OVI) and the Virtual Socket Interface Alliance (VSIA). For instance, the latter established in 1996, plays a key role in standards that enables exchanges of intellectual property rights. VSIA defines, ratifies and promotes open data formats, test methods and interfaces[25].

In order to analyze the economic roles of standards in the semiconductor industry, and more precisely those concerning the IP market, we use the classification established by Tassey (2000; 1992) who distinguishes four economic functions. The first, dealing with quality/reliability, specifies a minimum performance level or a given technical function. For instance, bus cores provide the interface between a standard bus structure such as a PCI bus, and the user's logic. However, the cores themselves are not standardized, they are not interchangeable because cores are available with different options (for instance PCI bus with 32-bit or 64-bit, running at either 66 or 133Mhz). We can also notice that the quality of additional services such as development support provided by IP vendors crucially influence the ultimate choice of the core provider. The level of support depends on criteria such as the degree of customization required by the SOC designer and the team's familiarity with this core. Furthermore, the core design varies depending on the type of application logic to which the customer is connecting the interface. Consequently, a quality/reliability standard does not imply compatibility. The second basic economic function is filled by a standardized interface that allows much closer links between system-level, logical and physical design. For instance, interoperability between tools is a continuing need in the SOC era, which has been fulfilled by design languages at different design levels (Verilog HDL, VHDL, RTL codes, etc.). These standards specify functional or physical properties that the cores must have in order to work with complementary blocks of IP on a SOC. Interoperability/compatibility standards 'provide "open" systems and thereby allow multiple proprietary component compatibility designs to coexist' (Tassey, 2000, p.590). Common compatibility standards consolidate the SOC as a modular system (Langlois and Robertson, 1995; Langlois, 1998; Arora, Gambardella and Rullani, 1997).

The third economic function of standards consists in providing scientific and engineering information related to measurement, test and verification. For example, VSI Alliance is defining and promoting open data formats and test methods standards. Finally, standardization may reduce variety and therefore simplify the assessment of the price performance ratio for customers, changing in this way the nature of competition (Foray, 1993). IP vendors will then compete mainly on prices and additional services.

Ultimately, as regards standardization, there is a delicate balance between when it is too early to create a standard, and when it is too late. If a standard is developed too early, the industry risks to abandon other technological varieties. Besides, any time a standard emerges prematurely, innovation suffers if the standard proves to be overly restrictive. On the other hand, if a standard is created too late, firms waste a lot of effort and resources. Design methodology is always changing, so this is an ongoing concern.

3.3 Money Flow and Business Models for IP Market

To understand the impact of IP vendors within the semiconductor industry, it is important to examine the purchasing money flow between the parties involved. OEMs represent the major source of money. They buy chips from fabless companies which make ICs for them, which in turn buy the pure-play foundries' manufacturing capabilities and IC design services from the design houses. Alternatively, OEMs buy the design services from design houses and also the chips from IC manufacturers which possess their own fabs. Moreover, IP vendors are the only parties to receive money from all other agents of the industry. This confirms their pivotal position in the restructured semiconductor industry (cf. figure 13).

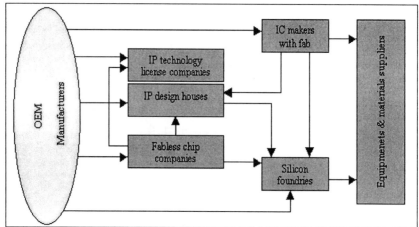

Figure 13: Money flow within the SC industry.
Source: McCleod (1998).

Given the very high costs of R&D design necessary to realize an IP, IP providers have to depreciate their up-front investments in several applications. Thus, patent sales seem to be excluded, as most of the transactions carried out by IP providers correspond to repeat licenses. Moreover, license fees are not generally the only source of revenue for IP providers, nor the most important, depending on the type of IP. With IP transactions, the licensor's revenue is staggered over the period. At the early stage it can stem from up-front licensing fees, then from non-recurring engineering (NRE) fees because most IPs require modification and adaptation for the chip's architecture in order to fulfill the specific needs of the customer[26]. Next comes remuneration from test services and maintenance and finally royalties for each unit incorporating the IP sold, this latter flow of money continuing for as long as the product is marketed by the customer. Moreover, the same IP can give rise to a flow of additional income if it is the object of a new license for the same customer but for a new application requiring modifications to the IP. In this case, the up-front fees will be less (generally reduced by half), but NRE fees will be higher.

The effective remuneration model which gives more or less importance to licensing fees in comparison to royalties, depends on the nature of the marketed IP. The more an IP requires new or key technological knowledge, the greater the freedom the IP vendor has when it comes to fixing a price scale. On the one hand, commodity IPs, which were launched on the IP market in the 1990s, represent functional circuit blocks in a reusable design (for example bus cores like PCI, AGP, USB). In this market segment, third party providers now opt for a royalty dominant business model with low up-front licensing fees, even free access in terms of licenses (free up-front fees). Indeed, the underlying technological knowledge is mature, and is moreover offered by many firms. In this case it is the market that essentially sets up the price. On the other hand, for strategic technology IP and branded IP[27], in which technological knowledge is respectively new and highly proprietary, the business model consists in demanding both up-front licensing fees and substantial royalties.

In the meantime, the IP value for the customer is not simply limited to its price. It is also necessary to consider the qualitative differences between what could be provided by the IP vendor and what the customer is able to do himself. In particular, complementary engineering, design and test services as well as the quality of the IP maintenance are crucial since customers look for particular qualities from IP vendors. They must demonstrate their know how and show that their IPs work according to customer's specifications, and moreover that they are able to differentiate their IPs for future applications. This interesting change which took place in 1998 means that some IP purchasers are beginning to consider IP providers not as a solution to outsourcing, but rather as an outside technology source. We must nonetheless underline that IP modifications are sometimes made by the customer itself, if agreed with the IP provider in order to avoid patent infringements.

3.4 A Case Study: ARM and the Embedded RISC Processor Market

ARM (Advanced RISC Machines), creator of the de facto standard architecture for the embedded RISC processor and one of the best success stories among the IP vendors, provides an instructive example of the semiconductor industry evolution and the focus role played now by IP vendors in the new and dominant SOC era.

The embedded processors market has benefited from the success of SOCs. Hence, customers now integrate processor cores rather than use processor chips. Less famous than Intel Pentium™ processors, these embedded processors are more pervasive in our lives. The main target applications include networking ICs and consumer ICs. For instance, this kind of processor can be found inside the anti-lock braking system of an automobile, the cellular phone and microwave oven, to name just a few. The market volume has increased approximately from 50 million units in 1995 to 180 million in 1999 and estimates for 2000 reach 220 million units. The market for embedded processors is very large, estimated at almost $50 billion worldwide in 1997 by Micrologic Research (Lexra Corporation, 1998). This market is projected to continue its rapid growth rate of 35% per year compounded annually at least until the year 2001.

RISC processors were first designed by Acorn Group plc and ARM, the joint venture created in 1990 by Acorn, Apple Computer (UK) Limited and VLSI Inc., introduced its first embeddable RISC core in 1991, the ARM6. ARM's market shares in this segment have been increasingly growing since then (cf. figure 14).

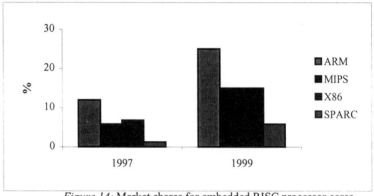

Figure 14: Market shares for embedded RISC processor cores.
Source: Adapted from Lexra Inc.

Since the first core generation in 1991, ARM has introduced incremental innovations using the same technological trajectory, thus introducing onto the market new derivative core families with new final applications. Although ARM's technological development is today favored by relationships with some partners, this has not always been the case. As the founder of ARM underlines 'ARM has learned from the mistake of ramping up full-scale licensing too soon, ... We have found that it's best to have a stable product with one or two lead partners. When you know you have a stable product then you license it widely' (quoted by Muller, 1999). ARM has thus successfully adopted a strategy aimed at imposing its architecture as a de facto standard thanks to its partners (EDA companies, OEMs, design service firms and operating system companies). So, ARM has to balance between reaping high revenues and having to ensure that its partners support ARM IPs. As noted in the first part of this chapter, the operating expenses assumed by an IP provider are highly targeted and are mainly related to R&D, sales and marketing. There are nonetheless other costs assumed by an IP provider, including product costs and service costs. The former are limited to variable production costs such as manufacturing costs of development systems and those incurred in making third party operating systems compatible with the ARM architecture. Service costs include costs of support and maintenance services to licensees of the technology as well as the costs directly attributable to consulting work performed for third parties (cf. tabie 8). As an intellectual property company, approximately two thirds of ARM's costs are employee related[28].

Table 8. The breakdown of costs

	Revenue (£ M)	Operating expenses (% Revenue)		Costs of revenue (% Revenue)	
		R&D	Sales & Marketing	General & Adm.	Product costs	Service costs
1995	09.7	-	-	-	-	-
1996	16.7	18	20	15	11	14
1997	26.6	23	20	13	13	12
1998	42.3	28	18	11	9	10
1999	62.1	27	18	12	7	8

Source: Adapted from ARM, Financial statements (1998, 1999)

The patents portfolio secured by the company extends to more than 200 non-US patents between 1991 and 1998. Patents secured in the USA are fewer (less than 10 patents at the beginning of 1994 to more than 70 at the start of 97). Nonetheless, as we indicated earlier, an IP provider does not sell its patents. With the growing acceptance of the IP licensing model, the greater part of ARM's revenues stems from license fees (65% in 1998). The ARM business model consists of giving greater place to license revenue and voluntarily underestimating royalty revenue. The experience of ARM shows that royalties are always smaller and later. Indeed, one important issue of the IP provider business is the balance between licensing fees and royalties. On an IP project model, ARM in effect must design and develop the core while the final demand is still uncertain. Also it chooses a strategy allowing costs to be absorbed solely through license revenue (cf. figure 15).

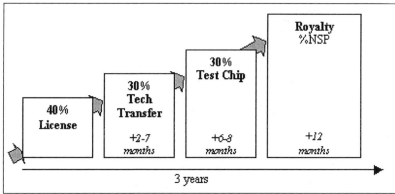

Figure 15: Licensing revenue model.
Source: Adapted from ARM

ARM thus escapes the risk run by its customers when their final products incorporating the ARM core turns out to be a commercial failure. Another major problem faced by an IP provider is the life expectancy of the IP. What characterizes ARM is that its architectures will still be shipped many years after their first shipment. ARM favors repeat business, i.e., it re-licenses the same core many times (cf. figure 16).

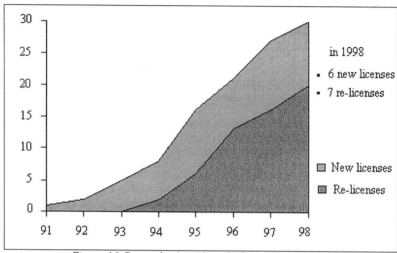

Figure 16: Repeat business is at the heart of ARM's success.
Source: ARM Financial statements (1998, 1999)

Repeat business accentuates the market for knowledge, because not only is the third party provider able to sell the same IP to several customers, it is also able to resell it subsequently to the same customers. Let us remind ourselves meanwhile that even if the IP sold is the same, it is later automatically adapted to the requirements of the customer. The company thus also provides consulting, support, maintenance and training services and sells software and development systems to accelerate the acceptance of its architecture and products (cf. figure 17).

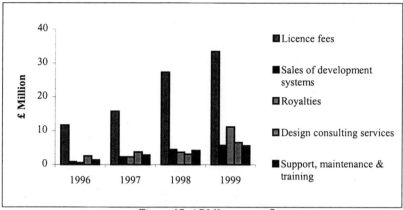

Figure 17: ARM's revenue flow.
Source: Adapted from ARM Financial statements (1998, 1999)

At the end of this case study, we notice that, even if we observe how a market for technological knowledge works, the absorption of the knowledge by customers is not an easy matter. In spite of efforts made by organizations such as VSIA to promote the reuse of portable designs, integration still requires the IP vendor's engineering services, and their interactions look like Von Hippell's (1976) and Lundvall's (1988) user-producer relationships.

4. CONCLUSION

The study of the evolution of the semiconductor industry organization has revealed a progressive division of innovative labor which operates on the basis of market relationships. New agents and new activities have emerged, bringing with them the fragmentation, on a worldwide scale, of productive and innovative activities as well as specialization of these agents. The major restructuring is due to the emergence of intellectual property providers, stemming from a clear separation between the locus of technological knowledge production and the locus of its use. These IP providers operate by selling licenses for the knowledge modules (cores) they design, on markets for knowledge. However, incumbents, in particular IDMs and ASIC companies, did not disappear. Although some of their activities are threatened, particularly design, these companies are gradually changing, leaving non-strategic knowledge creation to IP vendors, and keeping their design teams to differentiate a small part of SOCs through highly specific blocks of architecture. Thus the most strategic knowledge remains tacit for IDMs and ASIC manufacturers. On the other hand, some OEMs purchase the IP blocks they need, which are then differentiated by IP providers. The system on chip revolution marks a widening gap between the physical capabilities of silicon and the design capabilities. This design gap crisis is all the more accentuated due to new technological discoveries (nanotechnologies, etc.): the semiconductor companies already announce several billion gates per chip before the end of the year 2000. This gap between physical frontiers and in-house design capabilities make resort to the market more necessary than ever to acquire complementary IPs.

NOTES

[1] See glossary in appendix 1.

[2] In this case, the semiconductor is used within the firm which manufactures it and is integrated into the end product.

[3] Each SOC component is also designated by the terms core, macro-function, functional block, macro-cell or functional cell.

[4] Indeed, competition remains relatively strong in certain market segments such as microprocessors (cf. the struggle between recent generations of Intel's Pentium™ and AMD's Athlon™), but the increasing concentration limits the number of competitors.

[5] Thus nanotechnologies, on the border between chemistry and physics, involve carbon structures which behave like semiconductors. Their molecular size allows reduction in the size of the microelectronic system. These nanotechnologies (of the order of 10^{-9} m) also find applications in the textile and material industries. In the same way, neurochips (groups of neurones living on a semiconductor and electrically stimulated) already exist at the experimental stage (Ikonicoff, 2000; Pichon, 1998).

[6] In 1993, 3 billion transistors were mounted on a surface of 0.8μ (Pentium™ 60). Today the same number of transistors is held on 0.18μ.

[7] Among which a firm will progressively emerge on the world market, Applied Materials (Langlois, 1998).

[8] We can give the example of Chartered Semiconductor which has a close partnership agreement with Motorola and Lucent Technologies, and a joint venture with Hewlett-Packard.

[9] According to Donaldson, Lufkin and Jenrette Inc. (DJL) San Francisco, source: Quicklogic Corporation, Press Release, http://www.quicklogic.com.

[10] For example the leader TSMC left 74% of its sales in the 90s to fabless companies, the rest to IDMs. Source: TSMC, S2 Mag Conferences, http:/www.s2mag.com

[11] In 1998, among the worldwide population of 500 fabless companies, more than 300 were located in North America.

[13] Interviews were held with the engineers and directors of Groupe Cybernetix, Château Gombert, France.

[14] Companies that design, develop and produce electronic hardware.

[15] A reusable design in general contains two parts: a fixed unchanging portion and a flexible part which customers adapt to their application.

[16] A system company initially bought a PCI core from an IP vendor which claimed on the one hand a one-time license fee, ($100,000) and on the other hand a per-chip royalty of $0.10. As for engineering services, the cost of service for the first transaction is very high in order to absorb the cost of development, then it drops considerably for subsequent transactions. In our case, when the end product incorporating the first customer's IP – the chip – had hardly reached the production stage, other chip makers were buying the same IP block at a much lower cost, specifically for a license fee down to $10,000 and a per-chip royalty down to $0.02.

[17] According to a forecast by Wessels, Arnold and Henderson, an investments banker specializing in the electronics design field. Source: Lexra, http://www.lexra.com

[18] There is normally another form of protection which is the first-mover advantage at the moment of marketing a product but this means is only usable by companies designing and marketing their products (IDMs) or which only take on the sales and marketing (fabless

companies). In this case, it is less the knowledge that is protected than the tangible *artifact* which incorporates it.

[19] For a review of patenting procedures in different countries (Europe, US, Japan), as well as the use of patent indicators in the innovation field, see OECD, 1994.

[20] The cost of a patenting procedure (i.e. filing the application, research, examination) is approximately 38,000FF at the USPTO, 79,450FF at the EPO and 33,000 FF in Japan. The length of the procedure varies from 2 to 4 years (OECD, 1994).

[21] According to the International Patent Classification (IPC) semiconductors are classified in the sub-category H01L, that is the semiconductor devices and the electric solid state devices not otherwise provided for.

[22] At the time of cross licensing "firms agree one-to-one to license their IP to each other and retain control over their proprietary technology, which is used for competitive advantage via product manufacturing and further licensing" (Grindley and Teece, 1997, p.34).

[23] This technique remains rather costly and time-consuming. It costs approximately $500 for an SRAM memory, $50,000 for a mask-programmed ASIC and 400 to 500 man-hours per device (Hodor, 1998).

[24] The key standardization areas consist notably in (1) design methodologies including design tools and verification techniques, (2) advanced design automation tools (EDA tools), and (3) other standards such as (i) standards that allow much closer links between system level, logical and physical design. (VHDL, etc.), (ii) on-chip bus standards that enable the different blocks to play together. (PCI, USB, etc.), (iii) codes that provide design descriptions. (RTL code, etc.).

[25] This industry consortium is organized around 6 development working groups (DWGs): (1) Analog/Mixed Signal DWG; it is described as a practical document for designing mixed-signal blocks as VCs in a largely digital system. (2) Implementation / Verification DWG: identifies standards to help hardware design from the stage of RTL planning to final verification. (3) On-chip bus group: its charter is to recommend standards for design, the integration and testing of multipurpose blocks of silicon. (4) IP protection DWG: its charter is to define standards to make a compromise between VC (virtual components) security and its use by the customer. (5) Manufacturing Related Test and (6) System Level Design.

[26] Two scenarios are possible when modifying the IP. Firstly, if the IP provider bears the cost of these modifications, it then claims NRE fees to compensate. Generally, the IP provider also wishes to add modifications to its IP portfolio. Secondly, if modifications are made by the customer, legal problems arise. To solve them, either the IP provider uses diligence in ensuring the IP is free of patent infringement, or the IP provider generally offers some protection: designing a workaround (procuring licenses for the infringing IP), or defending patent infringement litigation in court (the most expensive), or returning the fees paid and terminating the contract after requiring the customer to remove the infringing IP.

[27] Strategic Technology IPs are IPs which rely on recent significant technological innovations. They thus represent high value cores, such as 1394, DSP, and MPEG microprocessors, or Rambus in RDRAMs. Typical fees can range from 1 to 8% of the average selling price of the chip. In the case of Branded IPs, the IP providers have invested in special relationships with other key agents in the industry such as EDAs, foundries and OEMs by offering their IPs at modest prices at the start of their life cycle in order to impose them progressively as a brand. This IP becomes thus a de facto standard, e.g., Dolby AC3 and ARM (Advanced RISC Machines) cores.

[28] This costs distribution shows the interest that these firms represent for financial markets; the market entry barriers and sunk costs are very low in comparison to the costs of new fabs assumed by IDMs and pure-play foundries.

APPENDIX 1
Glossary of Semiconductors, Acronyms

Analog (linear): An analog integrated circuit transmits information flows under its original form (continuous electromagnetic waves).

ASICs: Application-Specific Integrated Circuits. An integrated circuit designed or adapted for specific application. Traditionally called a custom circuit.

Bus: a path over which digital information is transferred from any of several sources to any of several destinations. The sources and destinations may be inside or outside the computer.

CAD: acronym for Computer Aided Design. Enables a circuit designer to simulate the performance of sections of the circuit which he designs, so that he can optimize the design without building a hardware prototype first. It can also refer to computer aided layout design.

CMOS: Complementary MOS, that is a variety of MOS technology (see below). CMOS devices generally exhibit very low power consumption and medium to high switching speeds.

Design House: a company that specializes in the design of integrated circuits but has no in house manufacturing and does not sell its design on the open market under its own brand name or trade mark.

Digital (logic): indicates the representation of data by a series of bits or discrete values, such as "1"s and "0"s.

DRAM: Dynamic Random Access Memory, a storage device which requires data to be continually regenerated. DRAMs are traditionally at the leading edge of semiconductor device technology and are sold in very large quantities.

DSP: Digital Signal Processor – a high speed, general purpose arithmetic unit used for performing complex mathematical operations.

EDA: Electronic Design Automation. The use of software tools to design, simulate, and verify a single chip or an entire electronic system. Using these tools, designers can verify that circuits work before production begins.

Gate: basic circuit which produces an output only when certain input conditions are satisfied.

Gate Array: an IC consisting of a regular arrangement of gates that are interconnected to provide custom functions.

IC: Integrated Circuit. Many transistors and other circuit elements "integrated" on a single silicon chip.

IDM: Integrated Design Manufacturer.

IP: Intellectual Property.

Mask: in the processing of semiconductors, especially ICs, masks (or photomasks) are used in much the same manner as photographic negatives. The surface of a wafer which has been coated with a photoresist is exposed through a mask which determines the size, shape, and interconnection of the various elements such as transistors of the integrated circuits.

Memory: stores needed facts, along with instructions on what to do with them and when.

MPU: Micro Processor Unit. The central control unit that directs the processing of data (arithmetic and logic functions) in PCs and other computer systems by directing the flow of electrical impulses, thereby coordinating the efforts of other parts of the machine.

Mixed Signal: the combination of analogue an digital technology on one IC.

MOS: Metal-Oxide-Silicon, one of two basic IC designs along with bipolar, is the fastest growing because it is cheaper, easier to use and consumes less power.

OEM: Original Equipment Manufacturer. A company that designs, develops and produces electronic hardware.

Optoelectronics: includes displays, lamps, couplers, and other opto-sensing and emitting semiconductor devices. It uses the optic technologies for light emission and reception.

Package: the container used to encapsulate a semiconductor chip.

RISC: Reduced Instruction Set Computing. Device where the number of instructions a microprocessor runs for a specific application are reduced from a general purpose Complex Instruction Set Computing (CISC) device to create a more efficient operating system.

Semiconductor: class of material which can assume the properties of either a conductor or an insulator. Common Semiconductor materials are silicon, germanium and gallium arsenide.

Silicon: a non-metallic element that is the most widely used semiconductor material today. Silicon is used in its crystalline form as the substrate of semiconductor devices.

Standard Cells: pre-defined logic elements that may be selected and arranged to create a custom IC more easily than through original (custom) design.

SOC: System On Chip.

TAP: Testing, Assembly, Packaging.

Wafer: a round slice of silicon crystal from which, after processing is complete dice or chips are cut.

APPENDIX 2
The Three Models of the Organization of the Semiconductor Industry

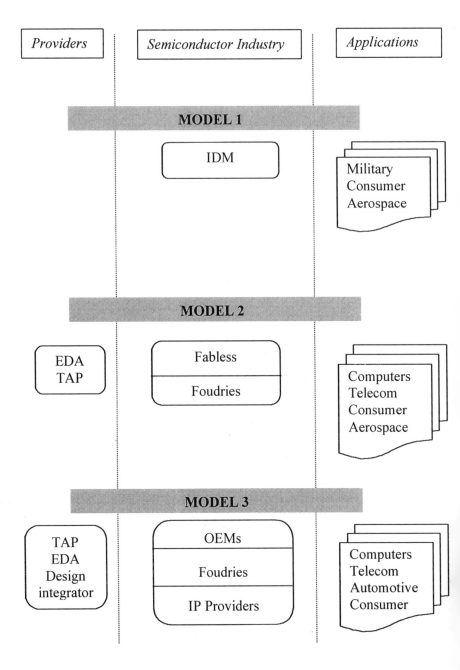

REFERENCES

Antonelli, Cristiano, *The Microdynamics of Technological Change*. London and New York: Routledge, 1999.

Arora A., Fosfuri A., Gambardella A. Markets for Technology (Why do we see them, why don't we see more off them, and why we should care). Working Paper N°99-17, Université Carlos III de Madrid. 1999.

Arora A., Gambardella A. The changing technology of technological change : general and abstract knowledge and the division of innovative labour. Research Policy 1994; 23:523-32.

Arora A., Gambardella A., Rullani E. Division of Labour and the Locus of Inventive Activity. Journal of Management and Governance 1997; 1:123-40.

Arundel A., Kabla I. What percentage of innovations are patented ? Empirical estimates for European firms. Research Policy 1998 ; 27:127-41.

Athreye S. M. On Markets in Knowledge. Working Paper N° 83, ESRC. March 1998.

Bresnahan T., Malerba F. The Computer Industry. CCC Matrix project. Cape Cod (MA). 1996.

Brunsvold B.G., Burgujian R.V., Pratt W.H. Protecting intellectual property: copyrights. Silicon Strategies 1998 ; June.

Cohen W.M., Klepper S. Firm size and the nature of innovation within industries: the case of process and product R&D. Review of Economics and Statistics 1996 ; 78 :232-43.

Cusumano, Michael A. *Japan's Software Factories*. New York: Oxford University Press, 1991.

Dauvin, Jean-Philippe, *Les semi-conducteurs*. Paris : Cyclope Economica, 1990.

De Bandt J., Ravix J.L., Romani P.M. Allyn Young : une approche de la dynamique industrielle. Revue Française d'Economie 1990 ; 5:85-109.

Dosi G. Sources, procedures and microeconomic effects of innovation. Journal of Economic Litterature 1988 ; 26:1120-71.

Duysters, Gert, *The dynamics of technical innovation – The evolution and development of information technology*. Cheltenham: Elgar, 1996.

Fernandez I. H., Fernandez D. S. Building a legally sound intellectual property portfolio. Silicon Strategies 1998 ; June.

Flaherty M.T. Field research on the link between technological innovation and growth: evidence from the international semiconductor industry. American Economic Review, Papers & Proceedings 1984 ; 74:67-72.

Foray D. Standardisation et concurrence: des relations ambivalentes. Revue d'Economie Industrielle 1993 ; 63 :84-101.

Gambardella A., Torrisi S. Does technological convergence imply convergence in markets ? Evidence from the electronics industry. Research Policy 1998 ; 27:445-63.

Geneau De Lamarlière, Isabelle. "Les déterminants des localisations dans l'industrie des semi-conducteurs." In *La dynamique spatiale de l'économie contemporaine*, George B. Benko, ed. Paris : Editions de l'Espace Européen, 1990.

Grandstrand O., Patel P., Pavitt K. Multi-technology Corporations : Why they have 'distributed' rather than 'distinctive core' competencies. California Management Review 1997 ; 39 :8-25.

Grindley P. C., Teece D. J. Managing Intellectual Capital : Licencing and Cross-Licencing in Semiconductors and Electronics. California Management Review 1997; 39:8-41.

Gruber H. The yield factor and the learning curve in semiconductor production. Applied Economics 1994 ; 26 :837-43.

Hayek F.A. Economics and Knowledge, Presidential address delivered before the London Economic Club; November 10 1936, Reprinted from Economica IV 1937: 33-54.

Hodor K. Adopting methods to protect intellectual property from pirates. Silicon Strategies 1998 ; February.

Ikonicoff R. Nanotubes: vers l'ordinateur microscopique. Science & Vie 2000; 989:130-33.

Integrated Circuit Engineering Corporation. Status 1995. Mid-Term Report. 1995.

Langlois R.N. Capabilities and Vertical disintegration in process technology. Working Paper, University of Connecticut. January 1998.

Langlois R., Robertson P. L. Innovation, Networks, and Vertical Integration. Research Policy 1995; 24:543-62.

Langlois, Richard N., Steinmueller William E. The Evolution of Competitive Advantage in the Worldwide Semiconductor Industry, 1947-1996. Report of the CCC Matrix Project, 3rd draft. Cape Cod: 1996.

Levin R., Klevorick A., Nelson R., Winter S. Appropriating the returns from industrial research and development. Brooking Papers on Economic Activity 1987 ; 3:783-820.

Loasby B. J. The organisation of capabilities. Journal of Economic Behavior & Organization 1998; 35: 139-60.

Loasby B. J. Transactions Costs and Capabilities. Proceedings of the XIe European Summer School on Industrial Dynamics ; 1996 September 12-16 ; Cargese.

Lundvall Bengt. A. "Innovation as an Interactive Process from User-Producer Interaction to the National System of Innovation." In *Technical Change and Theory*, Giovanni Dosi, ed. London and New York: Pinter Publishers, 1988.

Luther K., Graml B. Joining Hands in Memory Development. Siemens Review. R&D special 1996.

Macher J. T., Mowery D. C., Hodges D. A. Reversal of Fortune ? The recovery of the U.S. semiconductor industry. California Management Review 1998; 41:107-56.

Malerba F., Nelson R., Orsenigo L., Winter S. 'History-friendly' models of industry evolution : the computer industry. Industrial and Corporate Change 1999 ; 8 :1-36.

Malerba F., Orsenigo L. Technological regimes and firm behaviour. Industrial and Corporate Change 1993 ; 2 :45-71.

Mansfield E. Patents and innovation: an empirical study. Management Science 1986 ; 32:173-81.

Martinotti P. Microelectronics Towards System On Chip. Silicon Strategies Conference ; 1998 March 16-17 ; San Jose (US).

McCall T. Gartnergroup's Dataquest Says Worldwide Semiconductor Market Growth Grew nearly 18%. Press Release; 2000 January 6.

Mc Leod J. A sea change hits the semiconductor industry. Silicon Strategies 1998; June.

Moati P., Mouhoud E. M. Division cognitive du travail et dynamiques de la localisation industrielle dans l'espace mondial. Proceedings of the International Conference "La connaissance dans la dynamique des organisations productives"; 1995 September 14-15; Aix-en-Provence.

Menger, Carl, *Principles of Economics*. New York: New York University Press, 1981 (Original in German 1871).

Muller M. How to make Money in IP. Silicon Strategies 1999 ; May.

O.C.D.E. La mesure des activités scientifiques et technologiques - Les données sur les brevets d'invention et leur utilisation comme indicateurs de la science et de la technologie - Manuel Brevets 1994. Working Paper GD(94) 114. Paris: OCDE 1994.

Pavitt K. Technologies, products and organisations in the innovative firm: what Adam Smith tells us and Joseph Schumpeter doesn't. Working Paper, SPRU. May 1998: 1-21.

Penn M. Semiconductor Market - Trends & Analysis. Scottish SC Supplier Forum Annual General Meeting ; 1999a June 17.

Penn M. Semiconductors Market Drivers and profitability. SEMI Fab Management Forum; 1999b April 16; Dresden.

Pichon. A. Dossier spécial futur. Science & Vie Micro 1998 ; 166:58-123.

Quéré, Michel, Ravix Jacques-Laurent. "Proximité et organisation territoriale de l'industrie." In *Approches multiformes de la proximité*, Michel Bellet, Thierry Kirat, Christine Largeron, eds. : Hermès, 1998.

Ravix, Jacques-Laurent, *Production, Institutions et Organisation de l'Industrie, une contribution à la méthode économique*. Thèse d'Etat. Université de Nice-Sophia Antipolis, 1994.

Richardson, George. B., *Information and Investment, A Study in Working of Competitive Economy*. Cambridge: Cambridge University Press, 1960.

Streissler E. To what extent was the Austrian school marginalist? History of Political Economy 1972; 4:426-41.

Tassey G. Standardization in technology-based markets. Research Policy 2000; 29:587-602.

Tassey, Gregory, *Technology Infrastructure and Competition Position*. Northwell: Kluwer, 1992.

Teece D. J. Capturing Value From Knowledge Assets : The New Economy, Markets For Know-How, and Intangible Assets. California Management Review 1998; 40:55-79.

Von Hippel E. The Dominant Role of Users in the Scientific Instrument Innovation Process. Research Policy 1976 ; 5 :212-239.

Wieder A.W. Mapping the Future of Microelectronics. Siemens Review. R&D special 1996.

Winter S.G. Schumpeterian competition in alternative technological regimes. Journal of Economic Behavior and Organization 1984 ; 5:287-320.

Wright, Richard.W., "The role of imitable vs inimitable competences in the evolution of the semiconductor industry." In *Dynamics of competence-based competition*, Ron Sanchez, Aimé Heene, Howard Thomas, eds. Oxford, New York: Pergamon, 1996.

Young A. A. Rendements croissants et progrès économique. Revue Française d'Economie 1990 ; 5:85-109.

Technology and Markets for Knowledge

Internet Sources

ARM Financial statements 1998, 1999 : http://www.arm.com.

Future Horizons : http://www.future-horizons.net.

Gartnergroup : http://gartner11.gartnerweb.com.

IBM Patent Database : http://www. Patents.ibm.com.

Infrastructure: http://infrastructure.supersites.net.

Lexra : http://www.lexra.com

Quicklogic Corporation : http://www.quicklogic.com.

SIA/WSTS FactSet Research Systems :
http://www.bofasecurities.com/indices/content/factsheet2.html.

Silicon Strategies Magazine : http://www.s2mag.com.

Chapter 7

EVOLUTION OF MARKETS IN THE SOFTWARE INDUSTRY

Suma S Athreye
Manchester School of Management, UMIST, Manchester (UK)

This chapter analyses the evolution of the software industry into a market for technology and concentrates particularly on the evolution of segmentation within the software industry. The software industry is a good example of technology markets because it encompasses the two forms that a technology market may take. The first is that of a technology market that comprises outsourced demand, as is the case in its customized segment. The second is the possibility of a technology market that is arms-length and independent of particular consumers, as is the case in its product segment.

Analysts working on technology have often seen the context-dependence of technology as an important impediment constraining the emergence of anonymous, arms-length markets. Context-dependence of technological information imposes severe costs on the supply side for the buying firm making arms-length markets difficult to emerge. In this chapter, however, we have emphasized the role of the scale of homogenous demand. This is usually small for intermediate markets such as the markets for technology, and consequently it exercises an important influence upon market segmentation.

Favorable factors on the demand side encourage an idealized arms-length market to develop. Of particular importance here is the scale of homogenous demand which if large can encourage an independent market to develop around those attributes of the technology that are widely demanded. A small-scale heterogeneous demand can however, emphasize supply-side constraints, such as context-dependence. This encourages specialization around a narrow context of use and results in the emergence of niche markets, rather than arms-length markets. Such niche markets tend to characterize technology markets that are due to outsourcing. Demand and supply side factors can also be interrelated. Thus, heterogeneity of demand makes technology context specific but adequate standards can transform some kinds of heterogeneity into a manageable homogeneity.

In this chapter we try to illustrate all of these arguments through the history of software evolution. The evolution of the software market into "product" and "customised software" segments, we argue, reveals much about the way in which demand and supply-side factors influence market evolution and the subsequent segmentation of industry. Product markets are akin to arms-length markets for software technology, while customized markets represent a demand for software that is outsourced by particular firms. We draw particular attention to differences in the importance of the two segments of the software market across countries. These differences reflect, we argue, differences in the evolution of a homogenous demand for software. Furthermore, heterogeneous demand has often been managed by the creation of common standards.

The remainder of this chapter is organized in the following way. Section 1 briefly outlines the role demand and supply side factors in the emergence of technology markets. Section 2 describes what we include in our definition of the software industry and also contains a brief history of the evolution of the software industry. Section 3 outlines the demand side influences in the growth of the software industry and the (supply) constraints imposed by the needs of compatibility between different types of software. It also discusses the reasons for the segmentation of the software market into "product" and "customised" and the very different nature of competition in the two market segments. Section 4 concludes.

1. DEMAND AND SUPPLY SIDE CONSTRAINTS ON THE EMERGENCE OF TECHNOLOGY MARKETS[1]

For a subject preoccupied with markets and their functioning, economic writing on the issue of when markets emerge has been surprisingly sparse. At the same time, writing on technology markets has been preoccupied with the public good nature of technology, which it is argued may cause arms length markets to fail. In this section, we will set out some arguments for the emergence of markets generally and relate these to the emergence of technology markets in particular.

1.1   Existence of Exchangeable Commodities

Among economists in the classical tradition, Marx stressed that the most important aspect of capitalism and a market form of organization is commodity production. He additionally outlined the minimum characteristics of a commodity. Commodity production takes place when production is not for the direct use of the producer but for sale on the market, i.e. for exchange. Thus when baker bakes bread for his own consumption it is a product but when he bakes bread to sell in the market it assumes the form of a commodity (Bhaduri, 1986).

A product thus becomes a commodity when it can possess an exchange value, which is independent of its use-value. This defining feature of a commodity is important in the context of a market. This is because in a market products are traded at their exchange values in order to satisfy the use-values that the final consumer of product derives from the product. However, the fact that the use value of the product has nothing to do with the exchange value (prices) that it commands in the market is an important feature of both markets and commodities. Indeed there would be no production for a market if use values (for the consumer) did not exceed exchange values received by the producer.

Possessing this essential duality of exchange value in a market and use value for a consumer requires the alienation of the commodity as a prerequisite. Property rights are an important institutional necessity for such an occurrence.[2] It is only in the transfer of ownership involved in an act of market exchange, that both the exchange and use values are realized for the seller and the buyer respectively. Thus, the existence of property rights is sufficient to the condition of alienation.

Firms through their experience of production generate technology. For a market to develop in the technology it has to be more than the result of a firm's previous experience in production. Technology must acquire the status of a commodity. In other words, firms must to produce this technology for the use of other firms and with a view to selling it for a profit. It is also necessary that the use value (to the buying firm) of these technology goods must be larger than what the firm pays to acquire it from another firm.

1.2   Scale of Demand: Static and Dynamic Factors

Commodities exist with generalized exchange and generalized exchange already presumes markets have emerged. However, the continuous or frequent nature of such exchanges is also a pre-requisite for commodity production. If a producer is to be induced to produce for a market and in the expectation of a profit, then some frequency of transaction in the commodity must already be established. Put in another way, the "expectation" of the producer may be about how many units of a good he may sell, but usually it is not about whether he will find any customers at all.

Adam Smith gave the other important explanation for when markets emerge. Smith saw specialized markets emerging as a consequence of increased inter-firm division of labor due to the expansion of markets for exchange of final products. The extent of the exchange market for final goods in turn was positively related to population size and density, amount of natural resources and accumulated capital available (Book 1, chapter 3) the ease of transportation (Book 2, pp.259-61), extent of trade, and lastly the stability of the market. Smithian division of labor has usually been discussed in the context of scale of market demand and both Young (1929) and Stigler (1951) had recognized the scale of the market as the one factor, which ultimately determines the emergence of new industries through vertical disintegration.

It is also worth noting that the size of the exchange market is actually subject to two separate sorts of influences. At any point of time, the size of the exchange market is defined by the number of participants in the market multiplied by the frequency of exchange to any one participant. However, it is easy to see that an increased frequency of exchange transaction would in fact be the result of all the factors considered by Smith as the factors increasing the extent of the market positively, so that what lies behind the extent of the market is in fact an increased frequency of exchange.

At the start of a market emergence process, one may expect the number of participants to be small and unchanging. At this stage it is the frequency of exchange transactions that determines the emergence of a market. Once a exchange market has been established in one period, however, its continuance could come about by an increasing frequency of exchange or by an increase in the number of participants, or both.[3]

Once a market has emerged in a commodity, institutions may emerge to support the continuance of this market. These are likely to differ according to the volume of exchanges and also according to the differing social norms in different environments. They may also give rise to increasing returns in the process of exchange (North 1990). The emergence of standards in several industries is a good example of the role of institutions. Quality standards cut down the buyer risks associated with exchange and facilitate the continuation of the exchange process. Simultaneously by making for compatibility across different users and manufacturers they also facilitate the increase in the size of the market making seller risks low.[4] Thus, the emergence and existence of institutions is sufficient to the second condition viz. the maintenance of the reasonably frequent and continuing exchanges.

The above discussion suggests that the defining features of a market are both the existence of an exchangeable product and the existence of reasonably frequent and continuing exchange transactions in that product. On reflection it is also clear that theoretical conceptions of what a market is also implicitly assume these two characteristics. A "commoditisable product" alone is sufficient to define sporadic exchange and trading behaviour. Routine exchange is capable of giving rise to regular markets with stable behavioral regularities and the possibility that market prices reflect differences in quality or costs of production.[5]

Once markets have emerged they may be regular and irregular. Textbook representations of perfect and imperfect market distinguish between the spread of transactions on both sides of the market (in the case of competitive markets) or concentration of transactions on one side of the market (as in the cases of monopoly oligopoly, or monopsony), as a source of market irregularity. The effect of this irregularity is that make prices diverge from the costs of production.

The scale of market demand at a point of time and its growth overtime are both factors that may particularly constrain the emergence of technology markets. This is because the demand for technology goods is a derived demand from the demand for final goods. Derived demands are typically small. Thus, Athreye (1998) and Bresnahan and Gambardella (1999) argue that technology markets develop mostly on the basis of cross-sectoral demand – a possibility encouraged by the presence of technological convergence. Rosenberg (1963) argued that this was the most important factor facilitating the development of the US machine tool industry. In addition, the interchangeability of component parts ensured that an arms length market could emerge in some parts of the machine tool sector. The use of common standards has played the same role in the development of the software industry.

1.3   Boundaries of the Market, Bundling and Unbundling

In the discussion so far the term market has not been defined except as an organizational mode that facilitates production through exchange and the incentive for which is the profit from such exchange. In particular I have tried to avoid a product based definition of the market because if we think of the emergence of regular markets in more dynamic terms or over several time periods, it should be clear that the consolidation of the process of exchange and the considerations of profitability of the producers will also define the product which is being sold. What is exchanged between buyers and sellers in a market gets determined simultaneously with what can or cannot be alienated as a commodity and with what combination of products a reasonable frequency of exchange transactions might emerge to make it profitable for the producer to sell his product.

Two examples may clarify this last point. In several economies consumer durables are sold along with a guarantee of after sales service. This is a composite product with a product element and a service element. There is no reason why the two should not exist as separate markets by a product definition of a market. In several developing countries markets for repair often act as guarantors for consumer durables, or sometimes no guarantees are sold. Another example is that several developing country firms diversify into several lines of production because often markets do not exist in complementary products such as machinery. Here again is the case of a market that gets established in a composite rather than a single product. Excessive preoccupation with product-based definitions of the market could obscure the process and function of exchange which lies at the heart of the regular market abstraction and the organizational mode of the market.

Technology markets often emerge in composite or "bundled" products. An example here is the case of IBM, which initially provided both hardware and software till the threat of anti-trust legislation forced the firm to unbundle hardware from software. Partly this kind of bundling is a consequence of the natural evolution of demand. If demand grows in an unfettered way, the composite product is subject to specialization and a greater division of labor.

Partly however, bundling also reflects the difficulties of "alienating" technologies from their context. Alienating technologies from their context, imposes costs of codification and standardization upon firms. We turn now to a discussion of these cost considerations that prevent a market for technologies from developing.

1.4   Supply Side Views on Market Emergence

The question of when markets in technology develop maybe viewed from the point of view of a firm who decides when it will be profitable to make or to buy technology that it needs. Viewed in this way, the costs of buying the technology become the important determinant of when a firm will decided to buy the technology. If these costs are lower than what the firm would pay to produce the technology in-house, then a market for technology could emerge. Posing the question in this way should of course not blind us to the fact that buying a piece of knowledge is not the same thing as buying a component of production. Furthermore, the make-buy tradition is unduly static in its assessment of the costs of technology. It does not, for instance, consider what costs are incurred by the firm in using the market, nor does it consider the time that it takes for firms to produce the same technologies in-house.

Nevertheless there are some insights worth noting. In a through review of the existing literature in this tradition, Arora et al. (1999) [6]point to two important supply side constraints to the emergence of technology markets: the context dependence or "stickiness" of knowledge and the problems of writing contracts for knowledge type goods. Both these constraints impose large costs upon firms that in turn predispose them to produce technology in-house.

Arora and Gambardella (1994) argued that such context dependence affects the cost of information exchange, but that the new advances in information technology had reduced the impact of this constraint. This is because advances in computing capability have allowed the codification of previously context specific knowledge by the use of abstract and general principles. The costs of information exchange due to context dependence can be reduced thus leading to a growth in markets for technology.

However, they also point out that if these costs were like a fixed cost then supply side constraints would dissolve in the face of growing demand. Growing demand would ensure that the fixed costs imposed by say codification/standardization, would be lower in unit cost terms reducing the price of technology.

Another problem that is often raised is the difficulties of writing contracts in technology because of uncertainty, small numbers of participants and the ease of imitation. Arora (1995) argues that under some circumstances it may be possible to write contracts in technology, even if technology is largely tacit. The particular circumstance that he draws attention to is the complementarity of tacit and codified components and the possibility of the codified component being protected by intellectual property rights. In this circumstance, technology would be sold as a package. The licensor would always be able to withdraw the license on the codified part of the package and so control opportunistic behavior on the part of the buyer. This analysis again points to the importance of bundling in technology markets.

2. THE SOFTWARE SECTOR AND ITS EVOLUTION OVERTIME

Computer software is the stored, machine-readable code that instructs a microchip to carry out specific tasks[7]. Over thirty years of its evolution the software market has encompassed this basic functionality, across a differentiated range of uses. There are at least two ways in which data on the industry describe the different activities that constitute the software sector.

2.1 Classification of Software

One classification is based upon the function of the software and what sort of tasks it instructs the microchip to carry out. Here there are three broad categories: operating systems, tools and applications. Conceiving the software sector in this way defines the importance of particular computer science skills that are required to write those kinds of software.

A second classification is in terms of how software and its associated services are provided by producers. Thus there are "product providers" or "customised software/service providers". Each of these two kinds of producers may provide operating systems, tools or applications. Such a classification is useful because it emphasizes the associated differences in

188   *Technology and Markets for Knowledge*

the nature of markets and competition between the two segments (Mowery, 1996; Hoch et al., 1999). We use this second classification in this paper as it corresponds more closely to the two forms that technology markets can take.

Table 1. Domestic consumption of software and computer services in the United States, Japan, and Western Europe ($ billion).

	Package software		Custom software		Processing services
	1985	1992	1985	1994	1985
United States	12.60	28.46	4.17	35.60	11.1
Japan	0.27	5.96	2.74	5.95	3.77
Western Europe	5.21	23.85	4.72	26.57	5.33

Source: Mowery, 1996[8]

This current segmentation of the industry however, masks the fact that the software industry evolved overtime from being a professional services provider to providing software products. The evolution of the market segments we will argue is largely a consequence of the evolution of a homogenous or heterogeneous demand for software. Standardization played an important role in eliminating some sources of heterogeneity.

2.2 Stages of Software Evolution

Hoch et al (1999) argue that the software business unfolded in five stages. The first stage (1949-59) comprised the development of professional service firms in the US, who developed tailor-made solutions for several big software projects underwritten by the US government and later by large corporations. The SAGE and the SABRE systems were both products developed in this period. Nevertheless in the 1960s the demand for software came from a few large firms and the conventional wisdom was that software couldn't, by itself, make money.

1959-69 saw the emergence of the first two software product companies. Mark IV written by Informatics was one of the most successful software products. The other software product came about due to a failed contract. ADR produced the product *Autoflow* for another firm (RCA) who decided they didn't want it after all. ADR reacted by trying to recover its costs by selling the same product to other buyer. Eventually they rewrote the product slightly for IBM 1401 and later for IBM/ 360 series.

The decade of the 70s started with the unbundling decision of IBM. The immediate consequence was that a number of software product companies emerged, providing database applications across a range of business operations, for finance and insurance companies. These companies also called independent enterprise solution providers included firms like SAP, BAAN and Oracle- all established during this period.

The decade of the 1980s saw the rapid spread of the personal computer and the associated need for a different kind of software - mass packaged software that could be installed on small systems. The software market splintered into more areas of application. Even before the 80s there were two competing platforms for operating systems on personal computers, viz. the DOS system and the Mackintosh. In the 80s, Windows emerged as the standard operating system. Applications software for the personal computer were written based on the operating system it was to run upon, and this grew as a distinct area of software.

The spread of the PC created the possibility of replacing mainframe systems with networked PCs. This created a new kind of software market where PCs on different operating systems and on the same operating systems could "talk" to each other. The Internet is an extension of this same basic idea. The possibility of writing software that enables different microchips communicate to each other also opens up whole new areas of application – in telecommunications, in media and in "intelligent" consumer durables. These are also the important growth areas for the future of the software industry.

Figure 1, reproduced from Hoch et al (1999) shows the above history of software in terms of significant players and events. Two aspects of the figure are remarkable. The first is that the different developments described were periods in which new technological advances created opportunities for the entry of completely new firms. This is also a feature observed for the evolution of other industries, notably automobiles.

Second the figure shows the gradual development of new software languages as software applications developed. This aspect of software industry evolution is similar to that observed for the capital goods industry where the growth of the machinery sector in economic production was accompanied by the development of engineering and its sub-disciplines.

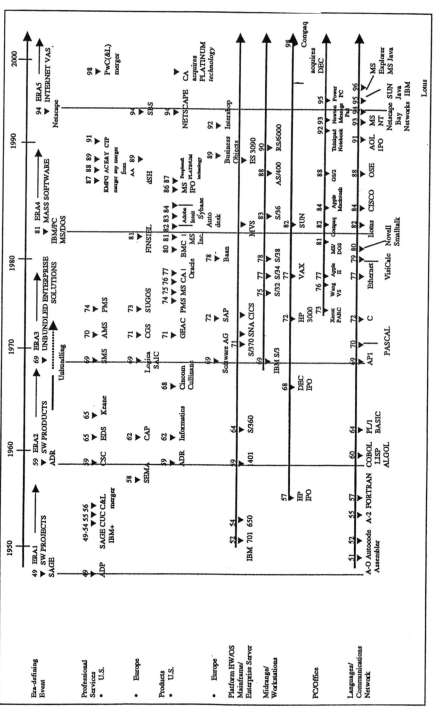

Figure1. Software history eras (including foundation dates of selected major players)
Source: McKinsey Research, as reported in Hoch et al (1999); page 264.

3. DEMAND AND THE EVOLUTION OF THE SOFTWARE INDUSTRY

The demand for software is a derived demand that has emerged as a consequence of increasing computerization of several administrative and production activities, and more recently the increasing digitization of different forms of data (numeric, graphic, musical). The factors that influenced the scale of computerization and digitization also had an impact on determining the scale of homogenous demand for software. In this section we will argue that the scale of homogenous demand, where large encouraged the emergence of product software. Where the scale of demand was large but heterogeneous, niche markets and customized software prevailed.

In the early fifties when the first computers were made, computer software was wired into the hardware. Software programs were very specific to the use to which they would be put to. In this early period of the software industry demand was heterogeneous and infrequent. Whatever software was written was sold with the hardware and was free. This is still the case in several other areas such as mobile phones and telecom switches to name just two examples.

For all of this early period, service firms that wrote one-off programs for large users populated the software industry. In the forties and fifties these large users were US Government departments. As big firms adopted computer mainframes to store their business data and files they became the big users that demanded software. The lack of standardization in hardware meant that the demand for software though similar remained fairly heterogeneous. The cost incurred was usually that of employing programmers and firms tried to maximize the use of these programmers by actively looking for new orders.

The idea that the same software program could be sold again and again to different users took some time to take hold. The repeated sale of the same software program was a relatively new way of doing business in the software industry. First the firm would undertake the fixed developmental costs of creating the program and de-bugging it. The use of the program would then be sold to recover the costs of writing it, rendering software production very similar to commodity production.

The early strategy of service provision was very different to the strategy of product providers. In terms of our discussion in Section 1, product provision in software is akin to the commodification of software, and as we explained commodification requires investment in anticipation of demand. In microeconomics terminology, the balance of fixed and variable costs changes for the producing firms. Service providers have very few fixed costs and can recover all their variable costs through utilizing their resources fully.

Software product providers however, have mostly fixed costs. The only variable cost that they incur is the cost of additional units, which for software is the cost of reproduction. When there is the large dominance of fixed costs standard economies of scale accrue to the producer. Total profits increase as market share grows.

3.1   Homogenous Demands and the Emergence of Software Products

The software product strategy could not have worked without a large enough scale of homogenous demand. A large-scale of demand was created by the continual introduction of cheaper and cheaper machines. In 1960, IBM introduced the IBM1401, a cheaper general-purpose machine meant for medium sized users. This was followed up by the successful introduction within a few years of the System/360 around a standardized operating system. The installed base of computers grew and so did the market in software services. The first software "products" were written to run on these IBM machines. Indeed the spread of computer usage and the growth of software markets is the best modern day example of the advantages of the increasing division of labor. Cheaper machines increased the usage of computers and created a demand for separate software. This trend was accelerated and replicated with the spread of the personal computer in the 1980s. The installed base of computers has grown ever more and for the first time a mass market for PC software products emerged.

Though software products needed a large scale of demand to which they could sell repeatedly, the areas of use in which software products emerged is also instructive. The package software industry emerged and grew around various applications that were usually cross-sectoral in application. Brady et al. (1992) argue that the commodification of software occurred when many of the smaller emerging software firms began to offer packages that reflected primarily 'the converging needs of large numbers of computer users across many sectors. With respect to application software specialization developed along two lines. Some software firms developed products for general purpose applications such as payroll or accounts where there was a commonality in the requirements of users across many sectors. Other firms evolved to sell to particular large vertical markets such as banking or insurance or the military'. However, where such cross-sectoral convergence of application needs did not take place, such as in the case of firm specific applications designed to achieve competitive advantage computerized systems were more likely to be produced internally, or be developed as bespoke software by software houses, as had been common during the earlier growth of the industry.

The growth of software products around particular applications was greatly helped by the emergence of common platforms. This in turn was caused by the early actions of IBM. Common platforms mean that one basic software language is adopted on a number of machines and programs. The IBM 1401 machine was sold with a new software language RPG that was available free with the machine. Software product companies could build their applications around this common and freely available language. IBM's motives in providing a common platform was to increased hardware sales, and create fresh demand by reducing the costs of switching for users. This increase in hardware demand of course had a dramatic influence on the potential demand for software.

3.2 Heterogeneity of software demand and the dominance of customized markets

Though there was a dramatic growth of demand for software- this demand was not all identical or homogenous. There were areas where software needs were fairly heterogeneous, and this heterogeneity could be usefully exploited to both blunt competition and make money. The growth of the customized software and services sector, both globally and within particular countries, can be best understood as a response to the common factors that underlay heterogeneous demand. These factors also varied from country to country.

There were many sources of heterogeneity in the demand for software. An important source of heterogeneity was linguistic and legal diversity across nations. This was particularly relevant to the spread of computerization for administrative uses in companies. Payroll software developed for one country could not very simply be used for another. Thus, localized software development was the first large source of software demand in every nation. The different waves of hardware installations created a need for software that was written differently but for the same vintage of the operating system installed. Software for mainframe computers could not run on minicomputers and software for minicomputer had to be rewritten for the personal computer and for PC networks. Again this created a need for bespoke software in niche markets. Lastly, industrial sectors were different in their administrative and production needs and procedures. Some firms specialized by sectors, such as finance, oil, or retail trading. Their aim was to provide all the software needs of their chosen sector.

All these different sources of heterogeneity are associated with segmentation of the market into smaller local or special markets where competition is low. The types of abilities and management practices that firms required to succeed in these markets are also different. Thus, in their survey of Western European software firms Malerba and Torrisi (1996) found that reputation and knowledge of user needs usually acquired through long term relationships with the customer were the important barriers to entry in the customized market. In contrast, the package software market demonstrated barriers to entry on account of marketing and distribution networks as well. The balance of skills needed and their variety is clearly evident in Table 2 below reproduced from Malerba and Torrisi (1996).

Similarly, Hoch et al. (1999) on the basis of their survey of 100 leading software firms around the world argue that the ranking of management practices in the customized and product segments of the software market are quite different. They found that customized software and services firms tend to place the highest priority upon human resources management, followed by software development strategies, marketing and sales and strategy. In contrast, software product firms ranked Strategy as most important, followed by marketing and sales, human resources and placed software development as the least important.

One implication of the different skills and management practices needed in the different market segments is that the transition of firms that serve niche markets into product market players though theoretically possible, is empirically less observed. The effect of initial heterogeneity in demand upon market segmentation is difficult to overcome, because the skills and management required to deal with mass marketing and the creation of homogenous demands through skilful marketing is less abundant in the economic system.

Table 2. Entry barriers for different types of European software producers (average scores).

Firm type	Software and services	System software and utilities	Packaged software	Services (EDP, Consulting / training)	Technical services (software development tools, expert systems)
Financial resources	2.83	1.50	3.50	2.23	3.50
Marketing and sales network	3.25	2.00	3.36	3.36	3.25
Knowledge of user's environment	3.64	3.50	5.00	4.00	4.00
Technological skills and capabilities	3.20	5.00	3.00	3.14	3.00
Image and reputation	3.68	4.00	3.45	4.36	2.25
Corporate culture	2.69	4.00	3.50	2.50	1.00

Source: Malerba and Torrisi (1996). Scores are from 1 'not relevant' to 5 'very relevant'.

The evolution of the software industry certainly demonstrates this kind of persistence in the aggregate. Thus, Table 1 showed us that American firms faced a larger demand for software products in the early stages of the industry. This early lead was a consequence of the larger scale of homogenous demand faced by American firms. Table 1 also shows that the pattern changes and package software consumption grows in Europe. This growth in demand for package software in Europe is however, served largely by US firms. Mowery (1996) estimates that US firms account for more than 80% of the US package software market and over 60% of the non-US software market.

3.3   Standards and the Reduction of Heterogeneity in Demands

An important element in the growth of the demand for software and its diversity has been the emergence of platforms and standards that has had many implications for the future development of the industry. Bresnahan and Greenstein (2000) argue that the emergence of standards and platforms have helped groups of firms compete with each other while helping them to avoid ruinous direct competition. However, the rise of a dominant standard is also akin to the emergence of sunk costs, albeit over a group of firms. This is because the emergence of platforms and standards is associated with other network effects that have important implications for demand for the standard, so that the expenditure on the standard affects both profitability and raises demand making it an endogenous sunk cost.

Our interest in this sub-section is to stress the demand-side implications of standards and their role in directing the evolution of the industry. As computerization proceeded in different waves and with different vintages of computers and operating systems, an important source of heterogeneity in demand was introduced. As long as the market was expanding with new participants entering the market this was not a serious problem. But when computerization was reasonably widespread further increases in the demand for computers could only come about by new buys from old users. In this situation the incompatibility of different systems introduced a new cost for the buyer- the cost of switching. A machine and operating system that was compatible with the older model reduced switching costs for the buyer and allowed them to transfer their data and files from the old machine to the new one.

For software producers who wrote applications around a particular operating system the existence of standards became even more important for similar reasons. Firstly, successful platforms defined their potential market in an important way. Secondly, upgrades of application software with new features or additional tasks, depended upon a compatibility with past software. For the buyer of software a common standard allowed her to have a variety of applications, which was desirable.

For all these reasons the importance of standards in software is similar to the importance of interchangeable parts in the growth of the machine tools industry. Interchangeable parts allowed heterogeneous production to proceed with the benefits of a homogenous demand. In software, standards achieve the same objective. The creation of standards however, requires coordinated costs to be maintained across a group of firms.

SUMMARY AND IMPLICATIONS

In this chapter we have tried to emphasize the role of demand and supply side factors in the evolution of the software industry and its important segments. Undoubtedly this is not the only way to read the evolution of the industry. However, it is an approach that usefully delineates the evolution of the two forms that technology markets can take. We argued that the evolution of these segments has implications for the nature of competition in the market segments, and also the potential benefits of technology markets.

Thus we have tried to show that the extent of homogenous demand has defined the existence of mass market commodities in software while heterogeneous demand has given rise to niche (outsourced) markets. The nature of competition in the two markets is quite different as is the nature of skills that firms require to succeed. Furthermore, these skills have shown remarkable persistence overtime. Software standards and platforms have played an important role in reducing the impact of some kinds of heterogeneity.

In many respects we have tried to emphasize the similarity between the evolution of software and the emergence of the machine tool sector in the latter part of the last century. Such a comparison also serves to highlight the nature of the advantages and externalities that accrue to the economy due to "economies of specialisation" in software.

By virtue of being intermediate sector efficiencies in software design and improvements in productivity that result from such developments in software are likely to be transmitted to a number of sectors. The scope of this transmission depends both on the extent to which software is used in the economy and the development of key user sectors for software. Two sorts of effects are evident. In the financial and information based sectors (newspapers, entertainment) and functions (administration in offices) the effect of software development has been in speeding up the production time and thus resulting in improvements in productivity. In sectors like manufacturing the development and use of software has given firms the ability to be consistent in quality and increase variety within arrange of products, as was noted by the flexible specialization arguments. As software expands in scope to include all kinds of digitization and communication, the improvements in software programming and development maybe expected to do the same kinds of things for other sectors - increase productivity by reducing production time, and keep quality consistent.

NOTES

[1] This section draws upon Athreye (1998).

[1] This is explained in the following passage about commodities, exchange and circulation, from Grundrisse: 'To have circulation, what is essential is that exchange appears as a process, a fluid whole of purchases and sales. Its first presupposition is the circulation of commodities themselves, as a natural many-sided circulation of commodities. The precondition of commodity circulation is that they be produced as exchange values not as immediate use values, but as mediated through exchange value. Appropriation through and means of divestiture (Entäusserung) and alienation (Veräusserung) is the fundamental condition. Circulation as the realisation of exchange values implies: (1) that my product is a product only insofar it is for others; hence suspended singularity, generality; (2) that it is a product for me only insofar as it has been alienated, become for others; (3) that it is for the other only in so far as he himself alienates his product; which already implies (4) that production is not an end in itself for me but a means.' Marx , K. (1857:1973; p.196). Alienation is usually discussed in a specific context popularised by existentialist philosophers, viz. the lack of control over the end use of its product by labour. However, Marx's discussion of the historical development of labour power as a commodity makes clear that the alienation of labour from the means of production was an important historical necessity in the transforming labour power into a commodity.

[1] The division of labour process is cumulative. The efficiency gains due to the division of labour ultimately lower prices, which should induce more consumption. Because this decrease in price does not happen at the expense of profitability but by cutting down costs, it also allows induces more production by existing firms or by new entrants.

[1] Yamin, M. (1997).

[1] Roncaglia (1985) discusses this point in the context of evaluating Petty's conceptualisation of the market as evidenced in The Dialogue of Diamonds.

[1] This brief sub-section draws upon their review.

[1] From Mowery (1996).

[1] Western Europe is defined as the seventeen countries of Austria, Belgium, Finland, France, Germany, Greece, Ireland, Italy, Netherlands, Norway, Portugal, Spain, Sweden, Switzerland, Turkey, and the UK.

REFERENCES

Arora A. Licensing tacit knowledge: intellectual property rights and the market for know-how. Economics of Innovation and New Technology 1995; 5:41-59

Arora A., Gambardella A. The changing technology of technological change: general and abstract knowledge and the division of innovative labour. Research Policy 1994; 23:523-532

Arora A., Fosfuri A., Gambardella A. Markets for technology. Mimeo. Carnegie Mellon University, Pittsburgh, 1999.

Athreye S. On markets in knowledge. Journal of Management and Governance 1998; 1:231-253

Bhaduri, Amit, *Macroeconomics: the dynamics of commodity production.* New Delhi: Oxford University Press, 1986.

Brady T., Tierney M., Williams R. The commodification of industry applications software. Industrial and Corporate Change 1992; 1:489-513

Bresnahan, Timothy, Gambardella, Alfonso. "The division of inventive labour and the extent of the market." In *General purpose technologies and economic growth*, Elhanan Helpman, ed. MIT Press, 1998.

Bresnahan T., Greenstein S. Technological competition and the structure of the computer industry. Journal of Industrial Economics 1999; 67:1-40

Hoch, Detlev J., Roeding, Cyriac R., Purkert, Gert, Lindner, Sandro K., *Secrets of software success*. Boston: Harvard Business School Press, 1999.

Malerba, Franco, Torrisi, Salvatore. "The dynamics of market structure and innovation in the Western European software industry". In *The international software industry: A comparative study of industry evolution and structure*, David C. Mowery ed. New York and Oxford: Oxford University Press, 1996.

Marx, Karl, Grundrisse (1857/58: 1973). *Foundations of the critique of political economy* English edition, ed. N.I. Stone, Chicago 1904; (translation M. Nicolaus). Harmondsworth: Penguin Books, 1973.

Mowery, David C., *The international software industry: A comparative study of industry evolution and structure*. New York and Oxford: Oxford University Press, 1996
North, Douglass C., *Institutions, institutional change and economic performance*. Cambridge: Cambridge University Press, 1990.

Roncaglia, Alessandro, *Petty, The origins of political economy*. Cardiff: University College Cardiff Press, 1985.

Rosenberg, Nathan, *Perspectives on technology*. Cambridge: Cambridge University Press, 1976.

Rosenberg, Nathan, *Capital goods, technology and economic growth*. Reprinted in Rosenberg, Nathan. *Perspectives on technology*. Cambridge: Cambridge University Press, 1976.

Smith, Adam, *An enquiry into the nature and causes of the wealth of nations*. Penguin Books, 1986.

Stigler, G.J. The division of labour is limited by the extent of the market. The Journal of Political Economy 1951; 59:185-193

Yamin, M. The dual risks of market exchange: the roles of marketing institutions and activity in the transition process. International Journal of Entrepreneurial Behaviour and Research 1997; 3: 1355-2554

Young, A. Increasing returns and economic progress. Economic Journal 1929; 38:527-542

CONCLUSION

Knowledge, as a technological input, progressively enters the market sphere. This movement goes along with the general evolution of contemporary economies, which are above all market economies. The analyzed process, on the theoretical level and trough four sectoral studies, can not be considered to have an atypical and transitory dimension.

The arguments suggested indicate that individual units of knowledge are subject to a market exchange in order to enter the knowledge base of user firms. These latter are able to manage increasingly complex arrangements and to reorganize the knowledge pieces they acquire so as to use them as productive resources. Whether they constitute new concepts of products or prototypes, elementary or more elaborated technologies related to specific contexts, different means of data processing databases patents or licenses. Only knowledge with a functional dimension can be exchanged. Markets for knowledge solely deal with a part of the knowledge held by economic agents. It means that soundly tacit knowledge, such as the one embedded in organizational routines and in work teams or in the beliefs and values of the firm, cannot be taken out of its context, cannot be exchanged.

Given this precision, we can consider that the analyzed knowledge process has a structural dimension. It is based on three main ideas we will quickly remind.

Firstly, markets for knowledge raise the fundamental question of knowing how economic agents acquire the knowledge they need. Up to now, economical analyzes were rather centered on the knowledge production issue. This approach examines firms able to produce and to develop this required knowledge and consequently to benefit from the externalities lying in their environment. The model qualified as institutional variety illustrates this step of knowledge production, which however remains, characterized by wastes, duplication of efforts and increased transfer costs, since it all depends on the externalities and firms learning capabilities.

The acquisition of knowledge is as important as its production when it is considered as a strategic asset. Knowledge gaps may be fulfilled by several mechanisms. We can consider that knowledge transfer between firms is realized through ownership, which may justify a large part of the mergers and acquisitions recorded nowadays. Economic literature has given a lot of interest to multiple contractual agreements (joint-venture, joint R&D agreement, co-development, co-marketing, etc.) based on the idea that firms do not need to fully possess assets in order to acquire knowledge. What is more crucial to a company is rather to know how to obtain a position at the center of a network as one of knowledge circulation. With regard to these transfer mechanisms, we have emphasized that intellectual assets can, under some conditions (increased complexity of knowledge bases, knowledge codification, information technologies, strongly established property rights), be purchased on markets. More precisely, quasi-markets for knowledge are efficient mediations for the organizations to function and innovate.

Secondly, the structural change process reveals deep changes concerning the industrial organization of knowledge production. The industrial logic henceforth imbues the knowledge sphere: inputs selection, definition of the targets, mastering the costs, shortening of research cycles, etc. The development of this logic implies an increased specialization process: the locus knowledge production becomes distinct from the locus of its use. The social distribution of knowledge is more complex than before since the deeper segmentation of knowledge blocks multiplies the locus of knowledge production. Also, we have to take into account that a large part of the scientific knowledge is produced in an application context. In this perspective, the KIBSFs act as an interface with the users. They represent an intermediate with fundamental research, the channel through which basic knowledge can be exploited. The knowledge base of some industrial firms thus gets enhanced due to these specialized inputs. But these inputs also represent specific application technologies. Surveys carried out on chemical sector, biotechnology, semiconductors and software reveal the relative importance of these mechanisms.

Thirdly, the institutional aspect was highlighted in order to explain the dynamism and specificities of markets for knowledge. This aspect was outlined through the issue of intellectual property rights and their recent extension to new fields (genes, genes fragments, etc.). It also appears through the notion of institutional architecture of an economy. We have borrowed the notion of institutional comparative advantage to show that markets are set up within institutional frameworks shaping webs of cohesion, which differentiate the national economies. The idea that technological specializations are linked to institutional structures, and particularly to national systems of innovation is not a new one. Along the same line, we observe that the intensity of market transfers is subordinated to the existence of institutional frameworks. A strong mobility of the skilled labor force, a buoyant and open capital market, substantial rewards to innovators, deeply influence the exploration strategies and the increase of KIBSFs as favoring connectivity and receptivity.

This collective research suffers from some shortcomings. The empirical analysis of markets for knowledge is strongly limited by the lack of information concerning exchanges between domestic firms. Besides, sectoral analyzes need to be improved by firms' individual data which would have made it possible to better understand the great recourse to markets for knowledge.

INDEX

absorptive capacity, 42, 49, 63
acquisition, 103, 109, 121-23, 126, 159
appropriability, 15, 22-23, 79, 144
asset, 15-16, 32, 34, 54-56, 58, 82, 90, 92, 116-17, 121-23, 138, 140, 159
capabilities, 32-33, 73, 88, 92, 123, 142-44, 146, 153, 155, 160, 166, 171, 194
codes, 5, 27, 35
codification, 6-7, 14, 41, 44, 49, 157, 186
codified, 6-8, 14, 23-24, 26-27, 32, 44, 46, 75, 93, 116, 187
collaboration, 15-16, 29, 31, 48, 74-75, 83, 120-123, 125-31, 150
competencies,15-16, 24, 32, 41-42, 46, 119, 127
competition,12, 19, 49-51, 63, 73, 76, 81, 92, 94, 100-02, 112, 126, 139, 143, 147, 156, 165, 187, 193, 195-196
complementary asset,10, 15-16
complexity, 53, 142-44, 146, 154-156
contract,8, 15, 28, 30, 32-33, 78-82, 118, 120-125, 146, 159, 186-88
cooperative arrangement, 72
copyrights, 11, 54, 162, 183-187
cost,4, 5, 7, 15, 22, 25, 33, 43, 47-50, 54-56, 73-74, 77, 80, 92-93, 102, 110, 113, 116, 122, 125, 140-141, 144, 149, 151, 153-154, 157, 166, 168-169, 191-193, 195, 197
demand-side, 14, 181-182, 195-96

design,14, 24-28, 31,33, 42, 46-49, 52-53, 57-58, 63, 75, 77, 80, 104, 116, 141-72, 196
disintegration, 17, 23, 28, 31, 42, 48
division of labor, (cognitive), 21-22, 27-28, 31, 33, 36-42
division of innovative labor, 110, 115-17, 127, 138, 142, 145, 152, 154-55, 160-61, 171
economies of scale, 21-22, 27-28, 31, 93, 141, 148-49, 151, 154, 192
economies of scope, 75, 138, 154, 160
entrepreneurship, 22, 47
entry barriers, 51, 100, 140-41, 156, 193-94
exploitation, 7, 10, 22, 32-34, 51, 54, 57, 89-90
exploration, 33-34, 39, 50, 52, 84, 109
externalities, 15, 22, 35, 42, 47, 52, 196
increasing returns, 27-28, 79, 147-49, 152, 184
incremental innovation, 43-46, 48-51, 168
indirect methods of production, 148, 152-53
information technologies, 31, 35-36, 43-46, 48-49, 56, 58, 63, 110, 116, 143, 186
innovation process, 15, 17, 22-23, 29-31, 35, 80, 110, 112-13, 116-18, 154
input, 4, 8-9, 16-17, 21, 23-24, 36, 118, 120, 125
institutional arrangements, 50, 118, 139, 153, 169
institutional variety, 22, 47
intellectual property, 137, 139, 155, 157, 159, 160, 164, 169, 171
(rights), 10-11, 43, 53-54, 155, 159, 162, 164, 187

Economics of Science, Technology and Innovation

1. A. Phillips, A.P. Phillips and T.R. Phillips:
   *Biz Jets. Technology and Market Structure in
   the Corporate Jet Aircraft Industry.* 1994   ISBN 0-7923-2660-1
2. M.P. Feldman:
   The Geography of Innovation. 1994   ISBN 0-7923-2698-9
3. C. Antonelli:
   *The Economics of Localized Technological
   Change and Industrial Dynamics.* 1995   ISBN 0-7923-2910-4
4. G. Becher and S. Kuhlmann (eds.):
   *Evaluation of Technology Policy Programmes
   in Germany.* 1995   ISBN 0-7923-3115-X
5. B. Carlsson (ed.): *Technological Systems and Economic
   Performance: The Case of Factory Automation.* 1995   ISBN 0-7923-3512-0
6. G.E. Flueckiger: *Control, Information, and
   Technological Change.* 1995   ISBN 0-7923-3667-4
7. M. Teubal, D. Foray, M. Justman and E. Zuscovitch (eds.):
   *Technological Infrastructure Policy. An International
   Perspective.* 1996   ISBN 0-7923-3835-9
8. G. Eliasson:
   *Firm Objectives, Controls and Organization. The Use
   of Information and the Transfer of Knowledge within
   the Firm.* 1996   ISBN 0-7923-3870-7
9. X. Vence-Deza and J.S. Metcalfe (eds.):
   *Wealth from Diversity. Innovation, Structural Change and
   Finance for Regional Development in Europe.* 1996   ISBN 0-7923-4115-5
10. B. Carlsson (ed.):
    Technological Systems and Industrial Dynamics. 1997   ISBN 0-7923-9940-4
11. N.S. Vonortas:
    Cooperation in Research and Development. 1997   ISBN 0-7923-8042-8
12. P. Braunerhjelm and K. Ekholm (eds.):
    The Geography of Multinational Firms. 1998   ISBN 0-7923-8133-5
13. A. Varga:
    *University Research and Regional Innovation: A Spatial
    Econometric Analysis of Academic Technology Transfers.*
    1998   ISBN 0-7923-8248-X
14. J. de la Mothe and G. Paquet (eds.):
    Local and Regional Systems of Innovation   ISBN 0-7923-8287-0
15. D. Gerbarg (ed.):
    The Economics, Technology and Content of Digital T V   ISBN 0-7923-8325-7
16. C. Edquist, L. Hommen and L. Tsipouri
    Public Technology Procurement and Innovation   ISBN 0-7923-8685-X
17. J. de la Mothe and G. Paquet (eds.):
    Information, Innovation and Impacts   ISBN 0-7923-8692-2

18. J. S. Metcalfe and I. Miles (eds.):
    Innovation Systems in the Service Economy:
    Measurement and Case Study Analysis ISBN 0-7923-7730-3
19. R. Svensson:
    Success Strategies and Knowledge Transfer in
    Cross-Border Consulting Operations ISBN 0-7923-7776-1
20. P. Braunerhjelm:
    Knowledge Capital and the "New Economy":
    Firm Size, Performance and Network Production ISBN 0-7923-7801-6
21. J. de la Mothe and J. Niosi (eds):
    The Economic and Social Dynamics of Biotechnology ISBN 0-7923-7922-5
22. Guilhon, Bernard (ed):
    Technology and Markets for Knowledge:
    Knowledge Creation, Diffusion and Exchange within
    a Growing Economy ISBN 0-7923-7202-6

KLUWER ACADEMIC PUBLISHERS — BOSTON / DORDRECHT / LONDON